Memories
of
Hammer

MEMORIES of HAMMER

edited by Gary J. Svehla
and Susan Svehla

Midnight Marquee Press, Inc.
Baltimore, Maryland

Copyright © 2002

Without limiting the rights under copyright reserved above, no part of this publication may be reproduced, stored in or introduced into a retrieval system, or transmitted, in any form, or by any means (electronic, mechanical, photocopying, recording or otherwise), without the prior written permission of the copyright owners or the publishers of the book.

First Limited Edition Printing January 2002, Luminary Press

First Paperback Edition, February 2009
ISBN 9781887664615
Library of Congress Catalog Card Number
Acknowledgments: James Bernard, Martine Beswicke, Catherine Birch, Joyce Broughton, Veronica Carlson, Beth Cavanaugh, Harvey Clarke, Jim Clatterbaugh, Sue and Colin Cowie, Cecelia Doidge-Ripper, Yolande Donlan, Leo Dymowski, Freddie Francis, Pam Francis, Kevin Flynn, Val Guest, Jeff Herberger, Phil Holthaus, Paul Jensen, Tom Johnson, Mitch Klein, Wayne Kinsey, Dick Klemensen, Cat Ledger, Christopher Lee, Suzanna Leigh, Bill Littman, Sydney Love, Mark A. Miller, Yvonne Monlaur, Caroline Munro, Barry Murphy, Scott Nollen, Mary Peach, Ingrid Pitt, Derek Pykett, Michael Ripper, Tony Rudlin, Jimmy Sangster, Barbara Shelley, John Stell, Yutte Stensgaard, Joe Treppe, Tom Weaver, Virginia Wetherell

for Veronica

Table of Contents

8	Introduction
36	James Bernard
61	Veronica Carlson
69	Veronica Carlson and Virginia Wetherell
82	Joyce Broughton on Peter Cushing
86	Freddie Francis
115	Val Guest
125	Christopher Lee
162	Yvonne Monlaur
166	Caroline Munro
168	Jimmy Sangster
191	Barbara Shelley
213	Veronica Carlson, Suzanna Leigh, Ingrid Pitt, Yutte Stensgaard
229	James Bernard, Martine Beswicke, Veronica Carlson, Val Guest, Ingrid Pitt
255	Afterword

INTRODUCTION

Being an intense horror movie fan growing up in the late 1950s and 1960s, Shock Theater and Universal Pictures were the classics first viewed late Saturday evenings on fuzzy channels that showed crackling and heavily spliced prints with tinny sound. In other words, these Universal treasures were "the classics" studied as works of ancient times, wonderful movies, perhaps, but movies that belonged to another generation, another time. But *not* mine!

For the baby boomers, who grew up during this emerging monster-kid era, Hammer Film Productions produced the horror movies of my generation, movies that were constantly appearing at neighborhood theaters, movies that featured a steady stable of talent (both behind the camera—Terence Fisher, Anthony Hinds/AKA John Elder, Jimmy Sangster, Michael Carrerras, Anthony Nelson-Keys, etc.—and before the camera—Peter Cushing, Christopher Lee, Michael Ripper, Oliver Reed, Barbara Shelley, Veronica Carlson, etc.) that created new icons to follow in the footsteps of Karloff and Lugosi. The new horror kings—Cushing and Lee—inspired magazine articles and fan clubs and became, as Calvin Beck once coined, the heroes of the horrors. For boomers, we had our own horror film factory filled with personalities and talent worth getting excited over.

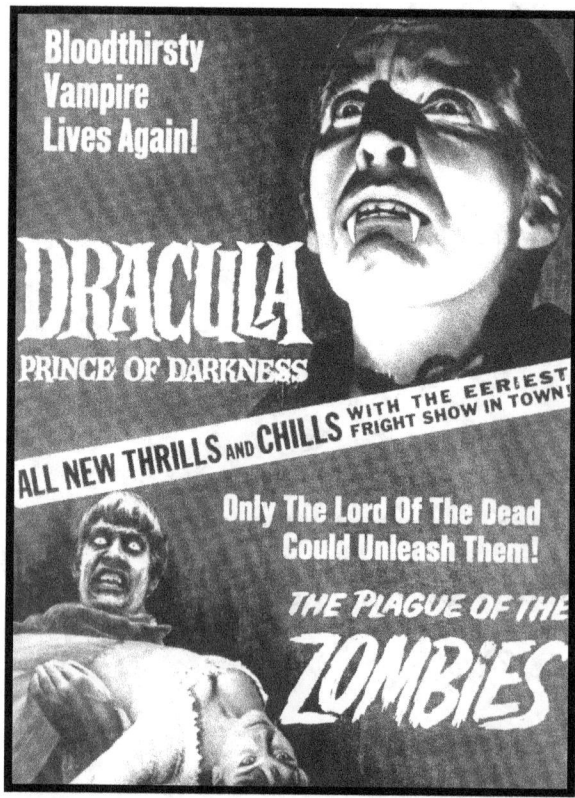

Universal Pictures was the Bible, these were the classics that we read about in *Castle of Frankenstein* and *Famous Monsters* magazines, but these movies were history... Hammer Horror was the vision of the new players, the new kids on the block, and their horror world view was filled with gaudy Technicolor, plunging necklines, blatant sexuality and graphically intense violence.

In this book, Susan and I turn to the numerous FANEX, Monster Rally and Classic FilmFest film conventions we sponsored since 1987, all of the shows held in the Baltimore/Washington area that we call home. Susan and I do not travel well, never have, never will, and we like staying within five hours or so of home. But after producing *Gore Creatures/Midnight Marquee* since 1963, Susan inaugurated the idea in the mid-1980s of sponsoring horror and classic film conventions where we would fly celebrities associated with movies we both love to our neck of the woods and in this way meet and honor them for all their marvelous work in movies. And now, in early 2002, as we are preparing our 16th FANEX, we have decided that most of the surviving Hammer film personalities who have endured from the late 1980s through the end of the century have appeared at our convention (or politely declined our invitation), many of them multiple times, to the extent that we no longer consider Hammer heroine Veronica Carlson a guest but rather a good friend. And last year it hit Susan and I directly in the face that the various guest talks and panel discussions these guests had appeared on throughout the years can now be considered history and well worth preserving for the legacy they offer. Some of these Hammer personalities who appeared at the show—James Bernard,

Gary and Richard Svehla with Veronica Carlson

Michael Ripper at Monster Rally with writer and major Ripper fan John Stell

Michael Ripper—are no longer alive, so their recorded testimony and reflections become even more important as the years melt on. Unfortunately, not every second of every guest talk has been recorded... too many people speaking and only one or two videographers, talks that went on longer than expected with video tapes that run out, mechanical equipment failure, etc. But in spite of all these challenges, the bulk of Hammer history has been salvaged and saved and this book is a testament to the legacy of Hammer films and the personalities that contributed to its success.

Sometimes the guest talks, the video tapes, do not tell the entire story. Susan and I also sponsor the guests, welcome them to the hotel, have a dinner or two with them, answer their frantic calls in the middle of the night, share stories out on sidewalks because the hotel had been evacuated because of someone pulling a fire alarm switch. We deal with the guests on the phone, book their flights, cater to their needs and celebrate victory at show's end with a convention-sponsored dinner. Most of these guests we get to interact with on a personal basis and we get to see the real human being behind the public exterior. Sometimes there is no difference; at other times, a great difference occurs between the public and the private personality. Before we allow the reader to dig deeply into this volume, to hear the words delivered before enthusiastic crowds assembled in auditoriums often times jammed-packed, I just wanted to share some of my most vivid reflections of meeting and interacting with some of the Hammer personalities who appeared at our conventions. Some stories will have to wait, but the following assembled reflections reveal that directors, screenwriters, supporting players and stars who appeared in Hammer films, both the classic earlier ones and the less distinctive later ones, share common attributes of politeness, humility, love of their fans and an enthusiasm for the movies they made so long ago. The Hammer people, unlike many of the Hollywood types, always gravitate together and become fast friends, even those stars who never worked together, and they always manage to entertain one another. The bottom line is this: Hammer personalities know how to have fun!

Ingrid Pitt and her husband Tony always have been enthusiastic supporters of our conventions and are willing to do whatever it takes to put on a good entrance for the fans. During Ingrid's first appearance at FANEX, during the Friday evening Guest Introductions, Jim Clatterbaugh wanted Ingrid to seemingly come out of a coffin wearing a sexy nightie under a black cape. Tony was nervous and wanted a detailed script that Ingrid could follow, and Ingrid, while excited to comply, also wanted to know about the physical parameters of the stage, the lighting, the sound, etc. They were professionals in every sense of the word and they wanted to do a good job, but they wanted to know that this new group of Americans they just met had the residual professionalism to deliver the goods and not embarrass Ingrid publicly with amateurish flubs. Susan tried to be comforting insisting impromptu stunts would warm the hearts of all the Hammer fans assembled, that too much rehearsal and preparations would simply stiffen the final effect. This was the convention where I blew out my knee the Thursday before the convention and I delayed surgery until the following Monday morning. Susan and I went to the local mall to buy a sexy negligee for Ingrid, and Sue purchased a white one. With so many responsibilities to carry out for the show, and with me on crutches hobbling around, we were glad to get that one task done and return to the hotel. However, once we returned and found Ingrid, to give her the negligee, problems developed immediately. Being the consummate artist, Ingrid was polite but visibly disappointed with the white negligee... she felt that black

Gary with Ingrid Pitt at FANEX 8

James Bernard, Martine Beswicke, Ingrid and Tony at the Inner Harbor in Baltimore. FANEX staffers got to spend the day with the guests but, as usual, Gary and Sue were at the hotel putting the finishing touches on the con.

better conveyed the evil of the undead and she insisted that we get her a black one. We knew that Ingrid was right, and so, under even more pressure, we ventured back to the mall to return one piece of lingerie and purchase another. That Friday evening, the Opening Ceremony was one of the best we ever presented. A local band had donated their wooden coffin for the cause; however, the hotel staff wouldn't allow us to light candles or use the band's fog machine (citing the fog would trip the alarm system), but the lighting, music and Ingrid's innate dramatic sense was nothing less than spectacular causing the audience to erupt into wild cheers and thunderous applause. To this day people comment upon the wonderful performance Ingrid delivered that evening. From that point on we bonded and became the best of friends. Tony, the consummate businessman, always picks my brain about sponsoring conventions, promotion, etc. Ingrid entertains us by proudly showing off the wedding photos of her daughter.

James Bernard, who recently passed away, was a true gentleman and worked overtime to make his convention appearance extra special. Bernard, a music composer, could not share stories of working on the Bray Studio set or share anecdotes of what it was like working with Christopher Lee or Peter Cushing... he composed his music after the shoot was done and everyone had gone home. Besides honoring the man, we did not expect James to be an exciting guest because of the nature of his contribution to Hammer films. However, we were dead wrong. Jimmy mesmerized the audience, sharing his private life stories of celebration and tragedy (his companion was brutally murdered) and translated the abstract process of scoring movies into something quite tangible and concrete. In one impromptu session, Bernard sat at the hotel piano which was set up near the Convention Entrance to the hotel and simply entertained the assembled masses by speaking of his work as he illustrated recognizable musical cues by playing them on the piano. What a perfect way to feature a film scorer... simply mike him at the piano and let him go wild. It was spontaneous and electrifying. During the convention's closing night dinner, Bernard sat at the table with Susan and myself, spinning many tales of interest for one and all. Bernard was very concerned with my injured knee and wished me luck with my surgery the next morning. He who wrote me a personal letter a few weeks later asking about my recovery and how I was doing. As I said, James Bernard was a true gentleman, a caring individual and a warm-hearted human being. His score for *Horror of Dracula* is music burned into my brain, *never* to be forgotten.

On the other extreme was lovable curmudgeon Jimmy Sangster, whose autobiography, *Do You Want It Good or Tuesday?*, was being premiered at our show. Sangster, who attended the show with his wonderful wife Mary Peach, was everything we could ask a convention guest to be, but he was the type of persona who always took charge and did things *his* way. I can remember when editing his book, Jimmy referred to the tragic fate of director Seth Holt. In the margins of the galley proofs, acting simply as editor, I implored him to tell us more, to give us an anecdote. It was common knowledge that Holt drank himself to death, but Jimmy never even alluded to that fact, so I felt further embellishment was required. In the margin of the galley proof pages, when it was returned to me, below my editor's notes, Jimmy wrote... "None of your damn business!" In other words, when Jimmy wrote what he wanted to say, that was it, there was no more! Sangster, while he was writ-

Jimmy Sangster at FANEX 11

ing the book, complained he did not remember too many specific things about making the Hammer films, and while he appeared at the FANEX show, he also, on stage, told the audience that he did not remember very much of his Hammer days. And while Sangster's book was the best it could be, we always wished he would have shared even more. But Jimmy happily complied with our wishes for him to sign a certain amount of books that we could sell after the show, and we spent over an hour up in his hotel room shoving him copies of the book while he labored away, never complaining, or at least never complaining without interjecting a joke or something humorous to the mix. When it came to appearing at the show, a huge line of people gathered in front of his table and he enthusiastically greeted every fan and personalized every copy of the book with his autograph. Sangster was the first personality whose book premiered at one of our shows, and while we were nervous over how Jimmy would respond and how sales would do, he always came through for us.

Veronica Carlson was nothing less than wonderful every time she appeared at the convention, and she has appeared at more shows than any other guest. Veronica, who first appeared a few times with her husband Sydney, more recently appeared solo while Sydney stayed home with their children, generously sharing Veronica with us and her fans. And Veronica effortlessly passed from the old FANEX era (bringing stills and signing them for fans for free) to the new era (reluctantly charging for her signature). Veronica, Susan and I bonded at that first show when we took Veronica out to dinner and shared the disasters of our wedding day. We went into detail about how the outdoor wedding was rained out, how the band canceled and how a guest stuck her hand into the wedding cake, just to name a few disasters. Within minutes, we had Veronica in tears from laughing so hard... she shared similar embarrassments from her life and became more like a friend than a Hammer heroine from the days of my youth. From the beginning, we assigned my father to watch over Veronica, who become her liaison, so to speak. My father Richard prepared by borrowing video tapes of all her films, watching and studying her work, and before long my father and Veronica became fast friends, he always volunteering to watch over her, especially when she began to travel to the show alone. Sitting shotgun with her at the hotel bar until closing time... Veronica would meet and greet her fans, share a drink and stories, holding court until the bar closed at 1:30 a.m. Many times my father would slip out from Veronica's table, and dash over to see Sue

Russ Tamblyn, Veronica Carlson, Acquanetta and Jim Danforth at FANEX 6

or me all in a tizzy. "This born-again Christian is trying to indoctrinate Veronica and won't leave her alone. I think you should call the hotel staff to take him away." My protective father, perhaps a little too protective, was on the right point: far too many fans have personal agendas that they feel a specific star or personality should subscribe to. And people like Veronica are just so kind and nurturing that their attentiveness and politeness is sometimes confused with genuine interest and acceptance. We did not need to call the hotel staff, but a suggestion to call it a night and to take Veronica up to her room was wisely followed.

Carlson is a talented artist, and once, a few months before a convention appearance, she asked about bringing full-size, full color prints of some of her art (usually of the nature or flowery landscape variety) and asked me if I felt movie fans would be interested in purchasing such prints with her autograph. I told her artwork illustrating Cushing or Lee would be of more interest, but if a fan is interested in *you* as a person, they would support a product that came directly from your heart and soul. And luckily, Veronica did very well that year selling her prints. As a gesture, she gave Susan and me one of them, autographed with a personal message, and that colorful painting today hangs in our home and is something very

Veronica signs an autograph at FANEX 4 for George Stover.

special, as is Veronica. Perhaps her Monster Rally appearance showcased the essence of her artistic talents—a gigantic oil painting of herself and Christopher Lee (simply gorgeous) which she asked permission of me to ask Christopher Lee to autograph. Mr. Lee was quite impressed and graciously autographed the oil. Veronica was beaming, and rightfully so!

Val Guest and wife Yolande, warm Brits to the teeth, had morphed into the stereotyped Hollywood couple, with Val taking to wearing bright print shirts and ascot ties and Yolande wearing huge Hollywood style sunglasses. Not that their outer wardrobe altered their kindness and sincere approach to the people they met... it just shows when one lives in Hollywood, one dresses in a specific Hollywood style. Val Guest was a special person for me to meet, as the Quatermass films, especially *Enemy from Space* (which I first saw with my father in 1957), greatly affected me in my youth and I grew up to adore these productions as adult, intelligent science fiction. I told Val that *Enemy from Space/Quatermass II* was an epiphany film experience for me, and Val was quite proud and

Val Guest, Yolande Donlan and Freddie Francis at FANEX 11

humbled by my praise. Disappointingly, Val shared the opinion that he enjoyed the first Quatermass film, *The Creeping Unknown*, more than the second, as he felt too much of the second film was rehash. But even directors are entitled to their own opinions. The Guests were simply charming and told stories of their settled-in life in Southern California and how much they enjoy living in the States. What impressed me most was Val's clear memory of the movies he made and his ability to verbalize anecdotes and thematic ideas he was trying to convey in his films. Simply as a cute couple, Val and Yolande are darlings.

Suzanna Leigh, another charming and quite beautiful Hammer starlet, thrilled the audiences with her reflections of working with Elvis Presley and making films such as *The Lost Continent* and others. Come Saturday night, I was sitting with friends at the hotel bar, ready to crash, when Suzanna Leigh and Ted Bohus came to sit down at our table. I was totally charmed to meet Suzanna and tried to stay attentive as she told some wonderful stories including her ambivalence over attending the show when her daughter was celebrating her 18th birthday that very week. I found my head getting heavier and heavier, and soon I was nodding off, much to my own embarrassment. Whether I was simply nodding out or totally asleep, I was abruptly awakened by the hearty chuckles and laughs of the assembled party, as Susanna cleverly muttered something to the

Suzanna Leigh (right) with Terry Moore at Monster Rally

affect, "Gary really seems enthralled by my stories!" Of course, I cherished the moments spent one-on-one with Suzanna, but as my wife can vouch, when I am sleepy, I will nod off anywhere at anytime. But Suzanna Leigh is the type of star who is effervescent and bubbly and who loves to talk to a collected crowd and spin her tales. She is ageless, youthful and never seems to run out of energy, something that cannot be said of convention organizers.

Michael Ripper, the man who appeared in more Hammer films than either Christopher Lee or Peter Cushing, was a special guest at our 1999 Monster Rally convention in Crystal City, Virginia. Working closely with Derek Pykett, author of Ripper's biography, and Ripper's wife, we knew that Michael's declining health would be a major factor for us to overcome. While in his early 80s and in good physical health, Ripper's memory was rapidly fading away and he could remember little of the past. However, he had never visited America nor did he ever have the opportunity to meet his American fans, so Pykett and Michael's wife felt it would be something special to premiere the biography at the convention, with Michael in attendance. Because of his age and lack of energy, everyone felt Michael would not be able to personalize the book while confronting a sea of fans lined up for yards, so the decision was made to have Michael personalize book plates six months before the show, so when people approached him to purchase a book, Michael could shake hands, say a few words, and the autograph would be ready-made. Michael was always dressed in a most dapper fashion, always pleasant and excited about meeting so many fans, but he never quite grasped where he was and what he was there to premiere. One time, resting alone with his wife, Susan and me in the convention suite, Susan asked Michael if he was having a good time, and without thinking, he snapped back, "No, I'm not." Ripper's wife, embarrassed by his comments, later unnecessarily apologized and explained that Michael was merely tired. But with so much sensory overkill for a kindly old gentleman, Susan and I understood he was merely tired and confused and most likely overwhelmed by the course of events. Even if Michael never fully understood the Monster Rally experience, by show's end everyone agreed that Monster Rally was a marvelous one for Michael, and Christopher Lee seemed positively thrilled to spend some quality time with his old Hammer buddy. When Lee appeared on stage during Friday evening's Guest Introduction, he voiced that meeting Michael Ripper, after all those years, was one of his biggest thrills of his American visit.

Michael Ripper and Christopher Lee meet again at Monster Rally.

Caroline Munro had always been a favorite with Hammer fans, having appeared in movies diverse as *Dracula A.D. 1972* and *Captain Kronos: Vampire Hunter*, among many other fantasy films. I met her and had my photograph taken with her back in the mid-1970s, attending a Pittsburgh Fantasy Film Convention. Now, 25 years later, I was the convention sponsor bringing Caroline back to the East Coast for another convention appearance. Strangely, Caroline had hardly aged and her personality was as sweet as always. While she was generally busy at her convention table meeting and greeting the fans, she had requested that her liaison Phil Holthaus take her to Toys-R-Us so she could buy some presents for her daughter back home. Phil reflected how charming and special it was to accompany a Hammer actress to a toy store and watch her "ooh" and "aaah" over all the special treats available. Caroline had been working on a music CD in London, with producer/performer Gary Wilson, and as Wilson had accompanied her over to the States for her convention appearance, we asked the duo if they wanted to perform live on stage. Wilson, you see, had brought along the backing musical tracks, minus

Gary Wilson and Caroline Munro perform at FANEX 11

the vocals, so all they had to do was provide the lead vocals. Caroline was very nervous about performing live, and even after she committed, she was unsure how her fans would respond. My gosh, we knew the convention audience would go wild, and when Gary and Caroline hit the stage, they owned the audience and performed a dynamic set. I don't know if the CD was ever released or not, but the music was vibrant and energetic and held the entire crowd transfixed.

Virginia Wetherell was more known for her dynamic performance in Stanley Kubrick's *A Clockwork Orange* and *Curse of the Crimson Altar* (with Boris Karloff and Christopher Lee) than her supporting performances in a few Hammer films such as *Demons of the Mind* and *Dr. Jekyll and Sister Hyde*. However, Wetherell was appearing more as the widow of Hammer star Ralph Bates and raising money for her charitable organization that is attempting to improve the quality of life with people who suffer with pancreatic cancer, a disease which claimed her husband in 1991. Wetherell, totally charming and without ego, was shocked to be so appreciated when attendees remembered her film work, but she constantly spoke on stage of feeling her husband's spirit among the convention goers and felt that Ralph would have felt quite at home here. Constantly informing people of her work to find a cure for pancreatic cancer, all the money donated at her autograph table and at the auction we sponsored would go to the cause, and it seems her convention appearance served as a way for her to reconnect with Hammer and the memories of Ralph Bates whom she met while both of them were filming *Dr. Jekyll and Sister Hyde*.

After many years of trying to locate Yutte Stensgaard, we finally found her on the West Coast. I can't remember who helped us locate her, probably Dick Klemensen. Fans were so excited to meet their dream vampire from *Lust for a Vampire* and the cover girl of Midnight Marquee #45.

Virginia Wetherell and Gary at FANEX 11

The same can be said of Martine Beswicke, it took a while to find her, but we did and she attended FANEX 8 along with Ingrid and Veronica. Like all the Hammer women, Martine charmed the fans and spoke with a witty shrewdness, proving beauty wasn't her only talent.

Freddie Francis is one of Susan's favorite guests from the standpoint of his overwhelming talent. Both a noted cinematographer (for which he will be best remembered) and a director, Francis and his wife Pam truly charmed the FANEX audiences. During one shared meal, Freddie was politely inquiring, in so many words, what Sue and I got out of sponsoring the FANEX shows every year. "Do you want to break into the business?" Freddie asked. Susan and I smiled at one another and said, "No, no, you don't understand. We love these films and simply want to host a party to honor you folks... to let you know how much we appreciate your work." To which a perplexed Freddie again questioned, "You must make

Ingrid Pitt and Yutte Stensgaard at Monster Rally

a profit doing these shows, right?" We told him that shows vary year by year... some shows come out ahead, some are money losers. But as long as we break even we are satisfied. We told Freddie, "It's meeting people such as you and your wife that makes all this worthwhile!" The amazing thing to consider is that our invited guests do not understand why we would sponsor a film convention such as FANEX... in the back of their heads they think we must have an ulterior motive or personal agenda, for why else would normal working people sponsor a film festival (something we often wonder ourselves)? By show's end, I believe Freddie and Pam understood our reasons why.

Freddie Francis was a person filled to the brim with funny, interesting stories, of working both in Hollywood and at Hammer. He had this

Ingrid Pitt, Richard Svehla, Martine Beswicke, Veronica Carlson at FANEX 8

Freddie and Pam Francis at FANEX 11

mischievous twinkle in his eye and really seemed to be having a grand time. Being in the Baltimore area, he was trying to get another movie into production which would tie in with Edgar Allan Poe, I believe, and he intended to film here in Baltimore, but the production, I assume, never got off the ground. Martin Scorsese's production company was involved, and the entire autograph line was stunned when Francis had to take a short break to respond to a telephone call from Scorsese concerning the proposed production. Another fabled director, David Lynch, had recently given Freddie a camcorder, a mini-job, that Freddie was using constantly throughout the convention to record his convention experiences. In fact, several photos of Freddie in this book show the director using the camcorder. It was the hope of Susan and me that Freddie would send us a copy of the impromptu video footage shot by an Academy Award winning cinematographer, but to this day we never saw the results of his creative efforts. But perhaps someday in the supplemental section of some DVD... one never knows.

Yvonne Monlaur was a special guest for me, since *Brides of Dracula*, along with *Horror of Dracula*, are my two favorite Hammer films. And Monlaur became the perfect damsel-in-distress to these 10-year-old eyes back in 1960 when the film was first released. Yvonne, who recently lost her husband and who still lives just outside of Paris, was visiting America for the first time and she was very, very nervous about her appearance, afraid few people would remember her. Yvonne was very sweet, very

Wow, Freddie Francis, an Academy Award-winning cinematographer, films FANEX 11!

quiet, and spoke in very broken English. But her shyness and vulnerability made her a favorite because she was "real people" and the aura of stardom had long faded from her life. Once Susan and I boosted her confidence by making her feel very welcome, she brightened up and was amazed at the interest shown in her film work. She graciously signed autographs and spoke at great length with each and every fan. One problem was getting her down to her table... she had been doing the tourist thing all day Saturday in Washington and returned home, hot and tired, the DC summer humidity an energy zapper. I constantly phoned up to her room, and when I finally reached her I was pleading desperately... "Yvonne, you have a long line of people waiting for you to appear. What should I tell them... they are getting more and more restless as the afternoon goes on." Yvonne, quickly pulling herself together, said give her a few minutes, that she would be right down, and she would spend as much time with the fans to autograph every poster or still they have, not to worry. And guess what, she came down refreshed and was enthusiastically greeted and stayed until the final fan had left. Everyone loved her to death. Having such a great time, Yvonne returned the following year, happily learning the hotel would allow her to bring her dog, a little yappy thing that she just adores. But by her second appearance Yvonne was even more confident and understood the routine better and had an even better time.

Barbara Shelly was the grand dame of the Hammer actress set, a beautiful woman who starred in films such as *Dracula—Prince of Darkness* and *Quatermass and the Pit/20 Million Years to Earth* back in the middle 1960s. Barbara's background was acting, the stage, but she did some modeling as did many of the other Hammer Glamour Queens. Barbara accepted our offer to appear at our show based upon the rave recommendation

Yvonne Monlaur and Veronica Carlson on stage at Classic FilmFest

from Christopher Lee who told her we treated him right by providing an entourage, security, a huge suite, etc. Barbara, who communicated to us via a third party until quite close to show time, was expecting the same treatment as we accorded Christopher Lee. However, after two money-losing years in Crystal City, Virginia, we had to adhere to a very strict budget. When Barbara and her sister arrived by car at the front of the hotel, I was luckily free to meet the ladies and accompany them to their room. When assistant Barry Murphy and I took them to their room, I could sense something was wrong... I looked outside the window and it overlooked the over-crowded pool area. Outside was very noisy and occupants of this room felt like they were living in a fish bowl. Barbara had insisted on a quiet room, so we knew we had to find another room pronto. To be honest, the second room offered by the hotel staff was still inadequate, but the third room was the charm. It was a regular room, not a suite, so I felt I had already lost points with Barbara, and adding

Barbara Shelley at the FANEX 15 Laemmle Awards

to my embarrassment was the ordeal of parading the ladies through the hotel from one room to another, both of them totally exhausted. Thus, a rough start was experienced by all! However, after this point I dare say that Barbara had a simply marvelous time meeting and greeting her fans. On her own she volunteered to speak off-the-cuff after the screening of her movies, sharing intimate anecdotes and reflections of working with other actors and directors. When she faced the autograph lines (for which she signed everything without charge), she willingly stayed well beyond her agreed upon appearance times, and her one hour Question and Answering session evolved into two hours or more. In other words, people during the show came up to me and said Barbara Shelley was one of the best FANEX guests we had ever had. Of course, we cannot pick favorites, but Barbara did everything expected of her, plus more, and when she appeared, she was the personification of culture and class. After a rocky start, the convention staff and its operation won her over, and she even shared the fact that because of her FANEX experience she is considering writing her autobiography in the future.

Barbara Shelley with her security team, Phil Holthaus and Leo Dymowski—they get the glory, we pay the bills.

Perhaps the real coup of our convention existence was enticing Christopher Lee to appear at our super-show, Monster Rally, back in 1999, right before his career re-ignited into high gear with major appearances in both *Lord of the Rings* and *Star Wars Episode II: Attack of the Clones.* Susan had another clever idea. Christopher Lee's autobiography was available in England in multiple hardback and paperback versions, but never was an America edition published. Enter Midnight Marquee Press who wrote and offered to publish an American edition. Taking several months for the legal work to be ironed out, a deal was struck with Lee's British agent, Cat Ledger. Up until now, we never contacted Lee personally, but Cat told us Mr. Lee expects you to phone him at such and such a time, on such and such a day. When that time arrived to phone, I was nervous thinking that this first impression would be a pivotal one, that I better not blow it (even though the book deal was agreed upon by all parties). When I phoned, I spoke directly to Lee who answered the phone and promptly informed me he was in the middle of his dinner, could I please phone him back in about half an hour. What would be ironic comic timing, whenever I phoned him in the future, two times out of three, I caught he and his wife eating, and my dinner interruptions became an ongoing theme.

During that first telephone conversation, which I will never forget, Mr. Lee spun stories and anecdotes and generally took the position of lecturer to my student, but I was a totally enraptured student enjoying every nuance of "the lesson." The conversation lasted almost an hour, and I spoke at most five minutes, mostly responding with "I agree" and "of course, as we agreed" and "no, no, no, you got my word on that!" But the essence of the conversation was Lee's stressing "promotion" as far as the success of the book goes. I of course countered with, promotion, say, we sponsor a film convention, so why don't we premiere the publication with your appearance at the show next summer?!!! Well, it never was that smoothly expressed and Mr. Lee's acceptance was not immediate, but for a person praising the virtues of promotion, how could he say no?

Mr. Lee wanted to spend some time in New York City before coming down to Washington, and at his request, we arranged a New York City book signing at the Virgin Megastore. In hindsight, this turned out to be a marketing error. First of all, not enough copies of the book were ordered by the store's management (against our protestations) and all available copies were sold out half an hour before the signing began. With Christopher Lee in attendance, no books, and long lines, security lost control (according to Mr. Lee himself) and the management said Mr. Lee will sign any video, DVD or CD related to him, as well as the books. Of course this was supposed to be exclusively our book signing, but all this broke down immediately. Many people who attended the New York signing no longer felt it necessary to attend Monster Rally, so we lost money on this New York proposition. To further add salt to the wound caused by the bookstore, Christopher Lee finished his Virgin Megastore experience when the management there offered him a free buying spree, having been given "carte blanche" by the store managers to take whatever he wanted. But unknown to Mr. Lee, the manager called us directly at the Crystal City hotel and wanted to bill his total buying expenses to our convention; well, Sue, who was so tired and didn't know what to say, finally agreed to split the bill.

Mr. Lee, taking the train from New York to Washington, was expecting to meet me at the station, and I brought along the head of Team Lee (his security team), Phil Holthaus. Unfortunately, I met his traveling companions but none of us could find Christopher Lee, who had jumped on a golf craft to retrieve his luggage. Desperately splitting up and scouring the massive Victoria Station, we finally gave up and returned to the limo to find Mr. Lee waiting patiently, wearing a touristy straw hat to protect his face from the sun and heat. It was literally a dream come true, but as I extended my hand, he extended his... and we made initial contact and all was well with the world. Now since one new traveling companion was offered a ride in Mr. Lee's limo, the limo was hopelessly overcrowded, and with my six foot-two inch frame trying to squeeze past Mr. Lee's six foot-six inch frame, we became quite intimate faster than expected.

Arriving at the hotel and ducking in through the special security entrance, I helped Mr. Lee and his gorgeous wife, Gitte, up to their room, a nice-sized suite. Mr. Lee was, as always, fascinating and a perfect guest and friend. "Svehla, is that a Czech name?" and answering it was, he continued, "Have you ever been to Prague... it's a beautiful city." He then spoke of some of his war experiences tied to Eastern Europe and simply mesmerized with his vast knowledge, experiences and insight. Mr. Lee is far more intelligent than the average actor and his mind reminds sharp as a tack, remembering everything with crystal clear clarity.

The next day, in preparing for the first autograph session Friday evening, Mr. Lee was dismayed at the fiasco at the Virgin Megastore and how the entire autograph process was handled. He told me, "Gary, first of all, there can be no photographs, it takes up far too much time. We must cut all the photos!" But our security team had thought everything through and we felt we could offer the fans a chance to get a book signed, shake Mr. Lee's hand and take a quick photo as he signs (not posing behind the table which would take too much time). I told Mr. Lee, trust us on this, let's try it Friday night, and if it doesn't work, we would adjust on Saturday and Sunday. Thanks to the efforts of Team Lee coordinator Phil Holthaus, the autograph session went off without a hitch and Mr. Lee was so pleasantly shocked at how well our autograph sessions ran compared to the negative experience in New York that he allowed the photo sessions to remain. Because of his faith in our security team, he loosened up and had fun meeting his fans and speaking to each and every one. I was to the left of Mr. Lee for all three signings, and everyone was having the time of their life.

What was wonderful was that at the signings on Saturday and Sunday, Mr. Lee, perhaps to rest his hand and to offer something special to the fans, built a tea break into the autographing proceedings where he simply stopped to enjoy a cup of tea, chatting informally to the fans assembled, answering questions and making the very formal structure of the autographing procedure something much more intimate and personal. Mr. Lee loosened up so much Sunday, that the very few people who remained after most of the crowd left, were able to form a circle about the front of Mr. Lee's autographing table and simply stand around and chat (and one or two had camcorders and made video recordings), almost one-on-one. It was an incredible experience demonstrating the fact that if handled properly (his last convention appearance was at Fangoria 10 years earlier where things also got out of hand when a fan rushed him), Christopher Lee was willing to get close and personal with the attending fans. This was demonstrated when his hour-long Question and Answer session evolved into over two hours of on-stage talk (and he even sang opera for the assembled masses). When Phil and Team Lee got him back up to his suite, he stood outside his door and held court for another half hour or so.

Forry Ackerman, Joyce Broughton, Michael Ripper and Christopher Lee at the opening ceremony at Monster Rally

On the final day of the show, Mr. Lee, who owned several older science fiction/fantasy hardcovers, wanted to raise some money for his personal charity, and wanted to find out what the books were worth. Mr. Lee called forth Phil Holthaus, and with one extended finger, smiled and pointed, "Sit down *here*." Phil said his knees were shaking when

Team Lee: John Miller, Dan Miller, Jack Bassett, Mr. Lee, Phil Holthaus, Ryan Christ, Jimmy Grossik and Dan McCoy

he sat down. Mr. Lee then told Phil, "I need to see Gary *now*. Can you find him for me?" Phil breathed a sigh of relief and fetched me and took me back to Mr. Lee's suite (sounds like a variation of many Hammer Dracula movies) and Mr. Lee asked if there is a dealer who could appraise the value of his books. I immediately thought of a vendor who supported all our shows, one hell of a nice guy, Sandy, of Bump in the Night Books. Mr. Lee sent me out to the convention floor to bring Sandy back to his suite. When I gave Sandy the "scoop," his jaw dropped and he got a friend to watch his table. Later, after completing their business, Sandy told me this was one of the greatest moments of his life, being a "broker" for Christopher Lee! Having achieved that pinnacle, Sandy soon closed Bump in the Night Books and returned to his former career... law!

By the end of the show, due mainly to brisk book sales and proper handling by Phil Holthaus and Leo Dymowski, Mr. and Mrs. Lee are enthusiastic about the entire experience, and one of the last bits of information Christopher shares with me is that he is hoping to hear from his American agent about the prospect of his appearing in a movie version of his favorite novel of all times, *The Lord of the Rings*, hoping to snare a major supporting role as a wizard! He is very enthusiastic over the scope

Christopher Lee has a cup of tea and talks with lucky fans during his book signing at Monster Rally.

of the production, the budget raised, the creative team involved and he is excited that he, then at age 77, might be part of a major blockbuster motion picture. We wished him luck and a healthy future.

It would have been wonderful to have hosted Peter Cushing at one of our shows, and even though we received a wonderful hand-written response declining our invitation, due to health reasons, just the fact that we heard from perhaps Hammer's greatest acting talent was something very, very special to us. However, Mr. Cushing's secretary of 35 years, Joyce Broughton, flew over from England to attend Monster Rally where we debuted the U.S. editions of Peter Cushing's autobiographies we had published. Joyce is a darling lady, soft-spoken and caring. Fans were honored to have her share her memories of Peter Cushing with them. We also came close to hosting Hammer producer Michael Carreras, but his declining health and death ended those hopes only months away from his convention appearance.

Sadly, even with all the talk of Hammer Rising from the Grave with expensive remakes of all their movies, this is now, and that was *then*. As spoken on our convention stage, Hammer Film Productions were specific people working together at a specific time making movies in a specific

Mr. Lee accepts his Laemmle Award at Monster Rally.

way. Producers can remake *The Devil Rides Out* or *The Creeping Unknown*, casting the film with new acting talent, hiring new screenwriters and directors, etc., but Hammer was Carreras and Hinds, Sangster and Francis,, Cushing and Lee, Carlson and Monlaur, Fisher and Baker, etc. Unfortunately, FANEX never hosted Terence Fisher, Peter Cushing or Michael Carreras, and it is doubtful we will ever host Roy Ward Baker, Anthony Hinds and other Hammer luminaries. But since 1987, we hope we have made our FANEX conventions an American haven for a reunion of all Hammer talent, allowing them to be meeted and greeted by adoring American fans, allowing them to experience American hospitality first hand. This book is a written record of those public appearances that Hammer actors, directors, screenwriters and musical composers made here in the Baltimore/Washington area. Meeting these people and getting to know them a little better is a dream-come-true for me, but now, for everyone who was or was not there, *Memories of Hammer* is another chance to understand, a little better, the heart, soul, humor and humanity behind Hammer.

Gary J. Svehla
January 2002

REPRINT INTRODUCTION

Many things have occurred since we published the first edition back in 2002. We did a few more small scale FANEX conventions before we had to face the fact that larger conventions with many modern guests and huge dealers rooms forced us to face the fact we were like the dinosaurs. Our time had passed and we were facing extinction.

Fans can't afford to travel as much, plus the travel restrictions since 9/11 make traveling a grueling experience, and not an experience we are willing to put aging film stars of the past through. And while we understand that actors and other film talent do not want dealers to profit from their signatures, we just find the whole signing-for-money distasteful. FANEX fans were truly at the show to meet the people who brought them so much pleasure through their work. To us the cherished memories are those moments talking to Freddie Francis about shooting *Dune* or to Robert Wise about working with Julie Andrews or listing to Roger Corman and his wife discuss living on the East or West Coast during her stint at NYU. A signature from someone we meet for 20 seconds is worthless—to us anyway. Fortunately for those stars hawking their signature, most people don't share our objections.

However, before FANEX died we did manage to bring over Freddie Francis and Edward De Souza to the U.S. We felt bad the crowds were so small.

Gary and Susan Svehla with Christopher and Gitte Lee following the Laemmle Awards. This photo hangs over our fireplace—a moment we will not forget.

Ingrid Pitt, Val Guest, Yolande Donlan, Veronica Carlson, James Bernard and Martine Beswicke with Gary Svehla in his wheelchair. An exhausted Susan and a ready-to-party Richard peek out from behind.

We thought having guests who had never done a U.S. show before would help draw crowds. But once again we were wrong. But our regular stalwart attendees had a wonderful time and got to spend some quality time with both Hammer stars, who gave wonderful talks and answered questions for as long as people wanted to ask them. Like all the other Hammer stars we have met, they were truly kind and so appreciative of their fans.

Sadly, we have also lost many of our past guests and others are in failing health. John Agar, Acquanetta, William Marshall, Peggy Moran, Freddie Francis, Val Guest, James Bernard, Lucille Lund, Robert Wise, Beverly Garland, Janet Leigh, Sam Arkoff, Robert Clarke, even Forry Ackerman, they have all gone to that big soundstage in the sky.

Fortunately, we have most of their guest talks on videotape and are in the process of producing a series of documentaries which feature many of our guests discussing their film careers.

—Susan Svehla
January, 2009

Joyce Broughton and Veronica Carlson at Monster Rally

Memories of Hammer

35

JAMES BERNARD

James Bernard composed many of Hammer's most impressive musical scores, including *Horror of Dracula, Frankenstein Must Be Destroyed, Dracula Has Risen from the Grave, Dracula—Prince of Darkness, The Devil Rides Out, Kiss of the Vampire, The Damned, The Hound of the Baskervilles, Quatermass II, The Curse of Frankenstein, X—The Unknown* and *She*. Mr. Bernard was a delightful guest, charming and warm and so appreciative of his American fans. He died this past summer, July 12, 2001. This question and answer was conducted by Bill Littman.

Start at the beginning. When did you first become interested in music?

I first became interested in music from when I can remember I was a little tiny boy and I would play about in my nursery. I can remember there was an old upright and I used to play about on it and made terrible noises on it and [I] begged my parents for music lessons. When I was at school I studied the piano. I thought I was going to be a concert pianist because I was the best pianist in school. Of course, as soon as you leave school you find there are lots of other players who are infinitely better than you are.

    At the same time I was getting very attracted by the idea of composing and at my—what we call a public school, but really a private school—it was the same school at which Christopher Lee was educated. It's called Wellington College and it was really founded by—I'm digressing but to let you know a little of its background—it was founded by Prince Albert, the husband of Queen Victoria, for the sons of Army officers. My father was an army officer and I imagine Christopher's was too. He was there just before I was.

    At that school, although we were all supposed to be military, there was a very strong interest in music and theatre and drama and I used to act in school plays.

    Benjamin Britten [1913-1976, famous British composer whose work includes many compositions for the BBC] happened to come to the school, that was in my last year of school before I went into the Air Force. He'd just written his great first opera *Peter Grimes*. Well, our art master, was simply teaching at the school during the course of WWII. He was a brilliant set designer. He used to design sets for the opera before the

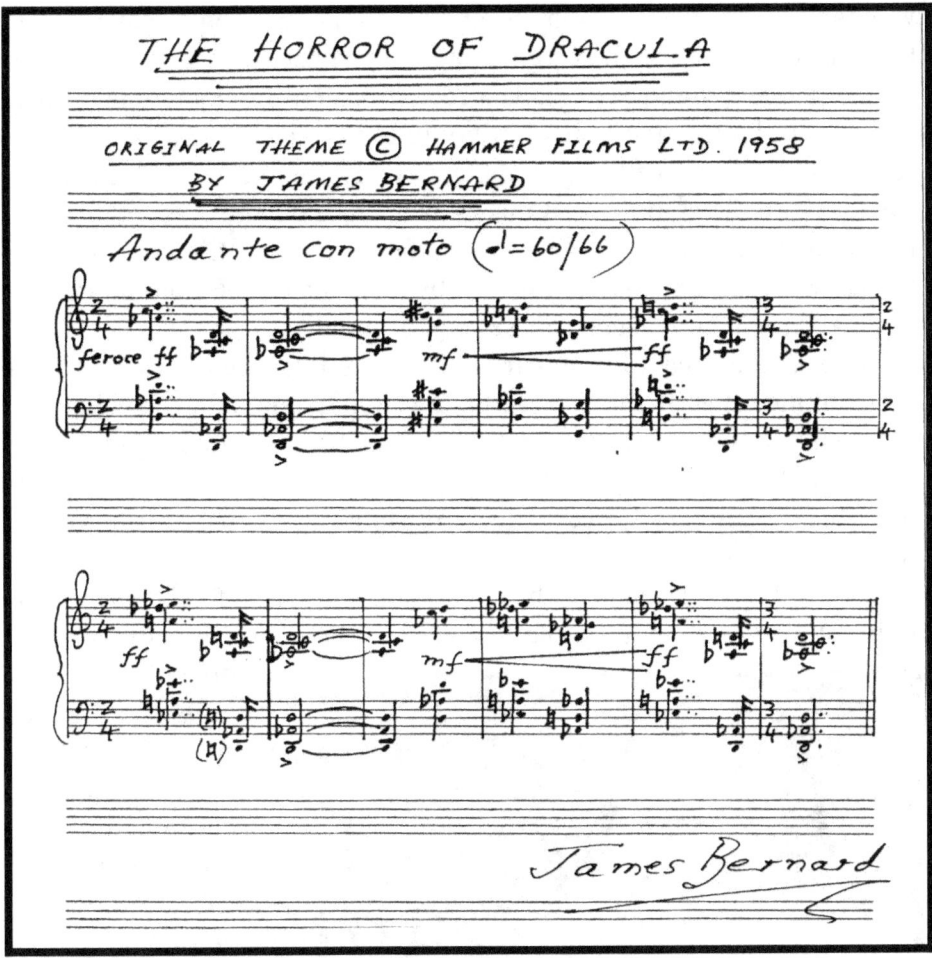

war. So, Ben Britten came to the school to talk to him and, naturally, he wanted to meet the boys who were considered promising in the line of music. So, I was brought to meet him.

I struck up a good friendship with him, I loved his music and still do. That's what really sort of got me going. That was how I started.

I gave him a couple of pieces I'd written for an inter-house music competition and I composed a piece for two pianos and an odd array of percussion. He helped me with this. I had a lot of boys in my house who wanted to take part. None of them could really play, so we had an array of percussion. That was my first interest in percussion because we use a lot in my film scores.

I do remember we invented a percussion instrument because we had one more boy than instrument. So Ben Britten said, "Well, we have to invent something. Let's have a little walk along the drive through the woods." So, we were looking to find anything that would make a noise that we could bang against something. He picked up two stones and he hit them together and they made a sort of flash of light and one of them broke. So, he thought that's not going to be the instrument. Then he saw a bit of drainpipe lying in the gutter. So, he picked that up and he tried it [with the stone] and it made a very nice clanging sound. So, we invented an instrument called stone and drainpipe. I still have my score to that, which is signed as composed by me, edited by Benjamin Britten. So, that's a much treasured possession of mine.

I spent four years in the Air Force doing intelligence work, all top secret at the time. It's not so secret now. Oddly enough, Chris Lee was also in intelligence. I didn't know him at the time. So, during that time I wanted to be a composer [and] I wanted to be an actor. Finally, I thought there are lots of actors, but not so many composers, so, I better go into that [composing].

I was always in touch with Ben Britten and I used to go see him and write him. I said, what is the first thing I do when I come out of the

Air Force? He said the first thing you must do is to go and get a basic grounding in the rudiments of music. You must go to the Academy of Music or the College of Music—one of the best ones. And, that's what I did. I came out of four years in the Air Force and went to the College of Music. There I studied with a very eminent composer, who would be a hundred if he were still alive, called Herbert Howells [1892-1983], who was a wonderful English composer. He wasn't doing a lot at that time, but he was very celebrated in England.

After I'd done my study there, he was a very gentle teacher, I simply learned the kind of rules of composing there, which are found to be broken. After I left him I went to work for Ben Britten as an assistant for a year, and that's when I really learned the kind of hard work that happens in composing. You think of your notes or tune or whatever, then putting it all down, and, that's where the hard work comes in. It's lovely when you have the inspiration or the flash or something, but then you have all that work.

Your credits list Seven Days to Noon.

I didn't do the music. I think the film came out in 1951 and we got an Oscar for it. Well, I shared a house with writer Paul Dehn, now alas, dead. He died in the 1970s [Sept. 30, 1976]. He became a very eminent screen writer. His last screenplay was *Murder on the Orient Express* [1974] for which he was nominated for an Oscar, although he didn't actually win. Robert Towne won the award for *Chinatown*. Anyway, Paul and I shared a house and we were crossing over Waterloo Bridge in London on a beautiful evening, in a taxi on our way to the railway station at Waterloo. It looked like a Caillebotte painting. Everything was beautiful, there were no clouds in the sky, the buildings were lovely. So, suddenly we turned to each other and said wouldn't it be terrible if this lovely London were blown up by an atom bomb? So, we had this idea for a story for a film and it turned into *Seven Days to Noon*. We sold it, the original screen story. Paul, at that time, was a actor rather than a writer. Later he became a screen writer and we sold it as a screen story. And, we won, to our amazement, an Oscar that year. We each got one for the Best Original Screenplay of that year.

The first thing we knew about it was when we bought the *Evening Standard* and we saw this headline about it. We had no idea. Nobody had told us. Everybody says to me, did you go over for the ceremony and all that. But, in those days, back in the '50s, they didn't have such a big thing. All that happened with our Oscar ceremony was that a member of the Motion Picture Arts and Sciences Academy rang us up and said, "I have your Oscars for you. Can I come over and deliver them?" We said, "Yes, please come tomorrow night and have a drink." So, he arrived in a London taxi with a big cardboard box and came in and said, "How do you do?" We gave him a large gin and tonic and gave ourselves each one and took out these two Oscars and that was our Oscar ceremony.

How did you begin with Hammer?

My first commercial work as a composer was writing music for radio plays, which was the thing much more than the television, because this was in the late '40s, early '50s and television hadn't really got started in England after the war. Radio was the big thing that was the equivalent of television today, and everybody listened. In those days we had a—we still do—have a channel, it's now called Radio Three, which specialized in classical plays like Shakespeare and Marlowe and newly written plays. So, I got into doing music for their plays. The head of drama for the BBC in those days, which was interesting, was Val Gielgud who was the elder brother of the eminent Sir John Gielgud, who, incidentally, is a friend of mine. And, Val was his brother and head of drama and I did a play for them. I did the music for a play—to show how long ago it was, we played the music during the actual broadcast of this radio play. It wasn't prerecorded or anything, so we couldn't do any of that timing.

That was my first work with John Hollingsworth, who, of course, became music director of Hammer Films. So, I continued to do various scores for radio and John knew I was longing to get into film. He rang me up one day and said, "Jimmy, Hammer is doing a film called *The Quatermass Experiment*." [US title: *The Creeping Unknown*, 1956] And, it was going to have a score by a composer called John Hotchkiss—I never knew him but he was doing quite a lot at that time but he'd been taken ill and Hammer rang up John and said, "John, have you anybody who can do a score? We need somebody quickly, John Hotchkiss can't do it." And, John, who'd just done a play with me and luckily still had tapes of it, said, "I think I have somebody who might be able to do the job." The play we had just done was a kind of restoration. It was written by John Webster in the late 17th-Century, early 18th-Century, I don't quite know the dates, after Shakespeare. But, it was a wonderful play, *The Duchess of Malfi*, which is a sort of horror play and it had an all-star radio cast. I can remember The Duchess of Malfi was played by Peggy Ashcroft, who was one of our great stage stars. And, one of the other main parts was played by Paul Scofield. So, it was an all-star cast and it needed a kind of horror score because it's a horror play and everybody ends up dead—they get stabbed or poisoned or the Duchess gets tortured. It's an appalling story.

So, I'd done this score for strings and percussion and John hurried down to see Tony Hinds at Bray presumably, and Tony said, "Yes, try him." So, I was to try and do it for £100, take it or leave it. I said, "Yes, I'd do it for nothing" and that's how I started.

The use of strings is really nerve-wracking in Quatermass Experiment. *The end comes to a wonderful build.*

It's called "Face the Unknown" I think, and, when the monster is up in the rafters or whatever in Westminster Abbey and they electrocute him, I was trying to think of an effect to use because Hammer never used an electronic instrument. Indeed, in those days they liked to have symphony sounds, symphony orchestra and, actually, that was strings and percussion. I was trying to think of a noise to go with this slaughter of this poor creature in the roof of the abbey and I suddenly sort of thought of the idea which had been used before and probably been used a great deal since, of asking all the strings to draw their bows up and down on the wrong side of the bow, on the very short bit. And it makes the most extraordinary noise. It's not musical at all, I suppose... as a sort of sound effect. This is on the other side of the bridge and it doesn't make any actual music notes, it makes all kinds of sort of squealing and extraordinary noises from the basses, sort of weird squealing. So, that's what they did and I simply wrote in the score. I put some sort of up and down across the stave and I said draw the bows across the wrong side of the strings and they did it. And, that's what made that kind of noise.

I had no idea that was made by the orchestra at all.

Well, I think it's a mixture, there were other sound effects.

Most of your scores seem to be toward the creatures instead of the humans.

I think so, yes.

Did you find science fiction gave you leave to experiment with different sounds?

In those first three films I did for Hammer which were *Quatermass Experiment*, *X—The Unknown* and *Quatermass II*, I was only allowed to use strings because John Hollingsworth knew I could use them effectively, and percussion, because I had done those on the radio. I was fairly limited, but it did seem a very suitable medium, the strings and percussion, to use for that type of film, science fiction. It was only when we got to *The Curse of Frankenstein* that I said to John Hollingsworth, "John, can't I now be allowed to, could you trust me, could I be allowed to use trombones or something else or some woodwinds?" He said, "Okay go ahead," and so I did. But I think these first three films didn't lend themselves to lyrical music, or I didn't think so at the time. There was no strong romantic interest, was there? It was very, very down-to-earth science fiction and brilliantly done by Val Guest. So, that's why the scores had to be like that, without much human feeling, I guess.

The first lyrical piece is in The Curse of Frankenstein. *There's a section when Frankenstein and his assistant try to cut the man down. There is an incredible string sound. It wasn't electronic?*

Brian Donlevy and Richard Wordsworth in *The Quatermass Experiment*

You know, I can't remember. I'll have to look at the score and see what I did. It was probably string harmonies where you can go much higher. I guess it was probably that. It obviously needed to be a bit like classical music, so I think I was modeling myself on Schubert. I was thinking of a sort of tune that Schubert might have written.

The man who rang Anvil Studios and was the recording engineer, Ken Cameron, was a charming man and now long dead and he loved that tune. And, ever afterward whenever I worked with him, the last time was *Frankenstein and the Monster from Hell*, he'd always greet me by singing dee da da dum da da dee and he loved that little tune. So, one day now that we're doing some records of it, I might be able to redo it. That was the story of that little tune.

I have you down for Pacific Destiny *[1956] and* Across the Bridge *[1957] for Rank.*

Across the Bridge, I don't know if anyone's seen it, it was directed by Ken Annakin, who went on to direct some very big films, *Those Magnificent Men in Their Flying Machines* [*The Longest Day, Battle of the Bulge, Call of the Wild*] and he went on to direct a lot of films for Disney.

This was a film [*Across the Bridge*] that starred Rod Steiger as a criminal on the run and it was a very good film, a very good script written by an English writer named Denis Freeman. I remember it had quite a moving score in that, because this criminal, who was on the run, Rod Steiger, was deserted by everybody because he's such an unpleasant man. He goes straight to Mexico. There is a bridge, I don't know where it would be because it is a rail bridge from the US into Mexico and the borderline was halfway across the bridge. The only one that Rod Steiger had left who loved him was his beloved dog, and so they managed to catch the dog and tied the dog halfway across the bridge. So, it was the dog who lured him from Mexico where they caught him when he rescued the dog.

In those days Julian Bream, the great guitarist, was willing to do film scores, and he was quite a friend of mine. So, he played the guitar in that. We had a guitar tune which was turned into a theme tune called *Across the Bridge* and was recorded by a well-known English singer called Vera Lynn, who was known as the Forces Sweetheart in WWII. She's still going strong. She's in her middle to late 70s.

The other one, *Pacific Destiny*, that was an independent production. It wasn't a Rank. Then I had Julian Bream again. It was set in the South Seas and we had to have South Seas–type music.

Tell us about Quatermass II *[US title* Enemy from Space, *1957], the tune Vera Day dances to.*

It was just a scene in a pub, so, we had to have some pub music and an Irish jig. I looked at it the other day and I thought it was quite convincing.

Dracula *[US title:* Horror of Dracula*], probably your most famous score. Were you under contract at that time?*

No, there was no contract to Hammer. They always liked to just ask one for an individual film. John Hollingsworth was the boss on the music side. He was a very good friend of mine. I used to think, "Why didn't

John ask me to do this one?" but I suppose he had to vary it a bit.

Can you tell us about your schedule?
About four weeks, if I was lucky enough, I might get four and a half or five, and sometimes only three and a half. It was real hell when doing it, because I always did my own orchestration, because to me orchestrations are very much a part of the composing. Only you can know the sort of sound you're after. There've been a few times in my movie scores when I have used an orchestration

The Curse of Frankenstein

like in the rock tune in *The Damned* [US Title: *These Are the Damned*, 1965], because I don't know how to score rock music. On the whole, I did all my own scoring. It was really a hard, a hard task because, okay, you'd seen the film. You had your music breakdown. You went down to the studio. You saw the film reel by reel. I'd probably seen it through about twice before, that when they were just showing it and getting it together. But, you can't really start on the music until the film is pretty well into its final cut, because of all the measuring and talking for the actor on the screen. So, then you had a music breakdown.

The director would be there if he were interested. Terry Fisher was never interested. He was so nice and charming and gentle. I used to worry that he didn't come to these, but he said, "Oh, well, my dear boy, we're happy with what you do. I don't know anything about music, so you go ahead and do it." Tony Hinds always came. He would see reel one and we would say now where in that reel do we need music. And we'd argue about it and we'd come to a conclusion and the task of the assistant editor [was] to write notes down everywhere in each reel. Here, there was to be music—exactly when it started, exactly when it ended—everything that happened during that sequence, when dialogue happened, when it stopped. So that you could bring the music down or hold it static. Then they would send me these lists of times and you went ahead from there. Sometimes I couldn't remember what happened in a particular sequence then I would ring up the editor, and they were very helpful. They would say, "Oh don't you remember, he gets up and walks across the room," or whatever. So, you could always ring them up and ask for help.

Then, you were just at it. There you were, in my case, with my piano and blank page of manuscript and a terrible feeling of panic because you'd think, "Oh my God, three and a half, four weeks, I've got to write the stuff and tailor it to the actor and orchestrate it and have it all ready." So, in my case, it was working round the clock. I cut out all social events, everything, and I just worked round the clock. Sometimes, I'd only have three or four hours sleep in a night. Sometimes I did only finish one the morning of the recording. The copyist would be down there at the studio copying the bits which we were going to do in the afternoon. In those days, there wasn't photocopying which there now is. The copyist had to really do every [page]. If you had six rows of violins he had to do all six. So, everybody was working flat out.

Where did you write?

I wrote at home. I used to live in this house with my friend Paul Dehn in a little house in Chelsea. Which, I still pass often after moving back to Chelsea after living in Jamaica.

It was quite cozy, one could work at home. I had very kind neighbors who didn't mind the noises emanating and one of them was a very eminent musician himself. He was called Dr. Thornton Lovehouse and he was a expert on Bach and he played the harpsichord and was a professor at the Royal College of Music. He must have hated the noise that he heard coming out, but he was terribly nice about it. I'm just digressing for a moment but he was this sweet elderly man, just like you think a sort of charming music professor of Bach might be, and he had this wife called Irene who was charming but she was very anti-booze. She didn't allow any drinking in the house. Dear old Thornton Lovehouse was dying for a drink all the time. So, if ever Paul and I saw him walking, we'd say, "Like to come in for a drink?" and he'd say, "Oh, yes, please," and rush in and we'd pour him a triple dry martini.

Bryan Forbes and Brian Donlevy in *Quatermass II*

Your score of Horror of Dracula *has a full orchestra and wonderful musicians.*

We always had top musicians. That was a luxury. In the early scores, the ones with strings only, John Hollingsworth, at the time, was chief conductor, or one of two, of the Royal Ballet. So, he used the string section of the Royal Ballet orchestra and then later on he branched out and we would always have players from all the symphony orchestras. I was in awe of them. I used to be terrified because, I'd never been taught orchestration, I sort of had to pick it up. I was terrified that what I'd written was going to be absolute nonsense to the players and that they were going to laugh at the score. I'd sigh with relief when they actually played it and it would sound all right. Especially when we got to *Horror of Dracula* and the fuller orchestra and brass and I thought, "Oh, God, is it all going to be awful?" They were such wonderful players they could play anything in any case, but they were all so nice and charming and encouraging. But, I was always kind of frightened of them. I really was. We did those early scores at some lovely sound studios. They were called Anvil. They were where all the early Hammer scores were recorded and they had wonderful sound there. I'm not sure if they exist anymore or not.

"Lucy at Rest" is a lovely piece of music, are you going to record it?

Well, I'm about to do that if can do some more recording of *Horror of Dracula* including those few quiet bits in the later Dracula films. I did get more of a chance to bring in the element of romance, which, is really what I love doing. I'm just sort of an old soft romantic at heart and I really love to write a romantic score. But, in these early scores they seemed to think I could do all the sort of horror stuff and the tension. So, it's like being an actor—you get so excited at times, and that's why I think I loved doing the score to *She*, which had a lot of horror and a strong romantic and fantasy element. That was one of my favorite scores. Any chance I get today to indulge in romance, I grasp happily.

She, the main title seems to split between romance and native music. That's annoying.

I must say that was not my doing, that was the powers that be who did that. When you've written your score you don't know what they're going to do and they can play around with it. I agree with you, I think it's a bit irritating to keep cutting between.

Tell us about Nor the Moon by Night *[US title:* Elephant Gun, *1959].*

That was a Rank picture. They were latching on to the idea we should have a theme song, which went with the title of the film. So, we were told to do a song called *Nor the Moon by Night*. There's not really much story to tell about it. I did a sort of African feel, a simple little tune.

The Stranglers of Bombay's *[1960] main title, is it based on Indian music?*

I imagine it must be. I haven't seen that movie for ages. They don't seem to show it on television. I suppose I took some Indian music and listened to it, but it was my own idea. I left myself be influenced. When I did *Elephant Gun* I had to have African sounding music. So, you have to be able to turn yourself into different nationalities. I think in *The*

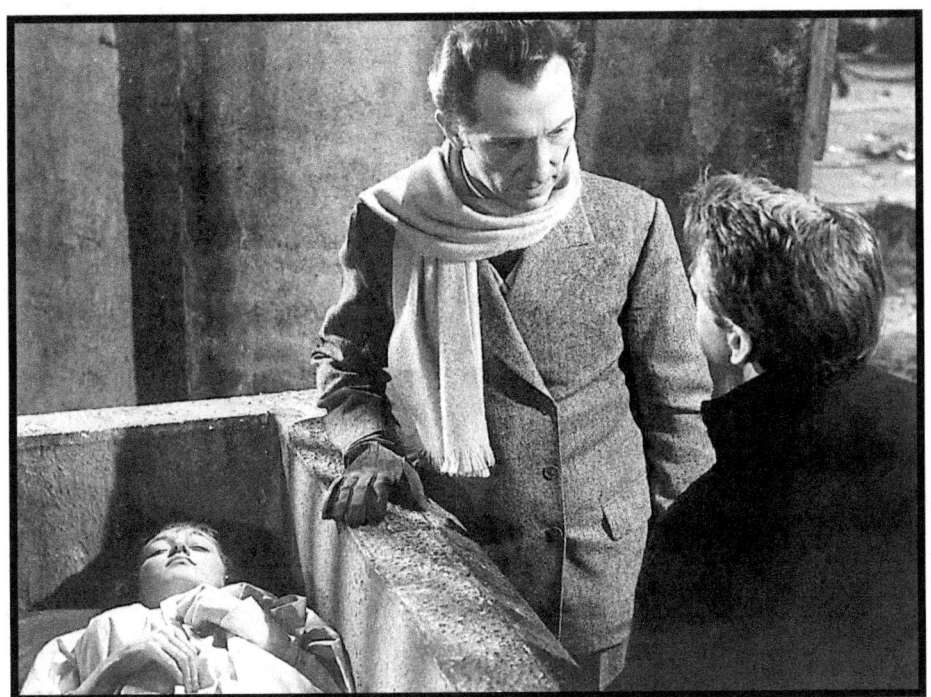
Carol Marsh, Peter Cushing and John Van Eyssen in *Horror of Dracula*

Stranglers of Bombay, that's what I did. In *She* in that opening in the nightclub there again they didn't want to use existing music. So, I had to listen to belly dance music. Phil Martell said you should use some kind of wind instrument. It was sort of related to an oboe. It was a kind of high clanging sort of oboe, so I used that. I did go down on the set to see how it was fitting. I thought, "Did I really write this? It sounds sort of authentic belly dance music."

Did you know the actors?

I would loved to have known the actors much more, because I've always loved actors. I have quite a few friends who are actors. As the composer on the films, I was called in rather late because the music is the last thing to go on to the films. It has to be, because the film has to be in a finished state so the music can be exactly tailored. They would only ask me down on the set for a particular reason. People are amazed that last night was the first time I'd ever met Veronica Carlson, whom I wrote music for. It happened like that. I did work briefly with Christopher Lee when we worked on the chant in *She*. I wrote the music and Christopher wrote the words. These were the times I might be on the set. Also [when] with *Kiss of the Vampire* [1963], the sort of convention of vampires at the masked ball had to be choreographed. It was choreographed by Leslie Edwards, who was a senior dancer at the Royal Ballet, who was a friend of John Hollingsworth. So, again, we had to have the music for the waltz scene on the piano. But, normally I wouldn't go down when they were shooting a film.

Who played the piano; did you coach the actor?

The person who played the piano was a wonderful pianist, a composer and musician himself, Douglas Gamley. He did several scores for Amicus. He did the piano for me. [Who coached] the actor—Barry Warren, I imagine Phil Martell, or was it John Hollingsworth? It was the last film John did and then he died, he had TB. I wasn't there. He played my piece. I should have been there. I don't know how it was done.

Frankenstein Created Woman *[1965] has a very end of life theme. Was that recently recorded?*

No. We hoped to put it on a subsequent record album, which Silva Screen is planning to make. I have done quite an extended orchestral version. I call it "Christina's Theme" because that was the character's name. One of the frustrating things that would happen during a film score—you think of the theme, I thought of Christina's theme, but then you come to a point where you have the middle section before you come back to the main theme. I thought of a middle section which goes into a major key and it's much more comforting, and there was no time for that in the actual score of *Frankenstein Created Woman*. So, now in the version which I've done for Silva Screen, I hope it will have that middle section.

One of the secondary themes of Dracula Has Risen from the Grave *is supposed to be based on a black mass.*

Yes, I think *Dracula Has Risen from the Grave*, at the end where some of the bells ring out and it's come to a sort of more or less happy conclusion for the time being. It comes in earlier in the film. It's a kind of plainchant tune which I thought I had written, but somebody told me about the use of the traditional [chant] which has been used in film a lot and classical music. Rachmaninoff used to use it in his variation for piano

Ursula Andress dares John Richardson to stab her in order to save the life of another woman.

Metro-Goldwyn-Mayer and Seven Arts Productions present "SHE" in CinemaScope and Color

and orchestra, and I'm told I used that theme at the end of *Dracula Has Risen from the Grave*. I didn't do it consciously and I'm not trying to hide that. I'd like to see [the film again] and compare it and see.

Your last film was The Legend of the Seven Golden Vampires *[AKA* Dracula and the Seven Golden Vampires, *1973].*

The score of *Seven Golden Vampires* was one of those odd things. As you know, it was shot in Hong Kong by Roy Ward Baker, who I saw the other day. He's still going strong, charming. When they came back to England a score had been attached to it by the Shaw Brothers, the Chinese side of that production, and they'd used apparently—I never heard it—a lot of library music that they possessed. Phil Martell heard it and said, "We can't possibly use this, it would be all wrong." And then, by then there was only two and a half weeks to do something before the deadline date and he rang me and said, "Do you think you can do something?" He said, "What we can really do on this occasion is use some bits out of previous scores because we really haven't got time to do an entire score." So, we did. We took part of previous Dracula scores, but I did about 25 or 30 minutes [of] original music including a chime theme which is part of my pretty music.

The Stranglers of Bombay **features mysterious disappearances and grisly deaths.**

What was your favorite score?

I was pleased with *She* because it gave me a script for a wider range of feeling and I have to be pleased with the *Horror of Dracula,* because I think it was one of these times [that] when we were doing it, nobody knew we were making a film which was going to become such a classic, but the muse of cinema if there was such a lady, shown upon us all and it just all worked out wonderfully. [But] I'll say *She* overall.

What makes The Damned so different?

I think the subject was completely different. It was more in line with the very early science fiction ones wasn't it? But, I always tried to do a score which would fit what was needed. I suppose the score had to come out like that because it's what I thought that [that] was what the film demanded. I was slightly in awe of Joseph Losey, as, everybody was. People say he was very difficult to work with. Actually, I had a very good relationship with him, but we worked together extremely happily. I have one little

Jennifer Daniel stumbles into a cult of vampires in *Kiss of the Vampire*.

story about working on that. There was one particular section, I can't remember what exactly, but I think it was one of those scenes with the children in their underground place by the sea where they were kept and we were doing the music which was required for that particular bit. At the end of it, Joe said, "No, I don't think that's quite right. I don't know how to describe it." Directors can never describe what they want because they're not composers or musicians. So, I said, "Okay, Joe, let me think about it." So I went to John Hollingsworth and said, "Whatever can we do?" He said, "I'll tell you what, go to the grand piano"—I wasn't a performer, so I was rather frightened—"and stand by it with your hand near the actual interior working strings of the piano, and when I give you the sign, go plink on one of the strings, any of the strings you like." So, we did that and we did exactly the same music that we'd done before and John did that [sign] and I went plink and at the end we said, "Joe, how's that?" "Perfect, exactly what I want."

Did any film composers influence you?

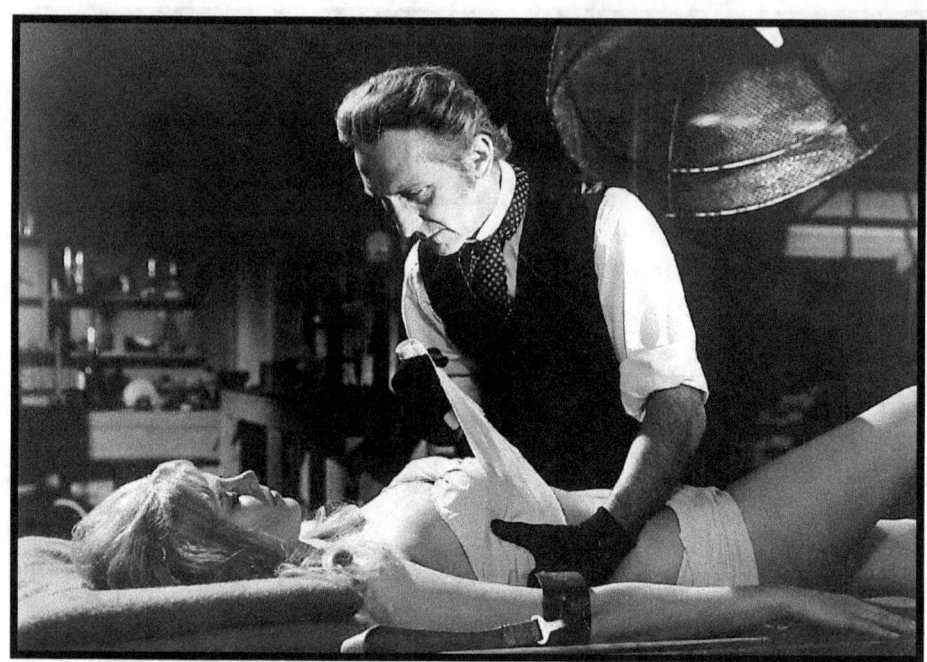

Peter Cushing and Susan Denberg in *Frankenstein Created Woman*

Well, I have certain composers that I love—I'm really eclectic, if that's the word. I love music from all periods and all composers, but I've always loved the romantic composers and I suppose Liszt. I love the music of Liszt, which is highly dramatic and romantic and I love the work of Ben Britten. I love Chopin, I love Mozart, although my music is hardly Mozartian, but I have a wide range.

Are you retired?

Well I'm not really retired. What happened was Hammer was doing very little. When was the *Seven Golden Vampires*, about 74? Well, just to put it briefly, what happened was my great friend Paul Dehn had written what turned out to be his last screenplay, which was *Murder on the Orient Express*. And, just before the premiere of that, it was a very wonderful Royal Garden premiere, he had been diagnosed with cancer of the lung. He always said, "I'm going to die quite early from cancer of the lung, but quite well off because, if I can smoke, I can write. Otherwise, I shall be quite old but I shall be a pauper because I can't write anything." So, he opted for the first option and, it was as he said, he didn't hang on for long. It took two years until it actually climaxed when he did come to an end, because the cancer—they'd kill it in one place and then he'd have

Legend of the Seven Golden Vampires

deep ray, the chemotherapy hadn't come in, but he'd have deep ray and they did an operation, but the cancer was always one jump ahead. So, if there'd been any work during those two years, it would have been really hard for me to do it. I was really looking after Paul and then he died in '76. And then I started going off to the West Indies. It had been a great strain at the time and I had a very great friend, Ken McGregor, who was in a few of the Hammer films. There was a close-up of him in *The Devil Rides Out*. He was an extra in films but he was a very good dancer. In the black mass scene/orgy scene there is a scene where you see him pouring a chalice of blood into the mouth of the unwilling Tanith. Whenever I see that film I think of Ken. Anyway, we used to go to the West Indies a lot, and finally, we bought a house in Jamaica, but that's a whole other story. To cut it short, Ken was murdered in the garden of our house, it was robbery. Jamaica, which I love, has a great drug problem, terrible poverty and terrible things; they happen everywhere. I was in England in '92 and I couldn't get through on the telephone at our house to speak to Ken. He was rather exclusive in those days and didn't like to have anybody up at the house, and I thought, "Is our phone down?" In the tropics things often would go wrong with the lines above ground. I suddenly had the kind of feeling that something had happened to him and I rang up a very good friend of ours. I said, "Have you seen Ken recently?" He said, "No, I haven't. I saw him about three days ago, he should have been down, shouldn't he? Should I go up and see if he's okay?" I said,

Brutal murder in Mobay

By Margaret Morris

KEN McGregor, Jamaican actor, singer, dancer-choreographer and playwright, was brutally murdered at his Copper Hill home in Reading near Montego Bay, on Sunday at about 10 a.m.

McGregor, 55, was found outside the back door by a neighbour who had gone to deliver a message.

Friends say his telephone had rung without an answer for several days but they presumed it was out of order.

The body was discovered face-down and chopped in the back; its bloated condition indicated that he had been dead for days.

A Toyota Corolla and satellite dish equipment were stolen. Police, led by Detective Inspector Morris mounted guard at the house and the body was not removed until Monday afternoon when forensic experts had completed their investigations.

McGregor was regarded as something of a recluse. Except for his two dogs, he lived alone, reading, listening to music and watching films. At the time of his death he employed no regular staff.

The Copper Hill residence, which he co-owned with James Bernard a friend and business associate, was built by hotelier Carmen Pringle when Montego Bay was the mecca of the rich and famous.

McGregor was born in St Mary but neighbours and police did not know the whereabouts of any family. His friend, composer James Bernard, is flying out from London to make the necessary arrangements. Both McGregor and Bernard were active in the Little Theatre Movement in Montego Bay.

McGregor worked as a policeman in Kingston before emigrating to England where he entered the world of show business. He appeared in West End cabaret and musicals, among them 'Finian's Rainbow,' and in the Burton-Taylor epic 'Cleopatra'.

Among the films in which he featured were 'The Wind of Change','House of Mystery', and 'She'.

He appeared in the TV series 'The Saint' with Roger Moore and was a regular in London pantomimes like Robinson Crusoe, Alladin, and Peter Pan.

"Yes, oh please do, Trevor." Trevor went up and he found Ken dead. Slashed to death with machetes. So, I thought, "Hammer horrors, this has caught up with me now." I had to go out to Jamaica, it was August '92, almost exactly two years ago. It was all horrific and shattering and it was purely for robbery. But that was the end of the Jamaica chapter for me. I thought, "Well, Jamaica was finished." It's funny how things can have a good outcome as well as Ken himself used to say to me, "Jimmy, what are you doing spending all your time out lying in Jamaica? You ought to be back in England writing your music. You're wasting your time out here." I think perhaps he was right. Anyway, I got over that tropical half. I always longed to live in the tropics and I lived there for 10 years and I lived it until it all turned sour at the end. So, now to bring you right up to track, I'm back in London, I'm back in Chelsea, very near my last house in Chelsea. I have a lovely apartment in old Chelsea very near the Thames. I've got my beloved grand Steinway piano back, which had been living in Jersey in the Channel Islands with my brother while I was in Jamaica, and I'm working on stuff for Silva Screen and I'm right here. I've seen Roy Skeggs and I've alive and kicking. I was in Hollywood last year, I went to the new Hammer offices and I'm meant to go again later this year, and if they want to use an elderly [composer], I'm here to be used.

TRIBUTE TO JAMES BERNARD
by Steve Vertlieb

Several years ago James Bernard told me that Silva Screen Records in England was planning an album of his music, proposing, among other selections, a suite from the Quatermass series. Jimmy asked my advice, wondering whether or not I thought anyone would be interested in hearing those early themes on an album. I excitedly assured him that I, for one, would salivate at the prospect. He shook his head in bewilderment and seemed profoundly startled. Such was the humility of the man.

James Bernard was a hero to me. For an admirer of symphonic motion picture music he was a legend, a genuine original. As much as Peter Cushing, Christopher Lee, Terence Fisher and Jimmy Sangster, James Bernard's music was an irreplaceable component of the classic Hammer films. More importantly, however, Jimmy was a wonderfully kind and gentle soul, humble and self effacing. The fact that he would admonish friends and acquaintances who called him James or Mr. Bernard was an ever present testament to his total lack of ego or pretension. "Please," he would always say, "just call me Jimmy."

I first met Jimmy in July 1994 at FANEX 8 in Baltimore. We went out of the hotel to an all night restaurant for ice cream with a crowd of fans and admirers. To my joy, Jimmy and I hit it off right away, becoming fast friends. We continued to communicate after the show by letter and by telephone. Every once in a while I'd receive a surprise telephone message from Jimmy. I remember one Sunday morning I was sitting on my living room couch talking with a friend on the telephone when my other line clicked in. I excused

> James Bernard, 75, who composed the eerie musical scores for some of Britain's most famous horror films, died Thursday in London.
>
> The British composer was best known for his work with Hammer Film studios, which made low-budget gothic horror films featuring actors Peter Cushing and Christopher Lee.
>
> During his nearly 40-year career, Bernard composed scores for "The Curse of Frankenstein" (1957), "Dracula" (1958) and "The Devil Rides Out" (1968).
>
> He won an Academy Award, but not for his music. Bernard shared an Oscar in 1951 with Paul Dehn for best motion picture story for "Seven Days to Noon."
>
> —News service reports

James Bernard, Phil Martell and Michael Carreras work on the score for *She*.

myself, putting the first caller on hold, answering the newly incoming call. I nearly fell off the couch when I heard a familiar English voice say, "Hello, Steve, it's Jimmy calling from London." Jimmy would telephone me often, always insisting that he pay the charges. He had a marvelous phone service, he explained, that allowed him to make calls to the United States for pennies so it made little sense for me to telephone him. At least, that's what he said. Even when I called him he'd insist that I hang up and allow him to call me back. Jimmy was a "night person" and would frequently make his telephone calls at midnight or at one o'clock in the morning. Consequently, I'd often hear from him early in the evening, East Coast time.

When his score for the restoration of Murnau's *Nosferatu* finally was released on CD by Silva, I couldn't wait to play it. I remember rushing home from work to collect my mail. I opened up the package excitedly, removed the telephone receiver from its cradle to avoid interruption, put on my stereo headphones and lay on the floor. As the first notes of James Bernard's first major score in years filled my ears, I begin to cry. I was astonished at how fresh and exciting the music was, reminiscent of the best of his work for Hammer, yet vital and exhilaratingly original. As far as I was concerned, the *Nosferatu* score was the finest new film music of the year, surpassing in quality any comparable work by John Williams,

Jerry Goldsmith or James Horner. When the album was done, I went into the bedroom of my apartment and wrote my feelings about the music to Jimmy. I conveyed that this was a brilliant score, one of the finest and most original compositions of his long career. I truly meant it.

About a week later I received a telephone call from England. It was Jimmy, of course. He appeared sincerely stunned by my words of praise for his work and said that he just couldn't wait to write a letter of appreciation. A letter would have simply taken too long to reach me. He had to telephone me to adequately convey his appreciation. I was equally touched by his gratitude and reassured him that he was truly a great artist who had created a remarkable work, for me a brilliant score.

After the critical success of *Nosferatu*, Jimmy had high hopes that his career would be on track, once again. He told me with pride that his romantic themes were his favorites and was confident that I shared his assessment of his artistry. I confess that I lied when I told him that I was most certainly in agreement with his own personal assessment of his work. I chuckled inwardly at the time since I, along with most of his other admirers, felt that Jimmy was better known for his more bombastic vampire themes. After that conversation I took the time to listen carefully to the quieter, more romantic scoring of films such as *Taste the Blood of Dracula*, *Scars of Dracula* and *Frankenstein Must Be Destroyed*. In

Ingrid Pitt, James Bernard and Martine Beswicke at FANEX 8

retrospect I discovered that Jimmy's love themes were among the loveliest, most sensitive sessions I'd ever heard. This was a sweet, tender side of Jimmy I'd never recognized before. My respect and admiration for him increased dramatically after that.

Jimmy's dreams of a major return to film scoring, sadly, never materialized. Despite an all too brief success with *Nosferatu*, writing assignments grew less and less frequent and Jimmy became more and more disheartened. I wrote Elmer Bernstein asking for his advice and help. He wrote back a very kind, thoughtful letter describing himself as a fortunate dinosaur who, miraculously, continued to work despite his own advancing age. He characterized film executives as blindly obsessed by youth, refusing to acknowledge or hire veteran artists in spite of experience and proven track records. Still, he offered the name of several agencies in the Los Angeles area specializing in film music and volunteered their addresses, telephone numbers and contact people. I happily forwarded the information to Jimmy who was profoundly touched by Elmer Bernstein's thoughtfulness.

Archivist, writer and producer Kevin Brownlow was producing a documentary for the Thames Group and Turner Classic Movies on the beginning of the horror cycle, entitled *Universal Horrors*, and he offered the scoring assignment to Jimmy. While most of the sound footage was accompanied by its own original music, all of the silent footage required new background scoring. Jimmy excitedly set about adding his own distinctive signature to the classic visualizations of Tod Browning and Lon Chaney, Sr. The completed scoring was strikingly evocative and richly textured, adding immeasurably to the atmospheric visual text of the televised documentary.

Jimmy was momentarily energized by the work and looked forward to working again with Brownlow. His health began to deteriorate, however, and when the renowned documentarian offered Jimmy an opportunity to score a second film for Thames and Turner Classic Movies on the life of silent screen star Lon Chaney, Jimmy was forced to turn down the lucrative assignment. Surgery, not film work, loomed large on his horizon and ill health seemed to take its physical and emotional toil. Depression, coupled with exhaustion, seemed 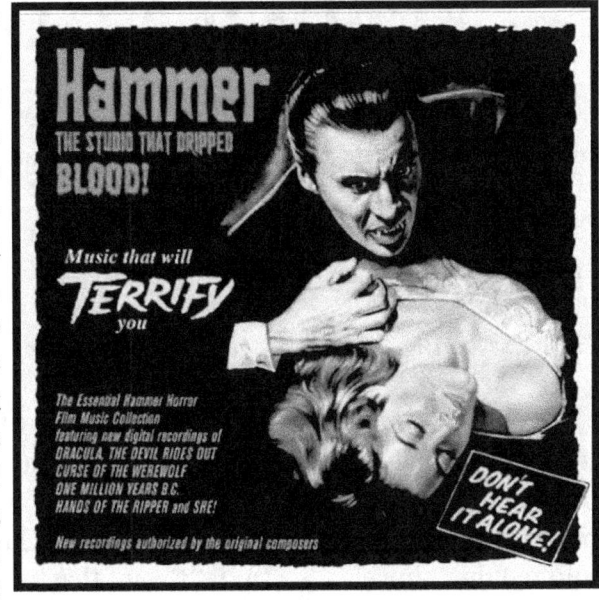 to plague Jimmy during his final years. Frustrated, he felt that he still had something significant to contribute, but Jimmy just couldn't seem to find either the energy or the venue.

On June 20 Jimmy wrote me what he described as the first and the longest letter he'd written to anyone in ages. He was suffering, he wrote, from extreme lethargy and hadn't had energy to do much of anything except lay around his flat. On Monday evening, July 9, 2001, at 10:30 p.m., Jimmy suffered a massive coronary and passed away quietly in his sleep. He would have celebrated his 76th birthday on September 20. A gentle, artistic soul had passed from our midst. He was my hero and my friend, and I shall miss him deeply.

VERONICA CARLSON

Veronica Carlson made her first appearance at FANEX 4. She is one of our very favorite people, someone we consider a dear friend. With each appearance, Veronica has charmed the entire crowd. Her fans are legion. The FANEX 4 questions and answer session was hosted by Bill Littman.

How did you get involved with Hammer Films?

I had a lot of small parts in varying films and I had a lot of publicity attendant with these parts. One of the pictures that they showed of me was on the front page of a tabloid in Great Britain which was the best selling one at the time—*The Sunday Mirror*. Jimmy Carreras saw the picture—he told me this himself—he said, "I want that girl in my next film."

I suppose most people would like to know what it as like working with Mr. Christopher Lee?

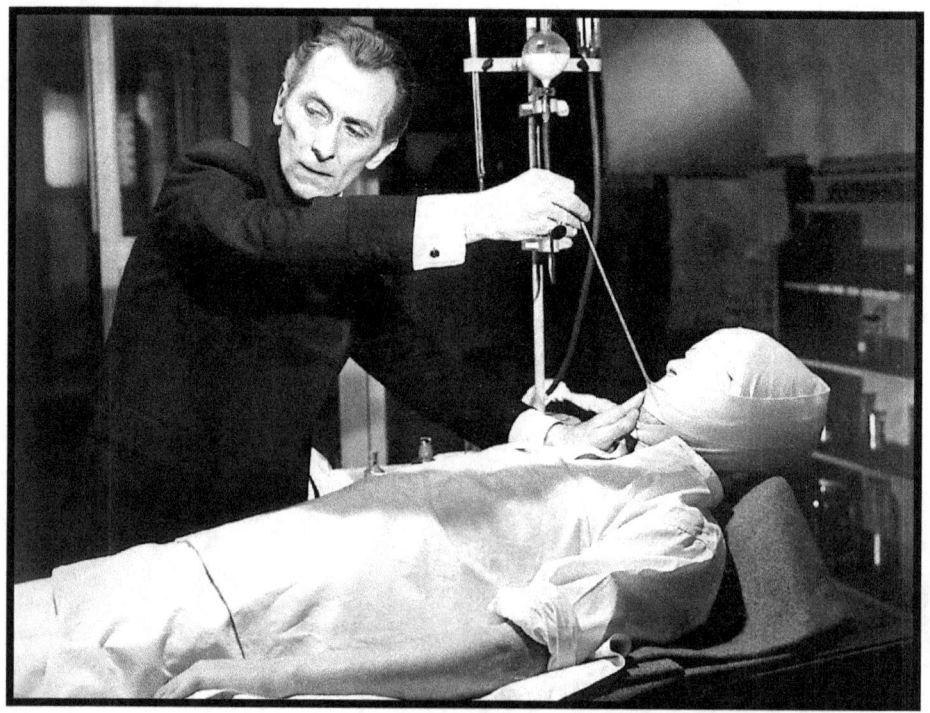

Peter Cushing in *Frankenstein Must Be Destroyed*

My first impression of Christopher was not just meeting him. I watched his films avidly, like we all have. I sat in the audience in England and I just loved being horrified by these films. So, I didn't expect a surprise. I was expecting someone very tall and very aristocratic, but he has an enormous impact in person. He's got a very strong presence that you don't expect in a small room. This man is wonderful—highly intelligent—speaks seven languages. He's a trained opera singer. He's endlessly interesting to listen to. He loves to talk about his life and we love to listen. He's got a lot to say.

I have you down here for a picture entitled Hammerhead *(1968, Columbia) with Diana Dors and Vince Edwards.*

That was another picture before I met Jimmy Carreras. I was going to be a dancer but then they had too many dancers. Well, I don't care to dance, so I said, "Well, I don't want to be a dancer anyway." So they put me in a waitress costume and that was that.

Frankenstein Must Be Destroyed—*for those of us lucky enough to have met Peter Cushing—I'm sure the impression is instantly everlasting.*

My favorite film. That was my favorite film to work on. I adored Peter. Everybody adores Peter. He's the nicest person in show business, I'm sure. He was very kind and thoughtful. The whole crew was just one big happy family. I think that's the happiest film I've ever made. I used to look forward to going to work every day.

I seem to remember one scene where you seemed to be drenched in water and mud. What was it like that day on the set?

That was the coldest day of my whole life. The firemen were in attendance because they'd taken the head off a fire hydrant within the studio so someone had to be in attendance because the power of the water was incredible. They convinced me that in order to keep me drenched they couldn't do it with warm water because I would react to the shock of the warm water and get very cold. So they doused me with cold water, very cold water, in order to maintain that low body heat so I wouldn't go from one shock to another. Well, after three hours of that I couldn't stop chattering. I couldn't talk—my teeth wouldn't stop chattering to let me talk. I was blue. I couldn't stand still. I was just a blurred outline in the studio. So they got the last shot and they said, "Well, I suggest you go to Roger Moore's dressing room." Which was lovely. Roger was abroad filming something else. I had the big tub he had. This was a very old studio. The tub was Victorian—very deep. I filled it up with warm water and I couldn't stand it. The heat was unbearable. So I had to make the water almost cold and for three quarters of an hour I just kept topping it off and the water kept getting deeper and deeper until it was up to here [her chin] 'til my cheeks got pink again. That was a day I won't forget. We tried to do everything in the first take but they had lots of different takes to do anyway. So I survived.

Peter Cushing in *Frankenstein Must Be Destroyed*

And you thought it was glamour.

It was not glamour!

I was going to ask you about working with Terence Fisher. What kind of director was he?

He was a very sensitive director and a very gentle director. He would discuss the scene that you were going to film with you. Hear what you had to say about it. See how you felt. Tell you what he felt and then let you go that path that you discussed without guiding you to it. What he was saying, virtually, "I've shown you the way to go, now do it all by yourself because I want to see what you put into what we've discussed." It was a privilege working with that man.

There was an actor in Frankenstein Must Be Destroyed *[1969] who was known for his larger than life performances—but in this one he gives a subtle, a very moving performance. That's Freddie Jones.*

I learned an awful lot from Freddie in the few days I had to work with him when I had to kill him by stabbing him. He's a brilliant actor. I'd seen him on many television productions before and many films. He helped me. If I had a reaction to him he would come to me immediately after the

Veronica Carlson in a very non-glamorous scene from *Frankenstein Must Be Destroyed*

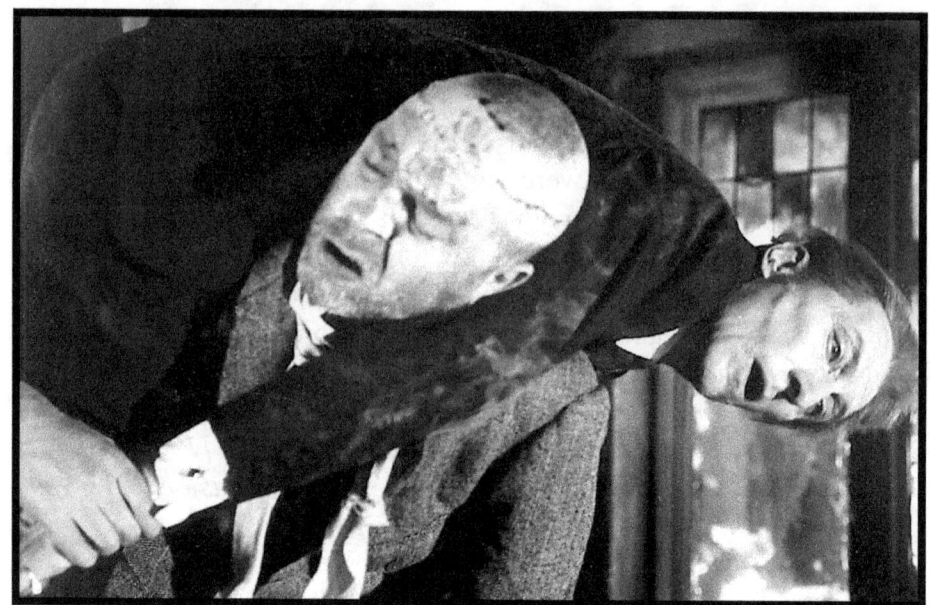
Freddie Jones and Peter Cushing in *Frankenstein Must Be Destroyed*

director had said cut and he'd say, "That was wonderful. I loved what you did. That helps me so." I wished I had more time to work with him.

How long did it take to film Frankenstein Must Be Destroyed?

All the Hammer films were 6 weeks long, and *The Ghoul* [1975] was six weeks long. So you did two rehearsals and you did the shot. It was very rare to have more than four takes.

And everybody listened when Jimmy Carreras came on the set?

Yes, Jimmy was loved by everyone. He was a real daddy figure. He was a lovely character. Michael, I didn't get to know. Michael didn't have the simpatico Jimmy had. Jimmy had a lot of simpatico. He seemed to know the mood people wanted. Michael was different. He was very eager to change it.

Tony Hinds?
I didn't have much to do with Tony Hinds.

Anthony Nelson-Keys?

The Ghoul (1975)

I liked Anthony. He was nice, always a doll to me. We did a lot of Hammer functions for charity, representing them. He was always kind and thoughtful.

It must have been a fascinating place to work at, with Bernard Robinson making those wonderful sets.

Wonderful sets. The atmosphere when you walked on the sets was there, he created it all. Brilliant sets.

Tell us about Jimmy Sangster.

He was a total surprise, he was a very mischievous man. He's got a terrific sense of humor and this took me a while to get used to. I wasn't used to this brevity just prior to shooting. Total discipline, total professional, but he had this outlet of irre-

The Ghoul **with Peter Cushing**

David Prowse and Ralph Bates in *The Horror of Frankenstein*

pressible fun. I remember once I was going to do this scene. I was sleeping in bed and I said to the lighting man, I'm going to stay here in bed, it's so comfortable. It would only take about 10 minutes to light. And there [Jimmy] was in beside me, hopped in bed beside me. But as soon as the camera was ready he was directing and he was good at directing. I think that was the happiest and most amusing film I worked on [*The Horror of Frankenstein*].

The person who played the Frankenstein Monster in The Horror of Frankenstein *[1970] went on to greater acclaim playing Darth Vader in* Star Wars, *that's David Prowse. What was he like on the set?*

He was overwhelming. I'd never met a man so big in my life. I stayed away from him. He was more a man's man and I didn't have too much to say to him. He was into body building. He used to talk to us about that. He was awesome.

I saw a photograph of you once doing a portrait of Christopher Lee on Dracula Has Risen from the Grave *[1975]. Are you an artist?*

Yes. I went to art school for four years—London Art School. I got my masters degree in life painting and fabric design. So, I am a professional. My mother insisted on it. I went to college when I was 16 and I left when I was 21. She said now you can do what you want to do but you always have something to fall back on. Which, of course, I've gone into in great depth now.

You moved over to Tyburn for The Ghoul?

Yes. Not good.

Christopher Lee, Veronica Carlson and Barbara Ewing in *Dracula Has Risen from the Grave*

What were the sets of Tyburn like?

The sets were wonderful. Freddie [director Freddie Francis] was wonderful. Freddie Francis was always wonderful. I adored Freddie. Kevin [producer Kevin Francis] and I did not get on. I don't think he liked me very much. He made it difficult for me. He wouldn't say good morning. Little things like that don't do very well. I mean when you're working and you've got all your ego up there ready to work, you need your ego to be built and when the producer comes on and

says good morning to everyone else and doesn't say good morning to you, you don't know why. So, Kevin came on one day and sat on his stool being Kevin and lighting up another cigarette so that he could look through the smoke. He used to lean back on the stool and, of course, the leg was off the edge of the podium in a heartbeat. He went flat on the floor so that was my cue to exit stage right real quick so that I didn't laugh or I would lose my job there and then. He used to come onto the set at odd times and just look around and disappear again.

I also show a title Vampira *which is known in this country as* Old Dracula *(1975).*

[Laughs] David Niven. He was wonderful. The first meeting I had with David, I had to wear a big headdress. So, David was brought over to be introduced to me or I was going to be introduced to David, whichever it was. As he stepped forward to take my hand he stepped on my toe — very

painful. I bent down forgetting my headdress and poked him in the eye with it. He recoiled in horror. So, he had a red eye and I had a red toe. We laughed about that. We got on ever so well. He was ever such a nice guy.

That was your last movie to date?

I did an episode of a television series called *Private Eye*. That was in 1974, the year I married and then I drifted to where my husband worked because he went abroad a lot. I drifted out of it [acting] then.

David Niven and Peter Bayliss in *Old Dracula,* which was distributed by AIP.

VERONICA CARLSON
VIRGINIA WETHERELL

Virginia Wetherell signs autographs at FANEX 11.

At FANEX 11, our second Hammer tribute, we were pleased to welcome back Veronica Carlson, as well as Virginia Wetherell. Virginia had appeared in several films such as *The Crimson Cult* [1968], *Disciple of Death* [1972], *Dr. Jekyll and Sister Hyde* [1971] and *A Clockwork Orange* [1971]. However, she was also happily married to Ralph Bates and now helps oversee a charity in her late husband's name. Mary Peach, who also sat in on this talk, had appeared in several films including *The Projected Man* [1967] and *Scrooge* [1970], is married to Jimmy Sangster.

Can you tell us something about Christopher Lee and was he a prankster?

Virginia Wetherell: Definitely not. Not a prankster. Certainly not with Christopher Lee. I found him probably the most non-humorous person I have ever met in my life. A joker, he wasn't. Ralph Bates, my husband, was a joker, but Chris Lee, definitely not. Whereas, somebody like Boris Karloff was absolutely wonderful and a gentleman and courteous. Well, maybe [Christopher Lee joked] with Peter Cushing.

Veronica Carlson: Yes, it was just between the two of them.

Virginia Wetherell: Definitely.

Veronica Carlson: They had a great camaraderie, and they were very secure in their ability to joke around with each other and keep it off the set. They were both very, very professional. But I, unlike Virginia—maybe because I was so green and naïve, and this was my first movie—Chris did help me. He was wonderful. He would stand and give me a line. He would say to Freddie [Francis], "I'll stand and give her a line," and he did, and he would give me the lines, and I found that to be immensely encouraging. I think if I'd maybe had more experience, he would not. I don't know. This is what I'm feeling.

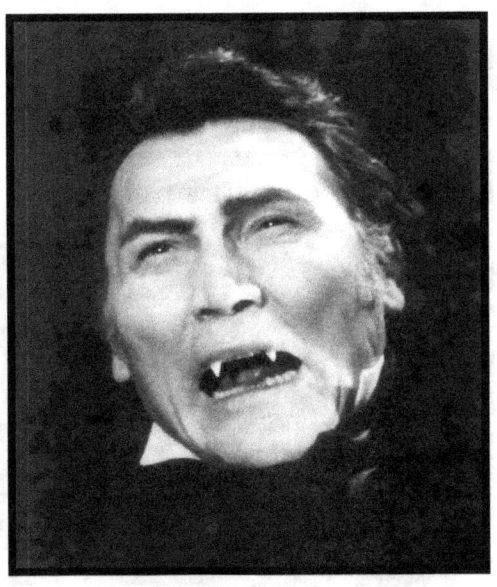

Jack Palance as Dracula

Virginia Wetherell: I think he fancied her and he didn't fancy me.

Can you tell us something about Jack Palance?

Virginia Wetherell: Well, when I worked with Jack Palance [in *Dracula*, TV, 1973], I was actually pregnant at the time, and he wasn't to know that. And there was a scene where I have to walk into a room playing one of the brides [of Dracula], and he has to push me around a bit. And on rehearsal—he's a very, very big man. I mean,

Veronica and Christopher Lee pose for a publicity shot for *Dracula Has Risen from the Grave*.

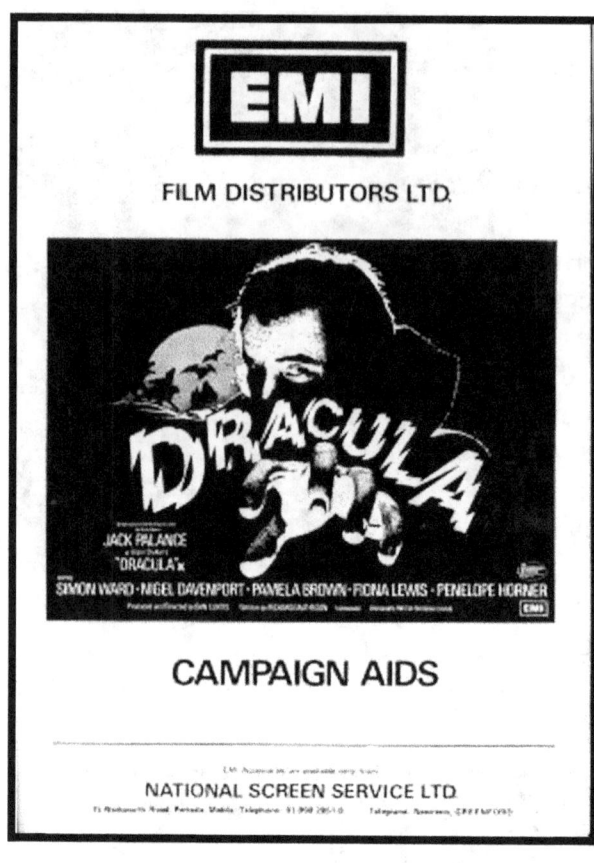

big this way and big this way, and I suppose, because I was pregnant, I was a little, sort of nervous and insecure. And on rehearsal, he would insist on pushing, like from here across the room—so much so that I was actually sliding down the floor—and I think that's somewhat unnecessary on a rehearsal, and we did that three times. He was just kind of showing how macho he was, but he didn't really have to convince anybody. He's very macho. But, aside from that, I'm sure he's really a very lovely guy.

Veronica Carlson: I can tell a very funny story about Jack Palance. I went to a film festival in Dublin and he was there... and you're right—exactly what you say—he's a very powerful man, and he's immensely strong. And I was sitting there in a room. I can't remember who else was there right now, but it will come back to me. He said, "Let's sing," so we all had to sing. And this is this big, powerful man singing in a very beautiful voice. And I said, "I don't really want to sing." So he said, "All right, so I'll recite poetry." So he was reciting poetry, and we had a wonderful time. He was very nice. I went back home, and the doorbell rings. I open the door, and Jack Palance is at the front door of my parents' house, and I thought, "Oh, my God!" And at that time I'd just gotten to know Sydney, my husband. Sydney arrived, and Jack Palance is there, sitting, having a cup of tea in the lounge. And he's never gotten over it. Every time Jack Palance is on TV, he storms out. "That bloody Jack Palance! Don't know what you ever saw in him! He's ugly!" He keeps saying how ugly he is.

Virginia Wetherell, Mark Eden, Ron Pember and Boris Karloff in *The Crimson Cult*

Can you tell us about Boris Karloff?

Virginia Wetherell: Wonderful. As I said earlier, a real gentleman. Totally, not at all what he appears on the screen. A very kind, gentle man. I can remember the first day that I met him, he was already on the set [of *The Crimson Cult*], and I walked in and sort of quickly went to the sofa—and as soon as I arrived, he stood up to shake my hand. And this was a man who was indeed at the time very sick—and he was very happy to rehearse, and was comfortable. He would make suggestions, and we discussed the script. I mean, he was just completely brilliant. Really, really lovely. A real gent, kind of old school. No mucking around, knew his lines, on cue, never fluffed. Great.

Especially in that film, there was a scene where we had to be outside. It was shot in November—and in England, November is pretty cold and damp. He was very, very sick, and he had a rug over him, and when he spoke, he wheezed like that. And if you listen—if you watch the film—you'll hear the music, he speaks, and then as he does that [wheez-

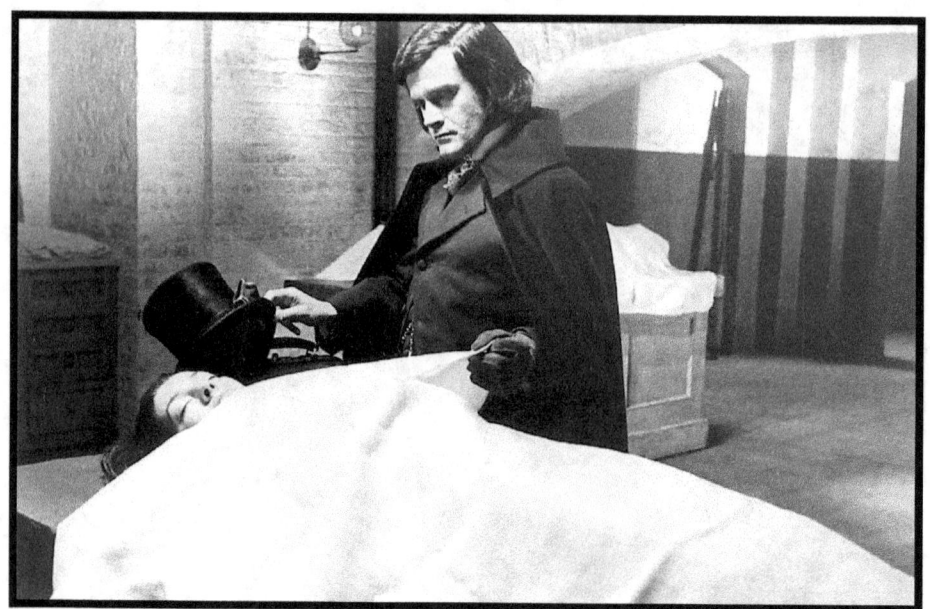

Ralph Bates in *Dr. Jekyll and Sister Hyde*

ing sound], and the music is played up. And he was a real pro. He didn't have to do it. They could have used a double for a lot of the scenes he was in, but no, he did it.

[Like Peter Cushing] exactly the same: The most wonderful, old school, just real gents and pros—like in the old days, when actors went to work, they wore a suit. This would not be heard of now.

Can you tell us about Barbara Steele and Michael Gough on the set of The Crimson Cult?

Virginia Wetherell: I didn't get to know Barbara at all, because we were never called at the same time, but Michael, I did, and I worked with him, did a couple of television shows with him later on, and he was a super guy. I mean really great fun—just lovely, nice guy.

Tell us about Disciple of Death.

Virginia Wetherell: When I made the film, it was called *Once Upon a Time There Was a Disciple of Death*, with Mike Raven, who sadly passed away about a month, six weeks ago. That was a film, one of these sort of low-budget, come down, it will all be over in three weeks and all the rest of it. And I have to say I had a lot of fun doing that film.

Ronnie Lacey... who was in the film, he played the guy who kind of dragged his leg... most people obviously aren't familiar with it, but he played a baddie. And we shot it in Cornwall, which is a very quiet village, a place called Buscastle in Cornwall. Very picturesque. And I remember on the first day, they put the so-called stars in little cottages. And, in those days, I was kind of used to living in London, in houses that were full of people, and rooms that were full of people—and suddenly there I was in the middle of nowhere in this really remote cottage, by myself. I was petrified. And all the crew and the extras were in the hotel. Anyway, I kind of checked in and was told where to go, and had to go down a long pier—and I was wandering down this pier by myself, and I heard somebody behind me, and I could hear the sort of steps in the pebbles. I walked a bit quicker, and this person followed and was walking quicker and quicker, and then I started

Veronica Carlson and Jimmy Sangster on the set of *The Horror of Frankenstein*.

running. I thought, "My God, I'm going to be killed." And recently there'd been a murder or rape or something—some lunatic who'd murdered his grandmother and family. And I don't know, I was very aware of this. Anyway, it turned out it was Ronnie Lacey. And I was beginning to scream—and that was the first time I'd met Ronnie. Again, sadly he passed away about five years ago. He was one of the nicest guys, and we became very good friends, and he and Ralph were great friends. Super, super man. Really terrific guy.

What do you remember about Doctor Jekyll and Sister Hyde*?*

Virginia Wetherell: Obviously, *Doctor Jekyll and Sister Hyde* was a very significant film for me, because that's how I met Ralph. And, in fact, the first day I met him, he stabbed me in the back. Two years later, I mar-

Veronica Carlson in the purple gown Peter Cushing admired with Simon Ward in *Frankenstein Must Be Destroyed*

ried him. Well, you know, you win some, you lose some. But that was Ralph. He was one of the best guys.

He would have been very good [as Dorian Gray]. There were lots of things that he should have done, but sadly—up there—they got him first.

I never met [Martine Beswicke], because, again, we were never called on the same day. But I know that Ralph liked her very much, and they had a lot of fun together—before I moved in.

Veronica, what do you remember about Dracula Has Risen from the Grave*?*

Veronica Carlson: I thought I was going to fall off [the coach]. The horses were just galloping on, and I had nothing to hold on to, except the edge of the seat... that was genuine fear.

How do you feel about being known for your horror films?

Virginia Wetherell: A lot of fun. Tremendous fun.

Peter Cushing in *The Ghoul*

Veronica Carlson: I looked upon it as an honor to be involved. I used to miss a few college classes to see the latest Hammer horror. We were all fans—I went to an art school—and to our absolute horror one day, when we were all in the intermission, waiting for the big Hammer to come up, then the lights went up, our lecturer was sitting right in front. And he stood up, and he counted all of us.

And he said, "You are all on detention and you will make up this work." And he promptly sat down and watched the movie with us.

And my body would travel through my eyes into the screen, and I would be with them. And it was my yearning to be a part of it. It was a dream come true for me. How was it for you, Virginia?

Virginia Wetherell: The same. The same thing, and always great fun. It was always lighthearted. It wasn't kind of, heavy. The only thing was, that they were always low-budget, and you did one take, and if it wasn't that good, well, that was tough.

Veronica Carlson: That's right. We had no rehearsal at all. We just walked through the line. "Stop there." And then, "Where's your mark?" "Where's your key light?" [that] you had to stand in.

Virginia Wetherell: You found it.

Veronica Carlson: But we were treated with utmost respect. We weren't treated like fools, and I enjoyed it.

Virginia Wetherell: Me, too. Enormously.

Veronica Carlson: I'd do it all over again if I could.
What are your memories of Peter Cushing?

Veronica Carlson: When I was working on [*Frankenstein Must Be Destroyed*, 1969], he invited me out to dinner, and he said, "Darling, I want you to wear the amethyst—the purple velvet"—he loved that gown. It was his favorite, with the beautiful hat. And he wanted to dress up as the Baron and take me out to dinner.

I did go to dinner, but I did not wear the gown. But he came to my hotel room. He was wearing white gloves. He presented me with a corsage, and I had one of the sweetest evenings I have *ever* had. It was just like stepping back into another era. And part of the reason he wanted to take me out was, at that time, we had the rape scene suggested, but how were we going to do it? Peter was tormented by this, as I was, and he kept saying, "Darling, What are we going to do? How are we going to do this?"

And we went back to his house. He showed me his—he had a toy soldier collection, model soldiers—beautiful things. And we talked about this, I think, for an hour. And it just caused us distress. It made him—his eyes teared—he didn't know how to do it. I didn't know how to do it. So it didn't really help.

The other memory, which was not a Hammer movie—it was on *The Ghoul* [1975]. He had to do a scene many times, talking about his wife's passing, the death of Helen. And I watched this man, take after take. Freddie [Francis] made him do it over and over again. And I saw the agony in this man, because always, the person to whom he was talking was Helen, his wife who had recently passed away. And he broke down.

And I looked around in utter dismay, and the crew were weeping. And everyone turned away, and he had to go to his dressing room. And he was there for a long time. He couldn't recover. He just couldn't get over it, and it just broke our hearts. Everybody was touched by Peter. Everybody loved him.

Ralph Bates and Jimmy Sangster

So that was a very fond memory, but a very bittersweet one. That sums up the man to me.

Can you tell us about working with David Prowse?

Veronica Carlson: A very big man. He's huge. He really is. He has an enormous stance, and I remember I upset David, because we had to pose for some stills, and the photographer asked him to hold a girl on each arm, and I thought that was downright dangerous. I didn't have faith in his strength to hold me. Which didn't say much, because, when I visited a circus one time, the trainer said the elephant would pick me up with his trunk. I didn't think that could hold me, either. So if an elephant couldn't do it, certainly David couldn't do it.

And I said, "No, I don't think that's right. I don't think that's fair."

And he was upset. He thought I should have more faith in him. And I went to apologize to him afterwards.

A very sweet man. Very kind, and I became very fond of David.

Christopher Lee, Veronica Carlson and Rupert Davies in *Dracula Has Risen from the Grave*

He's very soft spoken, and he's got that West Country burr. He comes from Bristol, that area. He's got a lovely, soft burr. And he is very quietly spoken—doesn't say very much.

Tell us about Ralph Bates.

Virginia Wetherell: As you may or may not know, Ralph died from pancreatic cancer. And after he died, we set up a fund—myself and [our] children and three doctors. And we have a research program going on at a big hospital medical school in London, called St. George's. And when Ralph was diagnosed, he was given six or eight weeks to live—and now I think people get about five years—and, who knows, one day we might even crack it...

Doctor Jekyll and Sister Hyde—technically I think it's quite a brilliant film—but *Persecution* [1974], the film he did with Lana Turner, I think he had a pretty terrible time on it. Although, I have to say, because of Lana's drinking problem, we went into overtime, and we got the carpet for the house, so I can't complain. But I thought he was brilliant in it. You know, I like them all. Have to.

How did you meet Jimmy Sangster?

Mary Peach: I had worked with Ralph [Bates]. I had done a few little television movies with Ralph—and I was on my own, and Jimmy was on his own. And Vig [Virginia Wetherell] said, "Come out to lunch."

And I went out to lunch, and there was Jimmy. I didn't expect him at all. And from then on, more or less, we haven't looked back. And, sadly, Ralph died afterwards.

I never really was involved in that [Hammer] world at all, I'm sorry to say. I wasn't a fan. I knew him [Jimmy] later when he was working in…American television. I never knew him in those days of blood and gore.

Virginia Wetherell at FANEX 11

How do you prepare for a movie role?

Veronica Carlson: I don't think I went into a movie with a preconceived idea. I don't think I did. Because you don't know until you see how other people evolve—the actors, their own characters—so that you know, really, that the weight is evenly distributed.

Virginia Wetherell: You work that out on the floor, don't you?

Veronica Carlson: Yes, you work it out on the floor. You meet these people, see how they treat the character. See how they bring the character to life, and that influences yours. It's best not to go in with a preconceived notion, because your reaction could be quite unexpected, as to how they are in that character role.
Virginia Wetherell: And, anyway, things change. You cut things. The director makes suggestions, and your character develops, and you get inspiration from the other artists.

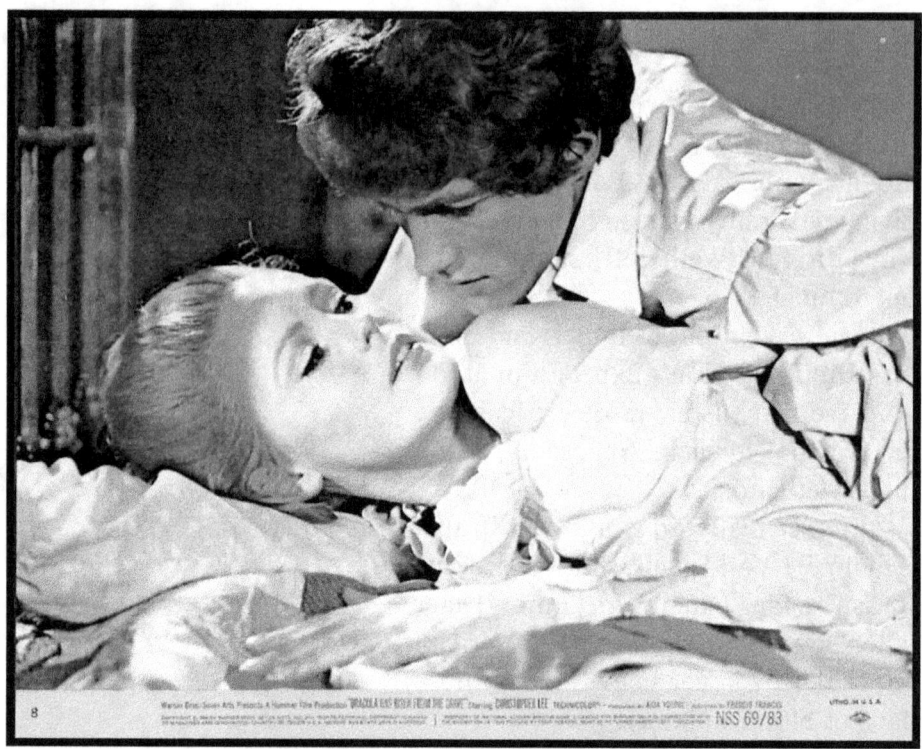

Tell us about Dracula Has Risen from the Grave.

Veronica Carlson: Freddie Francis was disappointed. Apparently there was a lot of Barry [Andrews] and me that fell on the cutting room floor, and he was really disappointed about that. Apparently he had taken time out for one week after completion of the film — and they had edited by the time he got back, perhaps because they had known what he had wanted to do. But he was very disappointed about that, and he wanted it put back in the movie if they ever redo it or put it on disc.

We were at the premiere, and we were all sitting, watching, and Ewan [Hooper] came on the screen, and first I didn't know who was talking. I couldn't understand, who this voice was coming out of Ewan's mouth, because I had seen bits of rushes while he was working, and obviously I worked alongside him and heard his voice. And everybody suddenly sat up a little bit taller in their seats.

And Ewan was sitting just in front of me, and he looked to the left and he looked to the right, and he said, "What have they done to my voice? Why didn't they tell me?" He was so hurt.

HORROR OF FRANKENSTEIN

And I think that's a shame—a shoddy way to treat an actor, because he had done a fine job on the set. I don't know what they found that they had to re-voice him for. I don't understand it. He was very hurt. Very embarrassing. It really is humiliating.

What about The Horror of Frankenstein *[1970]?*

Veronica Carlson: That was horrible. I still don't watch that. I won't watch that.

What can you tell us about Demons of the Mind?

Virginia Wetherell: I wasn't too happy about that, as it happens. There's one nude scene—the

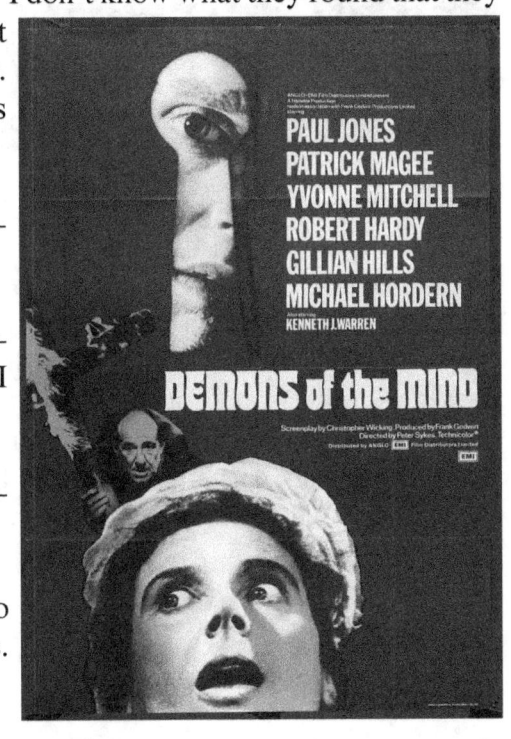

nude scene that obviously wasn't scripted. And I got a call from Peter Sykes the night before we were to shoot it, and he said, "Oh, Virginia, there's this little scene where you're trying on frocks. We want the dress to slip off and then you have nothing on underneath."

And I said, "You know, Peter, it's not in the script."

He said, "Well, it is now." So he did this whole thing. "We're going to take all day to shoot it, and light it like a commercial."

And I said, "Okay, I'm not happy about it. But okay, on one condition—no stills."

So he said, "Fine, no stills."

So we came to shoot it, and they built a little dressing room for me on the set. And I was made up and I was fit, and we did this whole thing. It was just with Yvonne Mitchell and Patrick Magee, and we had this scene, and I had to walk around the room and go, "Ooh, ahh" at all the frocks, in the nude. Well I did all the "ooh and ahhing," like I had to.

JOYCE BROUGHTON ON PETER CUSHING

In 1999 several people suggested we reprint the Peter Cushing autobiographies. We were great fans of Mr. Cushing and felt it would be wonderful to bring the two volume autobiography to U.S. readers. Tom Johnson helped us get in touch with Joyce Broughton, Mr. Cushing's secretary for over 35 years and holder of the copyright for the books.

Joyce Broughton is a charming lady and graciously flew over to appear at Monster Rally in 1999 and sign books and speak about the legendary Peter Cushing.

Can you tell us about some of his acting method?

I can only remember bits of them, you know. And he had to be a judge and he wanted to know what happened, where he looked, how he placed himself. And when he did—I think it was *The Masks of Death* [1984, television; U.S. Title: *Sherlock Holmes and the Masks of Death*], he had to play Sherlock Holmes and he had to play the violin and he couldn't play the violin. So he went and had lessons on how to hold the violin and the bow and how to hold his chin and everything. He was very good with things like that.

We're heard Mr. Cushing had a huge book collection.

Hundreds and hundreds of books, words were his favorite thing, quotations particu-

Peter Cushing and Joyce Broughton (photo courtesy Joyce Broughton)

larly, he'd spend hours looking up a quotation. He was a very, very well-read man.

Could you talk about Mr. Cushing's relation with the fans and the fan mail.

Well we did get a great deal of mail, and strangely enough, I still get a lot of it now. There wasn't one fan letter that he didn't answer personally. There wasn't one fan letter that didn't have his own signature on it. The fans were very important to him. We had some funny things, obviously. I can remember one, a family of four girls between 14 and 15 years old and they had these odd names like Merilee and Melody, really odd names, and they sent these photographs and sent along some papers and they said we really feel we'd like you to adopt us. And another one sent a photograph of a really voluptuous fan and she had said she'd heard that he needed somebody to clean the floors and scrub the floors and she'd be only too willing. Bernard [Joyce's husband] looked at the photo and said, "She can come clean my floors any day."

How much did Peter Cushing generally charge for autographs?

Oh, nothing, nothing, ever. (Enthusiastic crowd applause)

Did you visit Mr. Cushing on the Star Wars *set?*

No, I never did get to the *Star Wars* set. I did take my kids to see the Daleks when he did *Dr. Who and the Daleks* [1965]. It was very much in vogue then and they were real fans and they couldn't get over seeing

Peter Cushing in *Dr. Who and the Daleks*

the Daleks which had a thing that you plunge down the sink [on their costumes]. Their illusions were quite shattered then. I did go to many sets, but I didn't stay for too long. He was awfully busy and I never wanted to drag him away from business time.

Which American actors did he admire?

Well, he was a great fan of the Duke [John Wayne], of course. He loved him, thought he was great. I used to watch more cowboy movies than I watched anything else. We used to have to tape them all over the place. He did have admiration for many of your stars and he worked with quite a few. Alan Ladd he particularly liked. He did a film with Alan Ladd [*The Black Knight*, 1954], he was fond of Alan. None come to mind quickly, but he said he had admiration for the American stars.

Could you comment on his relationship with Christopher Lee?

Mr. Cushing used to make Christopher laugh very much, they had this wonderful way where Christopher would be Sylvester [the puddy tat] and

Peter Cushing and Christopher Lee share a quiet moment.

I'd come in sometimes when he was on the phone and I'd find him on the floor just laughing and laughing. They did have a great respect for one another and a great camaraderie. I'm sure Christopher misses him too.

Toward the end of his life when he found it hard to entertain, he never entertained, I always did. He had just a very small cottage. We would try very hard to ask stars that he was fond of to come to dinner because, although we had a great relationship, I didn't know the business. He missed it so much. We had Francis Matthews, Curt Jackson, Ian Richardson, so many of them, I can't really remember. He had a really great time, and he loved it too.

FREDDIE FRANCIS

Veronica, Freddie, Jimmy Sangster and the other guests sign at FANEX 11. Notice Veronica's painting of Cushing and Lee beside her.

think the art of the cinema is at times more interesting than the performances. Freddie Francis was a dream guest for me, he and his wife Pam were both delightful down-to-earth people. I remember sitting with him and discussing the beautiful shot of Meryl Streep on the pier in *The French Lieutenant's Woman* [1981]. I think it is one of the most impressive shots I've ever seen in a film. Freddie told me the weather was terrible and it wasn't Meryl Streep but a stuntman in her cloak. I can remember thinking, I'm sit-

Gary Svehla and Freddie Francis at FANEX 11

ting here with an Academy Award-winning cinematographer, a true genius, how lucky I am.

Freddie filmed the entire convention with a small video camera given to him by David Lynch. The convention was all abuzz on Sunday when we had to pull Mr. Francis out of the autograph line to take a call from Marty, Scorsese that is. Freddie Francis has a marvelous sense of humor, which you will notice during this question and answer session. This talk was hosted by Paul Jensen.

My name is Paul Jensen and I'm honored to welcome here at FANEX Freddie Francis.

Thank you very much now, but before we get this thing on the road, there's a question and answer session, isn't there, Paul?

Freddie Francis poses with the camera given to him by David Lynch.

I question, you answer.

Oh. It doesn't matter, just in case they start asking questions I'd just like you to know about me. I'm a filmmaker, I happened to have made a lot of horror films because I like making films. It doesn't matter to me, I'll make anything, any rubbish, I'll make it. I mention this because I'm always embarrassed when people start asking me questions about horror as opposed to horror films because it's something I don't understand. I'm a good fun loving boy and you know I'm very happy with everything I've ever done, I wish I had made a lot more comedies, but anyway having said that, I'll hand over to Paul, I know he's got a lot to say.

I'm going to try not to say it though; I'll ask you questions, later you may have a chance to. Freddie Francis has actually led two lives, renowned lives. The first life as a cinematographer and the second life as a direc-

tor. *The first life began as a cinematographer and then a director again, and then a cinematographer again; the two lives are intercut together. He first came to prominence, I would say, in the late '50s, early '60s as a photographer of a number of major British films, groundbreaking British films like* Room at the Top *[1959],* Saturday Night and Sunday Morning *[1961].*

I was known as the "darling of the kitchen sink."

The darling of the kitchen sink?

Because the kitchen sink started a new era, we thought, in British films.

Pauline Kael, the American critic, renowned critic and a difficult critic, wrote in 1961, when she was reviewing The Innocents *[1961], "I don't know where this photographer Freddie Francis sprang from, you may recall that in the last year every time a British movie is something to look at it turns out to be his,* Room at the Top, Sons and Lovers *[1960],* Saturday Night and Sunday Morning *and now* The Innocents. *Well she never perhaps had a chance to get an answer to that question, but where did this photographer, Freddie Francis, spring from?*

I sprang from, what are you laughing at? I guess I was, you know, a young kid and I didn't have a great deal of education as you may have gathered and in the last year of school we had to write a thesis on anything you could think of so I decided to write on films. Not necessarily from an entertaining point of view, [but] from equipment and all that. And during this period I scrounged a visit to the old Gaumont Studios in London and I was hooked and I wanted to make movies. I was also madly in love with Joan Blondell, so I thought will this—they laugh, they don't even know who Joan Blondell is—oh God, I'm so old. And I wanted to make movies and in those days it was easier to get into movies because the British film industry was a very strange industry. There were one or two great people like the Hitchcocks and that but the rest of them were sort of strange people who would come in, make a film usually featuring their girlfriend and then disappear completely. But this was very valuable because I suppose I was a bit bright and knew a bit about photography and filming and I used to benefit from seeing the mistakes these people made. And my advice to students when I'm lecturing to them is to benefit by other people's mistakes. However, I'm wandering off, you know, I got a job as a clapper boy and I'd tell you the films I made as a clapper boy but you're much too young to know about them. And, I went along happily until some idiot started a war and I was just the wrong age and I was called up at the beginning of the war, the first month, and I spent the entire war years in the Army, but once again I was very lucky because I was making films in the Army. So, that's how I started. I came out and I've done nothing since. Well, except films.

Would it be accurate to say you were not necessarily drawn to photography but it was at least your big chance.

I guess it was a chance.

But then you found an affinity for it?

Oh, I loved it. And as I say I enjoyed listening to people making ghastly mistakes and if I have any attributes as a cinematographer it's somebody who'll always help the director. And as I said, in the early days most of the directors were people who came in to make the odd film with their girlfriend and maybe the cameraman maybe in those days knew a little bit more about it than they did. I used to be astounded when I heard directors ask a cameraman to do certain things and the cameraman would say, "We can't do that," because the idiot directors believed that. So I vowed whenever I became a cinematographer or whatever, I would never say to a director "No you can't do that." The worst I ever say these days is "Yeah, we can do that, it will take a little longer but we can do that." So in answer to your question, I was interested in photographing movies because I feel that photographing movies is part of directing them as well. My idea of a cinematographer, which varies from a lot of cinematographers I know, is that when I get a film to do I do insist on spending time with the director before we start shooting the film because any director worth his salt has photographed the film in his mind before he starts shooting it. He doesn't know how to achieve that on film, but he's got this idea in his mind and I find it very interesting to sort of put his mind onto the screen.

I noticed after the war you spent about 10 years as a camera operator before becoming a cinematographer and during that 10 years you worked on 19 films. Interestingly 14 of them were working with two different cinematographers. There was a lot of consistency there. You made eight films with Christopher Challis and six with Oswald Morris so that's 14 out of 19. Plus there were four films directed by Michael Powell that you worked on and three directed by John Huston, all of which points to a lot of consistency, you were working with the same people. Do you think that's an advantage?

I think so, because, first of all, I can say this now, because I was a very, very good operator so the cameramen used to like me working on their films and also I had a great affinity with Mickey Powell and with John Huston. I consider those two my real mentors and, in fact, I had to sort of break away from John because he wouldn't let me go away and light anything, he wanted me there all the time so eventually I had to break with him but I didn't completely break because he knew I wanted to break and sort of allowed me to photograph and direct the second units on *Moby Dick* [1956]. But I do consider Mickey Powell and John Huston as my mentors. They were lovely guys to work with, every film was like going off to the great unknown on a great adventure and I like that, this was the spirit I tried to maintain in my own films to this day.

Is this one reason why in your own films you often don't preplan in detail but like to go on the set and discover things?

You see, you've observed me once, so he's telling me all the things I did wrong, you see. No, one of the reasons I don't like preplanning, one has to preplan a bit as a director of photography because, let's face it, the films on which I've been director of photography have been quite large films, the films I directed have been quite small films, and it's ridiculous to preplan too much because if you get too ambitious there's not the money there to carry out your ambitions, so I make a great point of thinking about them a lot but without planning, as you know.

I don't really understand what the distinction there is between a cinematographer and a camera operator. What's the relationship, what's the division with responsibility there?

Well, it differs. In my case, now, I have a wonderful operator, Gordon Hayman, and I know that when Gordon and I, when I speak to the director about the following sequence and everything, Gordon is always at my side and I know that he will get setups and camera moves almost the same as I would do if I was operating. So I know that that's something on my plate so I can spend more time with the director. In fact, in the sort of eight or nine years Gordon's been with me I suppose I've made him change his mind about three times. I also insist on having the chief electrician, and this again is a similar thing because he can sort of stand in the background while we're talking to the director and I can then turn around and tell him the sort of things I want so he can roughly prepare what I want to do. It's all, as I say, that my job is to make the director's job easier and to give him more time; therefore, if I've got a great staff who will do what they think I would do in the same situation, it saves a lot of time.

But it would be a mistake to envision the operator as somebody who pushes the on button. He makes decisions.

No it wouldn't be a mistake. It would be a mistake in the case of *my* operator but especially, it took American cinematographers, for whom I have a great regard, a great, great time to get the same idea of operators that we have in England. Some of them still want to be the boss.

Peter Wyngarde and Deborah Kerr in *The Innocents*

One of the films of yours that I think almost everybody admires, especially in this room, is The Innocents. *Certainly one of the points about that film that is so striking is that the images that include the ghosts had fear, well, you see them but they're not necessarily tangible. How did you go about achieving that quality, that ambiguity?*

It's difficult how I achieved, gosh I can't remember, but this was all part and parcel. Jack Clayton was a very close friend, we'd known each other since the war and we always knew that when Jack directed a movie I would photograph it, as I did with *Room at the Top*. We were very close and we used to speak always about the movies and I knew exactly what he had in mind; therefore, I used what expertise I had to create that in any given situation. One of the ghost things I think you're thinking about is Clytie Jessop, when Deborah thought she saw her in the rushes. This was a great time and I said to Jack, "I know what you want Jack, with this ghastly weather, let's shoot it now." It doesn't always happen but there should be that very close collaboration between the cinematographer and the director.

The wet rainy atmosphere in that shot wasn't created, that wasn't artificial, that was real?

Difficult to tell offhand. I know during the sequence we had the fire brigade from Brighton there, whether they were there for that shot—they probably were, but it was a very nasty English afternoon.

As a man who was a star as a cinematographer, you then after The Innocents *dropped that profession and took a turn to directing. What prompted that?*

Money. No, in those days a cinematographer in England, it was quite a good living, but you know if you wanted to live well you had to work all the time, and I suddenly thought, you know, I just got an Academy Award and people ask me to direct pictures, why don't I do that, so I did. And got even less money.

But you made a lot of pictures.

I made a lot of pictures, which is what I like doing, isn't it? I made too many. Most of my friends, you know, the late Jack Clayton, Darryl Ryerson, they made sufficient pictures.

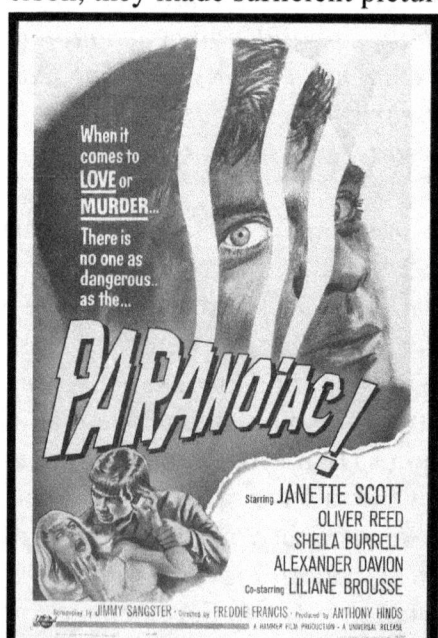

Every several years.

Every several years they said, let's get Clayton to do a picture. Almost impossible. The number of pictures he started on then got to do.

Too much of a perfectionist?

Too much of a perfectionist, absolutely. Are you inferring I'm not?

Early in your career as a director, you did become associated with Hammer and made a cluster of four films in a row.

Cluster being the right word, yes.

Evil of Frankenstein [1964], Paranoiac [1963], Hysteria [1965] and Nightmare [1963] and several years later another one. Tell us about that connection.

Yeah, I did a picture, why they asked me to do it [I'll never know], because, at that time, as a cameraman in England, I was rather expensive. [It was] a film called *Never Take Sweets from a Stranger* [1961, AKA *The Molester*], a very un-Hammer-like film, and I did it and I became acquainted with Tony Hinds who ran Hammer, so when I started directing he asked me to make a movie and I did and we had a lot of fun. You know, I like having fun when we work. I don't take it too seriously. We had a lot of fun and he asked me to do a movie and I did it, and he asked me do another one, then he asked me to do another one. I merely did it because it was so enjoyable.

But the connection initiated with Never Take Sweets from a Stranger?

Never Take Sweets from a Stranger.

Which was 1959, I think?

Well, it was before I stared directing.

You photographed it. What's interesting is, if you look at the credits, almost everybody connected with it is a traditional Hammer person except the director and the photographer.

That's right.
You know why they went outside the fold?

No idea, no idea at all. I suppose they thought it was slightly un-horror, but exactly why I have no idea. He was a very good director, Cyril Frankel, but he didn't do many films after that.

It's a film about child molestation. Straightforward and realistic and not a sensationalistic film.

A very straightforward film.

That led to the personal relationship with Hinds and then that led to directing with them.

Tony Hinds is still a very dear friend, as, in fact, is Jimmy Sangster, and it was a sort of family thing really. In retrospect, you know I come to these sort of places and you know I am delighted, but sometimes I wish I hadn't gone in that direction.

So you have Hinds to thank for that.

Hinds, yes, yes, I'll blame him for that.

Could you describe Tony Hinds?

He's a charming man, doesn't like getting involved in films. But he's always in the back room, hated to come on stage. In fact, the only time I remember Tony coming on-stage was when I was doing the fire sequence in [*The Evil of*] *Frankenstein* where the house burns down and, knowing me, Tony was afraid I'd have a real good fire and burn the studio down, so he came on the stage then and I remember physically restraining him while we were shooting because he was trying to cut the scene. He's a very charming man. When they sold Hammer he then retired to a quiet

country life and he now directs plays at the village hall, a dramatic club. Very strange, very rich, but very strange.

Many refer to Tony Hinds as Hammer. When Tony Hinds left, Hammer really lost its identity. Would you agree with that, and, if so, what's the nature of his creative influence?

Hammer—there's nobody from Hammer here is there? It was the most fantastic place I've worked, ever. Sir James, well, he was James Carreras, but then [he] became Sir James. [He] was a wonderful guy, could wheedle money out of anybody, and they loved him in the States because he was chief of Variety Club and most Americans thought if they flirted with Jimmy Carreras they were close to a knighthood, because he was very close to Prince Phillip. So the situation was, Sir James would say to Tony Hinds, "Tony, I'm going over to the States, get me some posters." He would go around the corner on Water Street to a little man who would design three or four posters for any films they could think of. They would think up strange titles and do posters, then go to Hollywood and get all his friends [to invest]. They used to sort of love him over there, he would produce the posters, he'd come back and say to Tony,

Oliver Reed in the Freddie Francis-directed *Paranoiac* (1963)

"I've got three of these films to make." Then Tony would write a script and then we'd make the film. They always came in under budget and it was really a great set-up. They never lost any money, that combination. The other thing was, Jimmy was an assistant director, they found Jimmy [Sangster] to write the scripts and they sort of waterproofed the whole thing. This is the reason why I did too many Hammer films. Because we had so much fun.

You made four in a row there.

Did I do four, yes, one later, you're right.

Three were of the psychological horror film thriller variety and one was The Evil of Frankenstein. *One was more of a monster film, similarly the other one you made,* Dracula Has Risen from the Grave *[1969], was a monster film.*

That was after the studio at Bray packed up and we made it at Pinewood. That's right.

Of those two types of stories, types of films, types of atmospheres, which do you prefer?

Oh, the sort of nightmare type film. I mean the only film I ever set up and made myself was a film called *Mumsy, Nanny, Sonny and Girly* [1970] which was a sort of black comedy, which, was the sort of film I really enjoy doing. As I say, I'm a fool, I'll do any film you bring me, because I love making films.

But the paranoiac type of thing appeals to you more.

Indeed, yes. But of all my Hammer films the one that really appealed to me was *Nightmare*.

Why more than the others?

I thought it was almost a straightforward story. After that, as you know, I went over to Amicus, who did a completely different sort of film which was fun enough that I enjoyed doing. The situation was not as nice as working at Hammer, because it was not as much fun as Hammer, but I enjoyed doing the Amicus films very much.

You mentioned that's a completely different type of a film, Amicus?
Yes, I suppose they come under the heading of horror.

Different in what way?

Softer, shall we say. That's the only way I can describe them. Hammer were really full into the sort of blood and gore stuff you know.

And that may be why you preferred the psychological Hammer ones?

Indeed.

The first of your Amicus films was Dr. Terror's House of Horrors, *also the first of Amicus' anthology films. And you later did* Torture Garden *[1968] for them and* Tales from the Crypt *[1972] for them. Did you like the idea of an anthology film or did that seem a disadvantage instead of a straightforward feature?*

Lee and Cushing in *The Creeping Flesh*

I thought it was great fun, because, it was sort of, you know, all these pictures were quite cheaply made. Somehow, if you could break it up into four different stories you didn't notice quite as much.

Didn't notice the cheapness?

Didn't notice the cheapness, and I suppose the audience thought they were getting their money's worth.

It was there too that you started working with Peter Cushing?

Well, I'd worked with Peter as a cameraman, let's see, what did I do with Peter? He had the tiniest part, but you've got to look quick to see him in *Moulin Rouge* [1952] and then he did the first film that Joe Losey did under his own name in England, *Time Without Pity* [1957]. He played a smallish part in that, not quite as small as the one in *Moulin Rouge*, but he was in that. Then I became part and parcel of the Peter Cushing entourage. We did so many films together I can't even remember.

Cushing starred in The Skull *[1965],* Dr. Terror's House of Horrors, Torture Garden *and quiet a few others. What was it like to work with Peter Cushing as a director working with an actor?*

Oh, it was wonderful because, the drill was, Peter used to live in Whitstable and whenever we're doing a film, Peter and I would arrange to meet, it was all very gentlemanly, we'd meet in the tea room at Charing Cross Station, because he'd come up by train, and we'd talk about it. We would talk about the film for about half an hour and we knew exactly what we were going to do. I knew exactly what Peter's views were and he knew what mine were and all I had to say was "Action" and "Cut," and that was absolutely wonderful. The luckiest two things that ever happened to Hammer were Peter Cushing and Christopher Lee, because these two guys were an absolute cakewalk for films, you'd just put them in and they would walk through it. Peter was wonderful, because Peter, apart from those sort of films, was a wonderful actor so he used to sail through them beautifully. I did a film later on, I tell this story because, as well I knew Peter, I was surprised. I had a script come to me, and in those days you didn't have [time] like today when you have a year to prepare them. They came to you today and you start shooting them tomorrow. A film called *The Creeping Flesh* [1972], and I saw this script, and these scripts were never works of literary genius. There was a scene there where Peter describes the whole process of this creature coming to life. I said to the producer, "Mike [Redbourn], you can't do this, nobody can get away with this, this is absolutely

Christopher Lee stars in *Dr. Terror's House of Horrors*

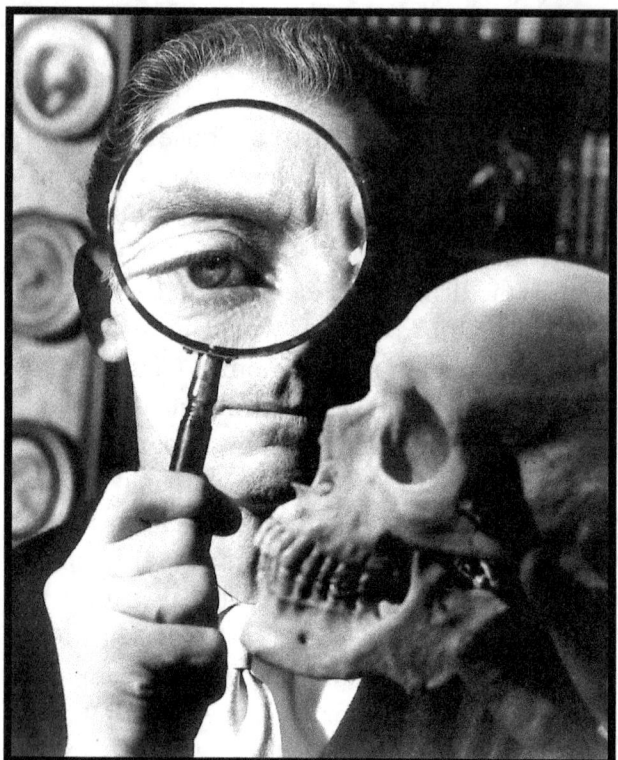

Peter Cushing uses one of his famous props in *The Skull*.

rubbish." A few weeks later, okay, turn over action and Peter starts talking and I suddenly realize he's playing this scene that I said was absolute rubbish, and it was absolute rubbish, but I was believing every word that Peter said. So this was the joy of Peter. Chris was slightly different, not that I ever had any trouble with Chris, but if I ever had trouble with Chris I'd say, "Okay, Chris this sequence is rather long and I'd like to do it all in one." That worried Chris, he didn't like doing it all in one take, so he'd go away and keep quiet for the next half an hour. They were wonderful, for Hammer to hit upon those two guys, it was an absolute Godsend.

I suppose that example with Christopher Lee illustrates one of the talents, skills of a good director, that is getting your actor or whoever, to do what you want him to do without telling him to do it. To understand his personality in such a way that you can say this and it makes him do that.

Yes, without actually fighting with him. I didn't really have a problem on that film until we came to the billiards scene, where Peter and Chris, a very nice scene, and I decided to play a bit into walking around the table and got to do it. And neither remembered to tell me that they couldn't play billiards, which was quite a problem.

So you never showed the ball?

No, no, no. They picked up the cue, prepared to shoot and then [I'd] go in close.

With Cushing you never had to rein him in.

As I say, a delicate English tea at Charing Cross Station before we started the movie and that was it. I could have gone through the movie without even speaking to Cushing.

Your relationship, working relationship, personal relationship with him, straddled the death of his wife. Did you find the methods of working, or his functioning on the set changed afterward.

Not really, no. The film I did after she died, we talked with him and said Peter would you mind if we used Helen's name as the name of your wife and do you mind if we have Helen's photographs around the set, which he absolutely loved. So one had to play with him a little bit that way.

That was your idea about the photograph?

Indeed. Yes. Actually, I asked Peter over our gentlemanly tea at Charing Cross Station.

And that appealed to him?

Oh he loved it, absolutely loved it. Well, without going too deep into Peter, he just couldn't wait for the day he'd join Helen up there or where ever.

That was Tales from the Crypt *you were talking about, where he was the junkman?*

You know better than I do. He's the old man whose father commits suicide and comes back from the grave. Yes.

I remember reading somewhere that that was not the role he was initially hired to play in that film.

I hired him to play that role.

There was an interview with him where he said, can I play this one instead, and between he and you, you worked out and built up the character more.

No, sorry Peter. No.

Okay, strike that interview. Milton Subotsky is to Amicus as Anthony Hinds is to Hammer.

No. No, let me tell you about Amicus. There's nobody here from Amicus, is there? Lovely guys, one of them's no longer with us, Milton is no longer with us. But this was a set up, there was Milton Subotsky, Max Rosenberg. Max used to stay in America to raise the money, Milton used to stay in England to make the movies. Max was the wheeler-dealer and they'd sort of get a script and they'd budget this roughly, and maybe they'd work out a budget. Let's take a figure from those days, I can't remember, budget figures were very different in those days, say they'd work out £100,000 to make the film. Max would go around the world trying to get it, and suddenly, we'd hear that he raised some money but he'd only raised £80,000 so we had to make the film for £80,000. In order for them to sort of live, dear old Milton had to write the script. Sorry Milton. Milton was not a writer but he had to write the script. I'd get scripts delivered to me, I remember one actual case, we were making a film with Margaret Johnson who played a crippled woman, *Psychopath* [1966], and first of all we haven't got enough money to make it, then the script came to me and I read it, and I said, this is very short. So, I said to my wife, "Pam, darling, time this script, I think it's very short." We were making an 80 minute film. So my wife, who's the greatest script timer in the world, she timed it—40 minutes and we've got a week before we start shooting it. We start shooting it on Monday morning and I've got a 40 minute script with about 20 minutes of ideas I can put in. Max came up to me on the set and said, "Great news, Freddie." I thought he was going to say we'd got more money. He said, "I've just heard from Columbia, they're going to do a television deal, they want 10 more minutes." But, they were great guys, but this was the way we went on. They were very different [than] Hammer. Hammer was really dead on the nail. They knew how much money they wanted, how much money

Judy Huxtable and John Standing in *Psychopath* **(1966), which was written by Robert Bloch and directed by Freddie Francis for Amicus.**

they had and the script was always right. Plus, [with Amicus] the fact that I always had the problem at the end of it. Milton used to always like being in the cutting room. So I used to have to shoot the film in such a way that Milton couldn't touch it. But they were good guys and I liked the films they made anyway.

How did you approach editing?

Well, I don't know if you remember things like *The Innocents* and films that I'd photographed, all done in rather complicated tracking shots and movements.

So that you'd stage a scene with a long continuous take involving camera movement and not involving editing.

Sure!

And therefore no editing is possible... So that wasn't an artistic choice on your part?

Well, I think I would have done it. I'd been so used to working with people like Jack Clayton and John Huston and Mickey Powell, who liked lots of moving shots. But, I guess I would have gone to that method anyway.

Certainly another challenge that comes from what you were describing is the fact that you have to keep making these films longer.

Absolutely. I remember one night we were so short on this thing, I thought I'd better write a little scene tonight to cover that. I said to Pam Davis, I said, Pam, please tonight write a scene about such and such a thing, and I said to my wife, Pam, will you write a scene about this and we'd be writing three scenes overnight to expand it.

One of the remarkable things to me is you look at the film and it doesn't feel that way. It doesn't feel added. It doesn't feel expanded. You've managed to hide the seams.

I suppose that comes not from being clever, but from having an idea about what the film is going to be about before you started. So, a little bit more doesn't hurt.

Certainly one of the most visual horror films I know of is your film The Skull.

I agree with that, I'm sorry to say.

Why are you sorry?

I agree completely.

How much of the last 30 minutes of the film, how much was your improvisation on the set?

If it was an Amicus picture, practically all of it. You know, one of the good things about that, we had a wonderful set designer and set dresser and he came up with an awful lot of good stuff to play around with. Then, I

was able to play around with this thing where we had the huge skull, and I used to have the camera, and I would be on roller skates with the camera mounted in front of me, so I was wandering around looking through the skulls eyes. We had a lot of fun that way. So I suppose having fun helped it as well. The visual things helped.

By the end of the Amicus period you were getting frustrated with all of this?

I think so, yes.

And were looking for other kinds of things and that's where Mumsy, Nanny, Sonny, and Girly *came in? Which is based on a play.*

A play that an agent rang me. An agent, who was Maggie Johnson, who, as an actress had been in *The Psychopath* and who decided she was going to look after me for the rest of my life. She used to always try to help me, and with Maggie's help you don't need enemies. Anyway, she rang me and said, "I've just seen this play at a night theatre in London and I think you ought to read it." I read it, and I liked it, and I got somebody to write a script, and, this was the strangest thing, it really spoilt my

life in movies because I didn't realize how difficult it was to set up a film. Because, something happened that was quite mad. I finished the script. I remember I picked up the script from the stenographer and took it to my agent and I said, there we are, get this going. He sent it to a man in London, an American who'd just been given a lot of money to start a leisure company and he read this overnight, spoke to the leisure company, and said I think instead of opening the leisure company, we should spend the money making this film. So the next day we'd set the film up. It's never happened again. I thought it happened like that all the time.

What was it that appealed to you so much that you would choose this as your first independent production?

Well it was a bit of a sick comedy. I like sick comedies.

Sick in what way?

Well, you know, these young kids who were about 20 and pretending to be about 12 and still went out and found new friends to play with them and then they built sandcastles and put their friends in the sand up to their necks and kept them there. It was crazy and the mother was crazy. I thought everything about it was crazy.

I remember one of the characters was beheaded. You don't see it happen but the head was in a boiling stew pot on the stove and one of the characters begins to think that maybe the head is in the stew pot and gets up and starts to look and his courage fails him and he can't look. You have a subjective shot where the camera is rising slightly until the camera can almost see but never quite sees it. This struck me, at the time, as being an extremely good example of a sort of discretion. You're not showing the head in the stew pot but you're playing with the idea.

We couldn't get anybody to play the head. I still like the film, not may people saw it. But, in my defense, I think we made it at a very bad time. We made the film and I made more money out of that than I'd made out of any other film, although it didn't do much business. On completion, the film was sold immediately to Cinerama, who then went out of business so the film struggled around, hardly got shown. But you can still pick up copies. I know I was trying for ages to get a video copy which somebody sent me one from the States. Anyway, nobody's seen it but I did enjoy it. Have you seen it?

I did see it and I recommend it. It is eccentric.

He recommends it. You have his word. You heard it here.

It's called Girly *over here, just* Girly. *Subsequently you did initiate another project—*Tales that Witness Madness *[1973]. Didn't you initiate that?*

Oh yes, yes, yes. Well, I made a film for—*The Creeping Flesh*—I made for this new company, and while I was doing it, you know, they were very happy and as the Max [Rosenberg] and Milton [Subotsky] films had been so successful, I thought, well, it would be a good idea to get a four story film going. So I spoke to the man who ran the company, John Haven, I got the script to him and, he said, "Come up and see me." So, I went up one day and he said, "How much money do you want to make this film?" I can't remember what I said, it was very little. He said, "I can fix that for you." I thought, "Yes, I've heard all this story before." It was the strangest thing ever. We were alone, it was a bank holiday, he walked out of his office into the teleprinter room, and I head him tapping something out. He came back and said, "Oh, I can get this fixed up for you in no time at all," and we spoke for about two minutes and suddenly the teleprinter started working, he went in again, he came back, he said, "That's okay, we got the money." He telexed to Frank Yablans, who was running Paramount then, and one of the films that I'd done for Max and

Milton had been shown over here and was a great success, and Yablans'd seen it was a success, so, he gave us the money to make that film.

You also had the stories written, didn't you?

Oh, I had an actress friend of mine, who had been in many of my films, Jenny Jayne, you've seen her. So she wrote it and off we went.

Did you originate the story ideas?

It's too long ago to remember.

I was particularly was struck by the one called "Luau" in which the Hawaiian hero has to sacrifice a virgin and feed her to her mother.

This was a children's film, yes.

As I recall, you treated it as a comedy.

Not that one exactly. No, we couldn't get a laugh out of that at all. But it was very enjoyable, because, we had some very good actors in it and we had a very dear lady, Rita Hayworth, come over to play the part, but she was too ill. So, she couldn't do it. She had this terrible Alzheimer's disease and it was starting then, so we had to replace her with another lovely lady we have, a very good friend, it was Kim Novak. We had a lot of fun on that movie. We had a lot of people in it. Other people too numerous to mention, quite a big cast.

After finally I guess reaching a point of complete disillusions in the films being offered you, you took about five years off. What where you doing in those five years between Legend of the Werewolf *[1975. AKA* Plague of the Werewolf*] and* The Elephant Man *[1980]?*

No, that's not quite true. I did take it off from feature films but, you know because I like eating or drinking, if anyone offered me a television show, I did things like *The Saint*. Another very good show, I thought, with Richard Bradford, *Man in the Suitcase,* I did several of those, *Black Beauty*s. I did those to keep body and soul together.

John Hurt as *The Elephant Man*

What prompted you to shift back to photographing films with The Elephant Man?

More promise. Well, David Lynch and Jonathan Sanger, who produced *The Elephant Man*, came over, they were looking around and they asked for a meeting with me, I met with them, and we hit it off immediately as, in fact, we still do. So I said if they wanted me to I would do the movie. There was a lot of opposition. People were saying, "You can't have Freddie, he hasn't photographed a film for 10 or 15 years," and David said, "Well you know, it's like riding a bicycle, once you can do it, it's just the same." So, it was a very funny thing. They finally got it down to two people, me and one other guy who is a friend of mine, so I won't mention his name, so they said, "Let's toss a coin. If it comes down heads we'll have Freddie, if it comes down tales we'll have the other guy." So a great friendship sprang out between the three of us. I've just come back from seeing David in L.A., but that's how I did that picture.

Which started you off.

Freddie and Martin Scorsese filming Cape Fear

Next thing I knew I was on *The French Lieutenant's Woman* and so on and so forth.

With a little bit of more directing in between, The Doctor's and the Devils *[1985], a very striking film which is missing one scene I understand, the scene toward the end where the doctor feels remorse.*

Oh yes, yes, yes. When I was doing *Cape Fear* [1991] I spoke to Martin [Scorsese] about it and he said, "Why don't we buy it and put the scene back?" But I couldn't go through all of that.

Was that scene shot and just cut out?

The idea was shot and cut out because dear old Mel Brooks didn't think it was necessary and as it was his money.

But the footage existed?

The footage existed but don't ask me where.

As much as I liked the film, there is a sense that everything happens too fast at the end.

The whole subject is the ends justifying the ends, and that's missing.

What's on your schedule at the moment?

Funny you should say that. I'm too old to run around setting up films, I'm also too old to work 18 hours a day on films. Not that I'm too old, it's not necessary, so I won't do films unless I'm really interested. I have a project. When I was doing *Cape Fear* with Marty a script came to me and Marty heard me talk to the guy who brought it, Henry Bumstead,

and I said, "Henry, I don't want to get involved in setting up movies," blah, blah, blah and Marty said, "Let me see that," and he took it home to read it. And, he said, "Freddie I think you should do this movie." I said, "Why Marty?" I can't tell you why, because it gives away some secrets. Anyway Marty said, "You direct it and I'll produce it," so we're trying to set that up at the moment and yesterday, I had a meeting with the Maryland Film Commission because I want to do it here. We'll see.

So there's still more directing in store?
I hope so, yes.

Regarding casting and working with actors:

It's strange, sometimes on the sort of films that I have done, I appreciate that I can never direct all the artists, because there's not time. So I'm very careful to cast them with friends or with people who have done so many films with me they've become friends and just get on with it. With Peter, you know, there's no problem, providing you let everyone know beforehand what you want to do with this movie. Fortunately, I've come across very few awkward artists. Chris, as I've said, used to need a bit of jockeying along, but Peter you could forget he was there. It's nice to have friends to play those smaller parts where you know you can't devote too much time to them. I have a very funny story. There was a very famous Irish actor called Jackie McGowran, he was one of the Abbey Theatre, and he was wonderful. I think it was the first film I'd ever directed, there was the part of a hotel porter or landlord or something. I said to the producer, "I'd love to get Jackie to play this part." I went with Jackie, I said, "This is a hotel porter, blah, blah, blah," just said a few words to him, and [told him] go ahead. Now this is a famous Irish actor, and suddenly, after two days, I was looking at the rushes and I suddenly realized Jackie had decided to play it as a Welshman, so you come across these snags occasionally. But one has to cast carefully because if you have a difficult artist in the movie, forget it.

Did Peter come to you with tidbits on how you wanted him to play Baron Frankenstein.

Very rarely, he'd played it before and we discussed it and [then] get on with it. Let's face it, Baron Frankenstein eventually becomes Peter Cushing.

You photographed a number of films in black and white. What are the advantages of it and do you think there's any future for it?

People are always asking me this question; they're always coming to say, you made something in black and white or color and they want to know was it a great artistic decision and invariably it was a commercial decision. Everybody always says what a wonderful idea it was to make *The Elephant Man* in black and white and who made that decision. It was not [an] artistic decision. It was a Mel Brooks film as you know and he didn't want to spend the money to make it a color film. Invariably those are the things. For my money, I love both black and white and color. I think I could have made *The Elephant Man* look just as period had we done it in color, it would have been more of a challenge. Very rarely is this an artistic decision. I think these days it's a bit rather difficult to sell a film to television if it is black and white.

Then, once the decision is made, that sets off a chain of thought about how to use black and white or how to use color.

Indeed. It comes down to the DP and designer.

So once you go down the road planning it for black and white, you couldn't just instantly change it to color.

I could. [laughs] I really mean that, you know. Once one's got the mood in one's mind you can create that mood in either black and white or color by different means.

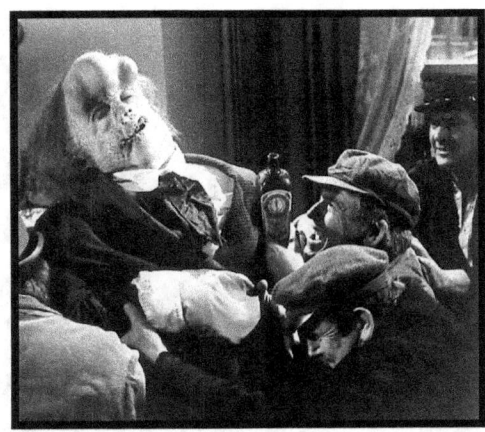

How were the Hammer films conceived when they were released, critically.

It depends on the press. The sort of high-class press sort of rather frowned on them. It's very strange because I directed a lot of these pictures, as you know, and most of my friends in the business would never dream of seeing them and eventually, in the early days of television they'd probably see these films and I know people like Jack Clayton and these people come visit and say, "I've see one of your films on television last night and it was very good, wasn't it?" But the press are very strange people. They have to hit a certain area and they're above all that you know. So not very well. The low class press, which, of course, I don't read, they viewed them quite normally but generally they [the films] were sort of frowned upon.

The films you're directed, did you have a choice of lighting and cameramen?

Not a great deal of choice because money came into it a lot. It's funny, the first film I directed, I'd seen a lot of films that had been directed by cameramen and I thought they had no soul, I thought they concentrated too much on the lighting. "When I do this I won't interest myself in the photography at all, I'll turn away from it." That was my worst mistake. And after about two films I said, "Oh to hell with this, I'm going to get friends to photograph them" and I would have long chats with them and tell them how I want this to look. Which I did and toward the end of those films I directed, you'll find I had one or two cameramen around all the time, John Wilcox and a guy called Norman Wooley.

You worked with David Lynch on two very different films, The Elephant Man *and* Dune *[1984]. How would you contrast working on each film?*

Dino and Raffaella De Laurentiis, David Lynch and Freddie Francis, on the set of *Dune*.

Dune *obviously cost a lot more money, but was it a more difficult film to make than* The Elephant Man.

Not really, no. I had my faithful companion Gordon Hayman with me on the movie. We loved David, and we realized that we would go into eternity on that film, and it was going on and on, and I can remember, I turned to David and I'd say, "One hour 40 David." "Aw, shut up." When I left the film, David said, "I'd like you to see the film before I go." That was the cut at the time which ran for four hours, so the film was in my opinion — I know some people love it — but I thought it was a very slow film. Also the sort of contrivance of having Mrs. De Laurentiis coming on screen every time and telling you the story, I don't think worked. But working with David is great, and, you know, those two films I enjoyed very much. David knew exactly what he wanted because he hadn't been used to studios, so, he didn't quite know how to go about getting it. So, I was able to sort of guide him a bit. Both the films are what David wanted, and I was able to help him get it, but, as far as I was concerned, I didn't think *Dune* was ever going to be a successful film, but it was very fun to work on with David.

VAL GUEST

Val Guest appeared at both Hammer tributes, FANEX 8 and 11. He is a very soft-spoken man, but very witty and the driving force behind Hammer's greatest science fiction films, *The Quatermass Xperiment* [1955] and *Quatermass II* [1957]. As with all the guests at the conventions, Gary and I seldom get to spend time with the guests, but we were happy to honor Mr. Guest, whose films are among our very favorites.

Tell us about your acting career/.

Well, I decided I wasn't a very good actor, and I was under contract to Warners, as a matter of fact. And I went to Warners and I thought I would tell them I wasn't a very good actor, and they told me, so I asked if they would release me, and they said they would release me, on condition that they had first call on everything that I wrote. Needless to say, they didn't use any of it.

You worked on the Hollywood Reporter?

I reviewed a movie he [Marcel Varnel] made with a character called Edmund Lowe. I believe it was called *Chandu the Magician* [1932], and in the brashness of youth, I wrote in my review, if I couldn't write a better picture with one hand tied behind my back, I'd give up the game. And Marcel Varnel got in touch with Billy Wilkerson, who was the editor and publisher of *The Hollywood Reporter*, and said, "If you're correspondent is so damn clever, let him write my next."

And Billy Wilkerson called me up, and I said, "Look, Billy, I was stupid. I shouldn't have said that. You know, of course I can't."

And he said, "Well, you can't make the paper look goddamn stupid. Go and see him."

So I went to see Marcel, and I said, "I'm sorry. I'm young and stupid... I can't write your next picture."

He said, "Well, I've read your column and I think you can." That's how we started on an 11-year partnership. I don't know how many films we did together.

And we had a contract that he couldn't direct anything I didn't write, and I couldn't write anything he didn't direct. That's how I really started, and when he went off to do other pictures with Columbia, I stayed... and they allowed me to write and direct my own. That's how that started.

How did you begin directing?

It's a rather strange story. It was during the war, and the Ministry of Information in England were wanting various documentaries done, Ministry of Information shorts to help the war effort. And one of them was a little subject about how to watch if you got colds and sneezes. It was "Colds and Sneezes Spread Diseases," which was a sort of slogan... a short to put 'round with all the feature pictures. Put them out in the cinema to help the war effort. And they asked me if I would write it, write one of

The Camp on Blood Island

these things. And I happened to find out that they'd already asked six other writers, and six other writers had written something, and they had been turned down. And so I gave an Academy Award performance and said, "Look, you've come to me sixth in line, and I think this is an insult. I will write one, on condition that if you like what I write, I direct it."

And they said, all right, they would. And I wrote it, and they liked it, so I directed it. And I had the very good fortune—it was shown in London at the Leicester Square Theatre on the same bill as Rita Hayworth's *My Gal Sal*. And the critics absolutely slaughtered *My Gal Sal*, and one of the top critics said, "The best thing on the program was a Ministry of Information short." And on this little review, I went to see the producer at Gainsborough Pictures, and I put it across the desk and I said, "Did you read this?"

And he said, "Oh, yes. If you're lucky, you might become the Ministry of Information's new director."

And I said, "How about I do one for Gainsborough?" And this was actually how I was able to write and direct my first feature.

Tell us about The Camp on Blood Island *[1958]*.

It was controversial because it showed the…soldiers in the camps… How it happened was that the front of house manager at the Lyric Theatre in London happened to have been one of the prisoners of war in the Japanese camp and had kept, written on odd scraps of paper that he could find, a diary. And it was from this diary…and he had sent something to Tony Hinds, told him about it, and they discussed it and everything, and they said, "What a hell of an idea. We can get a story out of this."

So it was actually from the remnants of a Japanese prisoner of war's diary. That's how that came about.

What about Yesterday's Enemy *[1959]?*

That was, again, controversial… there's quite an amusing story about that. We never went on location to Burma or anything like that. And we had a fabulous set at Pinewood Studios of the swamp and the soldiers going waist deep in all this mud with them holding the rifles up to keep them out of the water. And our art director was brilliant—made jungle sets that were on turntables, so that when you had finished shooting one section, you could swing these around and it was another part of the jungle. It was a brilliant conception—wonderful.

For the premiere of this film, they had it at the Empire Theatre in Leicester Square. And it was a sort of semi-royal premiere, and Earl Mountbatten, Lord Mountbatten of Burma, who was in charge of all the forces over there and everything, was the guest of honor. It was for him and for the Burma staff... and I sat next to him during the screening—and about halfway through one of the jungle sequences, he turned to me and he said, "I know that place. I know exactly where that was, and I can't think of its name." I didn't want to tell him... but he was absolutely convinced—that's how good the artwork was, and the camerawork. He was quite convinced, because he'd been in that part of Burma...

I had a terrible battle about that [the lack of music], because everybody was standing by to do a great war picture score, and I said, "Why don't we do a war picture without music?"

And they said, "You're out of your mind."

And I said, "I'd like to make a score with jungle noises, with jungle movements and the various things that you would get in a jungle." So we had reams and reams of jungle soundtracks, and from that we made it. And not an awful lot of people realized that there was no music. You'd be surprised how good background music is something that disappears into the background, until after the film and you hear an LP of it or something, and realize, "My God, it was a beautiful score." Sometimes you are aware of the music, but on that type of a picture, it is far better if you don't get held up by the music.

Tell us about directing Hell is a City *[1960].*

[Stanley Baker] was a very, very good actor. Very solid, very professional. You never had any problems with Stanley... the easiest person in the world to direct. What more can I say about him? He's sadly missed, and we had a lot of fun together… He was a no-nonsense man… there were certainly no airs and graces.

What can you tell us about The Quatermass Experiment?

I had never done a science-fiction or horror picture… that was way out of my canon. And I was probably the only person in the British Isles who hadn't seen the TV series, because it was an enormous success as a TV series.

And Tony Hinds called me one day and said, "We've bought the TV series and we're thinking of doing a film of it. Would you be interested?"

And I said, "Well, I'd like to read it." So we were just going on holiday. We were going to Tangiers.

And he said, "All right. I'll bring the script to the airport"…So he met us at the airport, as we got on the plane, with a packet this big: It was 16 TV scripts, which was all we needed on an aeroplane, as you can understand. And he said, "Read it while you're in Tangiers."

Brian Donlevy in *The Quatermass Experiment*

So I took this enormous, great package, and I put it at the side of the bed. And it was at the side of the bed for about a week. And suddenly, Yolande Donlan, my wife, said, "What's this?"

And I said, "Oh, it's something Tony Hinds wants me to read."

She said, "Well, have you read it?"

And I said, "No, this isn't my cup of tea. This is science fiction or horror. I don't know what to do with that."

She said, "Since when have you been ethereal?"

And I said, "Well, all right, I'd better read it then." And I did read it, and I thought it was very exciting stuff, and the greatest mystery of all was how in the world to get all these 16—I don't know if it was 13 or 16—episodes into one film. That was the problem. And I don't think Nigel Kneale ever forgave me for cutting a lot of the stuff. I had to. There was nothing you could do…to get it done.

And I said, "Yes, I'll do it." I made my first horror movie, or science fiction, or whatever you want to call it. When I first said I would do it, I said, "I will do it only if you will let me treat it as though I was making a newsreel…and we had a correspondent…and a lot of hand-held camera…At first they were very reluctant, but they finally let me do it…I thought…it would be unusual to have one of these kind of pictures done as though somebody had sent a newsreel…The character [Nigel Kneale] had written was a slightly ethereal professor who was really an intellectual, and that didn't fit in somehow with the way of shooting, as if you were covering a newsreel story.

I wanted someone who was so down to earth that he would be believable—and Donlevy…we had to take an American, by the way, because the distributors…wanted a bankable name they could put up outside… They said, "Here's a list," and I picked Donlevy out of the list because he was the sort of person I could believe involved in all this.

What can you tell us about The Abominable Snowman *[1957] and Peter Cushing?*

Peter was a dear friend… and he was a wonderful character… He was known as "Props" Cushing, because he adored props. But he wouldn't rehearse with these props at all. He would have it all worked out in his mind… and once I said, "Action!" and we were shooting, the props would come out in the actual shot.

Peter Cushing and Forrest Tucker in *The Abominable Snowman*

And I remember one in particular. He found the tooth of a Yeti. This happened so long ago, I can't remember. It was shown by the Llama in the monastery—the actual tooth of a Yeti that they had found... In the rehearsals, he looked at it, and he took a magnifier and looked at it, and I said, "Okay, we'll shoot it."

And in the take—we went through a perfect take all the way through—and Peter reached into his pocket and he brought out a nail file... but luckily we got through without anybody collapsing. They did the moment I said, "Cut!" of course. And he was literally always doing that... Not only did he take out a nail file, he took out a little tape measure and measured the thing, too. None of this was in the script. None of this was in the rehearsal... But he was a wonderful character, because here was a man who had started off... as a Shakespearean actor... and Peter worked in Petticoat Lane, which was the old market in the East End of London... and his wife... made him take elocution lessons... and he suddenly became a Shakespearean actor, and nobody knew this at all. And after a take, any particular take that we had trouble with, and we got it, and I'd say, "Great, that's a terrific take," he would suddenly break into a Cockney dance... It was so out of character, the whole place collapsed. He was a wonderful character.

How was it working at Bray Studios?

It was a family, probably one of the happiest studios I ever worked in. And second was Gainsborough Studios, where we were all around there for years and years. But Bray was really a family studio—and we were all working under the most incredible conditions. It wasn't really a studio. It was an old house, before they started building stages. And the [camera] operator had to get his backside into the fireplace to get a long shot. You were expected to come on the set every morning with instant genius... There was never enough shooting time, never enough money, nothing. Somehow we all got through... what was impossible was suddenly made possible, really.

I think that, during the Hammer period, we all learned how to make a few cents look like a million dollars. I mean sheer trickery, the whole thing. But it was a great family, and Jimmy Sangster was my production manager on my first picture.

Tell us about The Day the Earth Caught Fire *[1961]*.

Again, I did it almost newsreel, *cinema verite*... I must say that, with global warming, as it is today, we were ahead of our time... Again, I had terrible arguments about doing it in color. They all wanted it in color, and I said, "I think the essence of this is black and white." Because, in those days, newspapers were not in color. Newsreels were not in color—so that everything that was real news was black and white, and you had your black and white paper in the morning. And with this sort of a story, to give it the reality, just to keep it in black and white...

I had terrible trouble getting it made. I wrote the story of that about eight years before we made it, and every time we'd had a picture that was a success, they'd say, "What are you going to do next?"

"Well, I've got a story here" and I'd bring this up, and they'd say, "Are you out of your mind? Who wants to go see the atom bomb? We don't even want to know about them."

So we had a terrible time, and eventually we got it made, because I had done a picture called *Expresso Bongo* [1959], we'd won quite a few awards and things on it... Yolande was in it, with Larry Harvey. And we decided to put this up as collateral on it, because it was making a lot of money. We said, "Look. You let us make *The Day the Earth Caught Fire* and we'll put this up as collateral." So we turned the whole picture over to them... It was a tough picture to get made, and also a tough picture to make.

President Kennedy asked for a copy of the picture and screened it for 200 correspondents in Washington. And Eleanor Roosevelt asked for a copy, and there's a copy of it in the Archives.

We sold the remake rights to Twentieth Century-Fox, and I finished the updating... and it's now in what is laughingly called "pre-production." It could go on for years. We could be globally out-warmed before they remake it. But anyway, it's on their list... They sent a list of possible leads to play the newspaper man, and on that list was the name of Michael Caine.

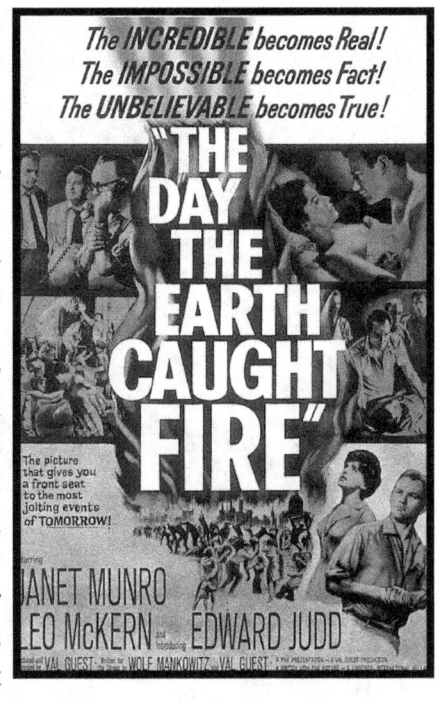

Now, what nobody may realize is that, in the film, in the one place where the leading man is stopped in his car going through rioting London—the water mains are out, and this and that and the other, and he's stopped by a cop who says, "I warn you, Sir. It's bad to go through here." That's Michael Caine." And we gave him the job because he was having a terrible time paying his rent. I think we paid him £15 a day... Not so long ago, I met up with Michael and said, "Do you know they're remaking one of your old films?"

He said, "No. What?"

I said, *"The Day the Earth Caught Fire."*

What do you remember about When Dinosaurs Ruled the Earth *[1971]?*

James Carreras... the head of Hammer, called me to come and see him in the office one day. And he showed me this enormous poster that he'd had drawn by the art department, of the dinosaur with the girl in its mouth and everything. And he had sent this poster to AIP, I think it was... He said, "What about this?"

And they said, "Yes, go ahead. Make it."

Victoria Vetri and Robin Hawdon in *When Dinosaurs Ruled the Earth*

And he said, "They're ready to make it."

I said, "Fine. Let me read it."

And he said, "Oh, Christ. You've got to write that!"

So this was written from a poster. That's actually how this thing started. And they had a writer who'd written out a story on it... and Yolande and I were on holiday in Malta. At that time, we had a holiday place there, and we were on holiday. And Aida Young, the producer, flew out to see me, and said, "Can we make this? Would you like to do this? Let's talk about it."

And we tried desperately to see if we could make it in Malta, so I wouldn't have to leave our place. But there weren't any mountains in Malta, and there weren't any lava rocks and things, so we thought, "Well, we have to go abroad to do it."

It was a sort of cobbled together picture. We did the best we could with that. I wasn't all that happy with the final cut. I had done my final cut and went off on another picture... There was re-editing... and I was not happy with it.

CHRISTOPHER LEE

One of Gary's favorite films has always been *Horror of Dracula*. I'm sure he never imagined he would meet Christopher Lee, let alone publish the U.S. edition of his autobiography, *Tall, Dark and Gruesome*. Christopher Lee was everything we expected and more. He was regal, tall, handsome and refined. But he was also warm and charming with his many fans who showed up at Monster Rally, shaking the hand of everyone in line and posing for photos. I can never forget many grown men coming out of the book signing with trembling hands and more than a few had a tear in their eye. Mr. Lee was scheduled to speak for an hour on Sunday. He spoke for over an hour and a half to an enthralled audience. I hope Mr. Lee will always remember Monster Rally and the effect his work and presence had on his many fans.

Currently, Mr. Lee is appearing in two mega-blockbusters in 2001 and 2002—*The Lord of the Rings: The Fellowship of the Ring* and *Star Wars: Attack of the Clones*. Happily he will beget a whole new generation of fans.

Of *The Fellowship of the Ring* Gary notes: Last Saturday [Dec, 8, 2001] at 9 a.m. at the premiere theater in Baltimore, the historic Senator Theater, I was honored to attend a special press screening of *Lord of the Rings* under pristine viewing (and listening) circumstances. Simply stated, as *Entertainment Weekly* notes, the film is a solid A, and it is my favorite film of the year. I could go on and on, but just to hit a few major points...

The film begins with a *Gladiator*-style epic battle sequence, but under the direction of Peter Jackson, the sprawling visuals are simply awe-inspiring and jaw-dropping. And this is only the beginning. The film seems closer to two than its actual three-hour running time. The visual contrast between the *Brigadoon*-style Shire and the horrors of Saruman's domain is again quite incredible. The thing that impressed me most about *Lord of the Rings* is its quotient of pure horror that I never expected. The spectral riders on horseback seeking out Frodo and friends makes Tim Burton's headless horseman seem quaint.

But let's talk about Christopher Lee as Saruman. In his two major scenes in the movie, he is at the top of his form, perhaps in this very important supporting role submitting one of his best performances bar none. In one sweeping visual sequence, Lee is outside atop a tower with his arms raised. The sweeping steadicam flies through space and zooms in on the imposing presence of Lee, but the camera does not stop there. Instead the camera swoops past the wizard and follows him, moving away, from behind. What a sequence. I can just play it over and over again in my mind. In Lee's best scene, and one of his all-time greatest performances ever, in a one-on-one sequence, Lee has a wizard's dual, throws Ian McKellen against the walls, up into the air, etc. Imagine AIP's *The Raven*, with Vincent Price and Boris Karloff as the dueling wizards, done seriously, expensively, and with great special effects. It is almost as though Jackson wanted to create an homage to Lee.

In another great sequence, Lee is allowed to mesmerize the audience with his Lugosi-esque elongated extended fingers magical stance. Christopher Lee must have thought he died and gone to heaven, as this is his favorite novel and the role is among the finest of his career. For his fans, its seeing Lee the way we always dreamed of seeing him... at the top of his form in an artistic movie with a big budget to do it right.

Lord of the Rings is a triumph in every way, and the intensity Jackson gets from PG-13 rated violence seems almost R-esque, but supposedly on DVD, Jackson will finally get his wish to have an R rated version released. But the PG-13 packs a visceral wallop, believe you me. Ian McKellen, working under heavy costume and makeup, submits the performance of the movie, working mainly with his face (Jackson does some incredible things with tight facial closeups) and his subtle, quick reactions. It is a performance far richer than it first may appear. Much more natural and subtle than his James Whale.

But I am babbling on far too long. Bottom line is this. *The Lord of the Rings* is the type of fantasy film that we wished could still be made but knew deep in our hearts that it never would be. Well, think again. The film on every level is a triumph (and the horror sequences are classic horror sequences... just wait until you see Lee with his army of Gothic demons!). The film of the year!

On being an actor

When I made the decision to be an actor, to learn how to be an actor, the first person I told who could stand paying for my mis-surviving...was my mother. My mother was the greatest dramatic actress I've known my entire life, though she was not a professional. And her reaction was straight out of Victorian melodrama. She reeled back, with her hand to her brow, like that, she really did, with the other one holding onto the door, and said, "You can't, you can't, you can't. Think of the shame you'll bring upon the family. And—think of the people you'll meet."

What she meant—and it has indeed been true—is the people you have to deal with in this business, not the public—but the sort of people you have to talk to, tell them who you are, and make the decision, ultimately, to

"Have you ever played any wise, mysterious characters?"

offer you the job. And the haggling starts, and the offers go on, and the contracts go wrong, and all sorts of things. So when she said, "Think of the people you'll meet," she certainly wasn't wrong there, sadly.

It wasn't like that when I started, but it has become like that in the intervening years. Now it's just figures in the ledger, which is very sad, because people of my generation, actors and actresses of my generation, and the next one, and maybe even the next one—actually anybody 30-35, 40-45, onward: We love our work. We meet some of the most loyal, talented, devoted and hard-working people in the world on both sides of the camera. And we, of course, meet the marvelous and the appreciative people all over the world who make up the public who watch our work and hopefully are entertained by it. You are the public, and we do what we do for *you*. We do not do it for some executive sitting in an office.

Not all that long ago, I was in a certain studio in L.A., and they asked to see me in regard to possibly being in a certain film. I obviously can't name names or titles. And I went into this studio, one I have worked in quite a bit, because it was during the time I had lived there between '76 and '85. And I parked the car and went to the office. The first thing that happened was this rather embarrassed-looking lady said, "Would you mind if I take a Polaroid of you?"

And I said, "Polaroid?" I was getting really confused. And I said, "Why do you need a Polaroid of me? I'm standing here."

"Oh, but it's customary now. I just took one of Jack Lemmon the other day."

And I can't believe what I'm hearing. She was obviously quite embarrassed about this. Then I was told I was going to meet the chief administrator of the executive casting division, and I thought to myself, it's presumably the casting director—all of 20 or 25. And I went to this little area—all these doors were open, so there were people in these offices, I knew that, of course. So I started making rather extremely tactless remarks, deliberately. And eventually the summons came and I went into a room, and there was a man sitting behind a desk. He didn't get up. I didn't expect him to. He didn't really even look up at me. And all the floor was covered with folders and folders and stacked with photographs of actors and actresses, all around the room. I can't tell you his name, which I have not forgotten. And I sat down, without being asked, and he said, "What have you been doing?"

And I said, "Well, I've just had a Polaroid taken of me."

His face kind of changed. He said, "No, no, no, no. What have you been doing?"

I said, "You mean this morning?"

And he said, "No, no, no, no, no. Mr. So-and-So and I are very interested in you playing something in our film."

At which time I had become a little, let's say, irritated, and I said, "Something? Is that one word or two?"

And actually this has got nothing to do with the beginning of my career, except that it hasn't changed all that much. They do ask you what you've done, when it's their business to know. And they should do their homework, not just with me—anyone. And I went to see a director on a film that again has to be nameless; and he talked about everything getting away from it, 15 or 20 minutes, that goes without saying, just to put me in my place. And some young boy, [who looked] about 15 or 16, he said, "What was your name, again?"

I very nearly said, "Lon Chaney," but I didn't.

And there was this man. He actually did get up, until he saw how tall I was, then he sat down again. And, of course, came out with his remark, "I didn't realize how tall you were." That was said to me in New York, only four or five days ago, when I was lucky enough, and privileged enough, to see *Death of a Salesman* with a man I consider to be one of the finest actors around today, Brian Dennehy. And I went backstage, and Gitte was with me, my wife. And I don't know how he does it, because it's an exhausting part. And the first thing he said: "I didn't realize how tall you were." Lots of people say that to me. Which just shows that obviously I don't look so gigantic on the screen. The screen actually widens you rather than lengthens you, at least that's what they tell me.

Anyway, I went in to see this director. He said, "I'm going to do such-and-such a picture."

And I said, "Yes, I believe that's why you asked to see me." And so on. And then he talked about everything except the film. He was waiting, I suppose, for the producer, because the door opened and a man came in in shorts, trainers, baseball cap and said, "I am the producer."

So I said, "Fine. Okay."

He sat down with a sheaf of papers and kept turning them, saying, "You've done a lot of movies. You've done a lot of movies. You *have* done a lot of movies." And so on.

And I said, "Well, a few, you know." And I thought, "This is ridiculous."

And then the director turned to me and he said, "Have you ever played any wise, mysterious characters?"

And I said, "Yes, I think so."

"Can we see something?" I assure you that is what they say to just about everyone. "Can we see something?"

And I said, "Well, yes. It might take a little time to see over 200 films, but I'm sure it can be arranged."

"Can we *see* something?" and I said, "In other words, what you are asking for—is you are asking for film of me playing the part you are thinking about casting me for in your forthcoming movie. I'm going to show you something on film of myself already playing it." This is the thinking. It is. And I said, "Well, actually, the wisest, most mysterious character I ever played was a character called Prospero." No reaction. I said, "In a play by William *Shakespeare*."

"Uh huh. Uh huh. *Shakespeare in Love* and all that sort of thing. Uh huh. Uh huh. Right, right, right."

I said, "The play was called *The Tempest*, not *The Twister*."

It's not what you know or what you've done. It's so many different things which really have no meaning at all, as far as I can see.

When I started, I knew nothing. I suppose that could apply to all of us. When you start a profession, you are going to learn. Now, if they said to me, which they did in England after approving my contract through Rank—which nearly finished my career. If they said to me, "You have no experience." Right, no argument. If they said to me, "You have no name." Right, no argument there. If they said to me, "You don't know much about acting," I would have said, "Yes, you're absolutely right." All these would be valuable. But when they turn around to you and they say, "You're too *tall* to be an actor," and too foreign-looking, because of my Italian blood, it's like saying to someone, "You're too red-haired to be a pianist," or "You're too thin to be a sculptor," or whatever, you make it up. You can think of anything yourself.

It is actually half-witted, because it isn't valid. The reasons, apart from the fact that I knew nothing about acting, and I was terrible—if I thought acting meant acting *all the time*—I'm reminded of my first play, called *The Constant Nymph*. I played the butler. I still have that review: "Christopher Lee, as Roberto the Butler, here gives a remarkable performance." I certainly did, because at the end of the first act, the producer of the play came 'round to me and said, "I'm sending the rest of the cast home. You can finish the play by yourself."

And I, of course, took it very seriously, and was very alarmed. "What do you mean, home?" I didn't know what to say.

And he said, "Well, you're already playing all the roles."

And, of course, I was, because nobody told me. And I knew somebody on the stage said, "Oh, it's an absolute tragedy. My father passed away..." and somebody said, "It's terrible weather outside. I'm going to go get my umbrella." And I did everything they said, which of course was very distracting and extremely unprofessional, but I didn't know.

The real reason that I wasn't used was a very different one. The average British leading man of that time, in '47, '48, '49, '50, etc., the first 10 years, really, of my career, was not tall. There were some very fine actors. John Mills was one, Kenneth More, Richard Todd, the list is very, very big. But they were certainly shorter than I was. But the ladies, generally speaking, were shorter than the men.

But the other men who were supposedly the giants, very tall men—Stewart Granger, Vincent Price, Michael Wilding and many others—were still shorter than me. And there was no way I was going to be put on the screen with these people, even if I didn't say anything. It's understandable, if you're me—different coloring, different size, different shape or something. No matter who you are, if you are different, the attention of the audience wanders, and they look at you and, of course, as I said rather pointedly on some occasions, said, "This is the star. See that he concentrates the attention of the audience on himself, and not worry about somebody who's coming over there and putting up the wall." That was the real reason, and I'm already a determined person. The more they said that to me, the more my poor mother said, "You should give it up. You should give it up. This is a terribly dangerous profession. You're not earning any money, anyway. You won't earn enough. You won't do this and you won't do that." And the more people said, "You're too tall. You're too foreign looking. You're too this. You're too that"—the more I said, "I'll *show you.*"

It took 10 years before I got the chance—but *during* that 10 years, something happened of such value that I cannot exaggerate it too much. I *learned.* I watched. I did everything I could possibly do, suitable and unsuitable. Traveled around Europe on a bicycle, getting a job in a crowd somewhere. I *learned.* Swept the floor of the stage, assistant stage manager, et cetera., prompter. I did everything, everything I could lay my hands on, in any language, even those I didn't know very well, but I learned—and that does not happen today. Sad, and it's very obvious, too—although I'm obviously not going to go into details—it's quite clear when somebody really knows what they're doing or when they don't. And the sad thing is, today, more than ever—and it's been going on for the last 20-odd years, and longer... obviously they come and they go, the "Golden Boy" and the "Golden Girl," flavor of the month, making millions...

But with people like myself, who really aren't what you might call "leading men stars" or anything like that, not in the sense the giants were—I met most of them, worked with some of them—I don't think there's a name you could mention I haven't met at one time or another—they kept going because they had *learned*, and they could do almost anything. And they were giants.

There are no giants today. There are some very fine actors. I'll go and see anything with Gene Hackman—anything. There are some marvelous actors, like Jack Nicholson, a tough opponent at golf. I remember when I was trying a short putt, he said, "Don't chip it. Don't chip it." And he also told me that when he did these pictures with Roger Corman—with Boris, Vincent, Peter Lorre—that Roger Corman said to him, "Don't try and be funny as they are." Wise advice—and Nicholson, Pacino, DeNiro, Mel

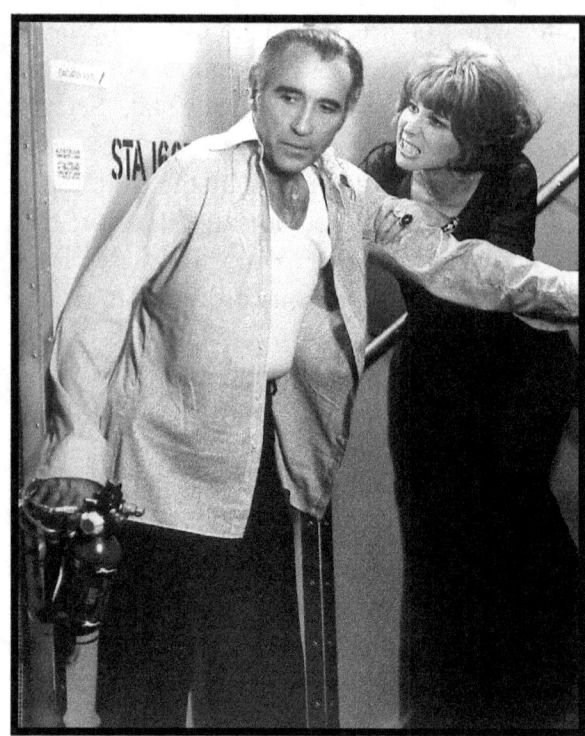

Airport '77 with Lee Grant

Gibson—there's some wonderful actors around. And actresses. To me, Jodie Foster, wonderful actress...there are many. You have your favorites, I have mine. Jack Lemmon. That's the only reason I did *Airport '77* [1977]. I had a scene with him. That's the only reason.

And there are some other wonderful actors around, and there are some stars, but they're not giants, not in my opinion.

Sheila Graham, whom some of you have heard of, she was a very well-known journalist, and certainly the lady of Scott Fitzgerald for many, many years—I knew her, and in London, she made a quote—and this is 35 years ago—she said, "There are no giants anymore. Only dwarfs with long shadows."

But, anyway, that's how it started, in 1947, when I thought, "Well, I'll show you," and I think I did.

The Warrior

Because of Churchill's famous quote, "Never was so much owed by so many to so few"—the pilots of the Spitfire Iron Squadrons—all my friends, sadly, tragically, *all* gone. Men with the equivalent of the Medal of Honor... And going up into the North African desert, spending two years there, getting into all sorts of strange aeroplanes, dropping leaflets, dropping bombs and getting into some very, very strange units... Popskey's Private Army—I shouldn't think any of you have ever heard of that—P.P.A., commanded by a Belgian Russian called Vladinya Penyikov, called "Popskey"... number one demolition squadron, 120 full strength, they were very scary people. I was much more frightened of them than the enemy. Well, you felt like you do about Wellington's remark at Waterloo, when he looked around at the British soldiers and he said, "I don't know what effect they'll have on the enemy, but, by God, they frighten me." And he did say that.

And, of course, I had the great good fortune to survive for quite a long time with the British equivalent of the American O.S.S., "Oh So Secret." So... I spent a great deal of the last year of the war with Tito and his partisans, and also with a unit, on and off over a period of about two years, which most of you probably think was an airline, called the S.A.S., but actually it's not an airline, it's called Special Air Service, and it's still very much around. It's the British equivalent of the Delta. So, I guess I'm lucky to be here.

Dracula

He said he didn't know he spoke for the rest of the audience, but he would like to see me play a *certain role* again. There's Forry Ackerman sitting there, who kindly gave me a copy of Lugosi's ring, for which I am very grateful, as you know.

I have mixed feelings about this. I've always said, contrary to what you may have read in the papers—couldn't help saying it that way—I never said that I would never do another horror movie. I've never said that. I always said, "Come with something I haven't done before that was worth doing." And somebody would come up with another role which was bait—which was the best I have ever seen—and, of course, you saw nothing. I would certainly do it.

Playing this part was a tremendous launching pad for me—and very important. I wasn't a name. I wasn't a face, although I'd been around for 10 years. And it was *The Curse of Frankenstein* [1957] that sort of "did it," because I realized that nobody was particularly interested in my name or my face. And I thought, "If I make myself totally unrecognizable and it *does work*, people will think or say, 'I wonder what he really looks like?'"

Well, I more than showed them subsequently that that was a very important part for me, an enormously important part, but strangely enough there was a gap of eight years between the first one and the second one. As you well know, I didn't say a word in the second one. As you, of course, will see for yourselves, I am a very taciturn, remote, withdrawn individual who doesn't like to say very much, cowering in fear from the sun [laughter]; but in that film I did not say one word, because I frankly refused to. I'd read the script, and I said what I always say, "Why don't you use Stoker's words?" And they never did, practically—hardly ever. But there was no way I was going to burst into a room and shout, "I am the apocalypse!" Unbelievable. So I never said a word.

Subsequently, I did play the part again. I did not play it in France, contrary to popular belief. A film came out with the title of *Dracula, Father and Son* [*Dracula, Pere et Fils*, 1976]. I did not play Dracula in that film. I *did not*. I played a mysterious, rather odd nobleman from Eastern Europe. I had... a confused young man who refused to follow in the family tradition. It was a comedy, and a lot of it took place in the open air. It was *not* a Dracula movie. I did not play that character, because I've never parodied it. And the one I did in Italy, and a little in Russia, I did *not* play the part of Dracula, because I would never parody it. It's been parodied, but I wouldn't do it.

I subsequently played Dracula, I honestly don't remember how many times, I think for Hammer maybe four more times, possibly. And in one film which unfortunately was not good, I actually, I think, I'm the only actor to have portrayed that character *physically* as Stoker described him:

Dracula and Son

as the old man in the black clothes, white hair and mustache, getting steadily younger. Well, the film [*Count Dracula*, 1970] really was unworthy for a large number of reasons I won't bore you with. But Herbert Lom played Van Helsing and Klaus Kinski played Renfield, so I was in good company but I never even met them. We shot the film: It was all long shot, medium shot, close-up, zoom. I never did rehearsals or anything like that. But at least I did try and I managed to get some of Stoker's actual words in, which was a miracle... It's all wonderful writing and a wonderful book.

But I turned down every single one of the subsequent films after doing the first two. I said, "No" every single time. Maybe you do not know this. I can say that now because all of the people to whom I said it have left us, so it doesn't really matter and I have put it in my book. But I said, "No," and it wasn't a question of money. There was never any money—at least that's what they used to tell *us*. And I said, "No," because I said, "You've got a great character here—heroic, erotic, romantic, whatever you like to call him. You have a great character. You are writing these stories and then you don't know where to put the character." This is exactly what happened: They wrote the stories first and then scratched their heads and said, "Where do we fit him in?" Well, of course, that's exactly the wrong way around.

And I read these scripts and I thought, "Oh, no, this is deterioration." I'm talking from my point of view. Obviously, fortunately, the audience did *not* react like that, because they were entertained, which is what we're here for. But I said, "No, no, no," and I then used to get these terrible phone calls from Colonel Carreras, Jimmy Carreras, who was the boss of Hammer. Brilliant promoter. Great entrepreneur. We need them like that today.

And the same conversation took place every single time. "You've got to do this movie. You've got to do this movie."

And I said, "I haven't got to do anything at all. I don't *want* to do it."

"You've got to do this. You've got to do this!" Voice going up the scale. "I'm on my knees, begging you. I'm 62-years-old. I can't stand the stress and the strain! ...You've got to do it! You've got to do it!"

And I said, "Jimmy, I haven't got to do it."

And he said, "Yes, you have!"

And I said, "Why?"

"Well, I've already sold it with you in the film, to the distributors." ...Think of the people you'll put out of work if you don't do it."

That's not very nice. There's a word for that: blackmail. And that is actually the reason why I did those subsequent films, because if I had said, "No"—they did do one without me—but if I'd said, "No," a lot of people would've been out of work. What can you do? The sad thing was—and I'm not attacking the movies—there are some very fine performances and some very fine actors and actresses in these films—but it wasn't *Bram Stoker*.

Francis Ford Coppola is one of the great filmmakers of our time—remarkable filmmaker. He makes a film called *Bram Stoker's Dracula*. You've all seen it. Looks wonderful. Of course, people ask me and say, "What did you think of it?"

And I say, "I can't answer that question."

And then they say, "Why not?"

I say, "Well, if I said I thought it was the most wonderful, marvelous, incredible, fantastic, brilliant picture I've ever seen in my life, people would say, 'Well of course he says that, he wants to work with Coppola.'" If I said, "I thought it was terrible, embarrassing, it was this, it was that, I didn't like it at all," they'd say, 'Of course he says that—he wasn't in it.'" So, you see, you have no answer in a situation like that.

But, to answer your question, briefly... I have said, "Yes, I would, *but only* if it was Stoker's book. What he wrote. What the characters said—not word for word, but using his lines and his story, because it has never, ever been done."

Peter Cushing

I've been asked to tell you stories about my old friend Peter Cushing. I find it extremely difficult to talk about Peter without becoming really very emotional. I was, last night, actually, reading part of his autobiography—I can hear him speaking.

I first met him—we'd already been in two films, but not together. He, of course, had a *real* part in *Hamlet*, as Osric, in which he was superb. Of course, he'd had an enormous amount of theatrical experience, which I hadn't had. I simply had carried a spear, which wasn't authorized by Laurence Olivier—he never found out.

The Curse of Frankenstein

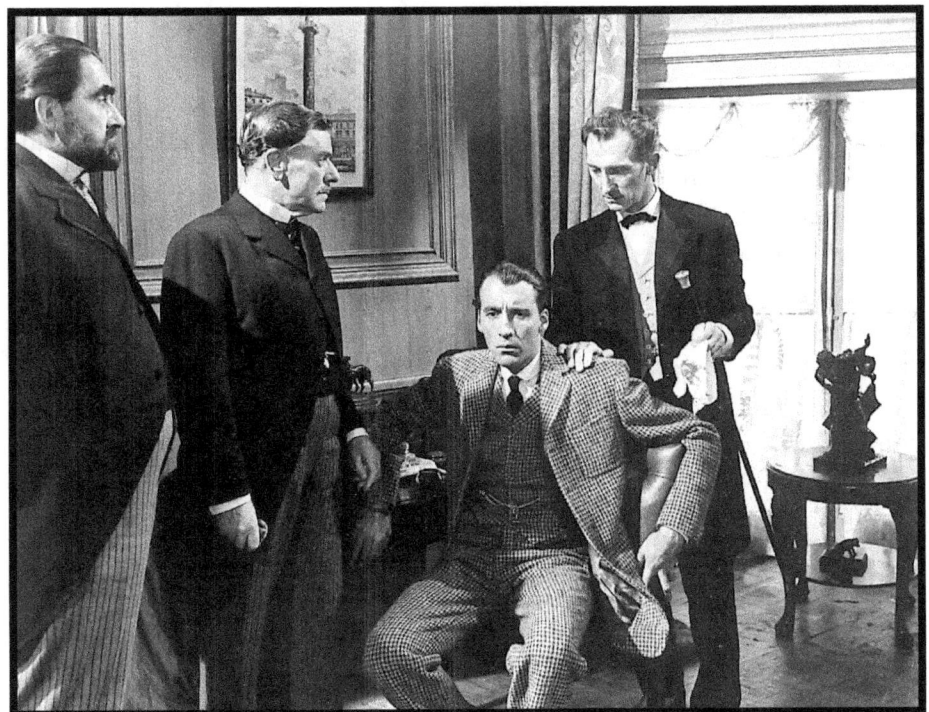

Francis DeWolfe, Andre Morell, Christopher Lee and Peter Cushing in *The Hound of the Baskervilles* (1959)

Just to watch him directing. Then we were in *Moulin Rouge*, both in small parts, but we didn't meet.

We met at Bray Studios, where we did *The Curse of Frankenstein*, and I met this quiet, rather reserved, extremely courteous, delightful man whom, of course, I had seen a lot. Notably, in *1984*, on television, live, which was one of the most brilliant performances for which he got whatever the award was at the time—I can't remember—my first reaction was, "This man is a real actor and I can learn a lot from him." And the second reaction was, "He's an easy man to talk to." And the third reaction was, "Well, we'll do it together."

He said that I burst into his dressing room, looking like hell on Earth, literally—shaking the thing—and saying, "I haven't got any lines"—shaking the script—"I haven't got any lines. I've got nothing to say."

He said, "You're lucky. I've read it."

Well, gradually, over the years, we developed a professional partnership... and I came to love him, dearly, because he was one of the most remarkable human beings I've ever met in my life. He was a superb actor, I mean *superb*. I was simply agog at some of the things he managed to do. The precision. The marvelous intensity. If you don't have that, you don't have the imagination, you don't have the power of invention, you aren't an actor. *Think* about what you're saying, *listen* to what the other people are saying, *stand still* and don't do anything unless it means something. If there's a secret to acting, that's it.

But he had abilities which I just envied. He was brilliant with props. I'm hopeless with them, and always have been. And I used to say to him, "Will you stop doing all this, because you're distracting me. You're lighting your pipe, reading the *Times*, drinking your whiskey, throwing something in the air and doing, 'What, thou?' all at the same time. I really wish you'd stop doing this, because I'm just sitting there, looking at you, and I've got nothing to do—and I want to do something."

And he said, "Oh, my dear fellow, I am sorry." And he was absolutely wonderful in that respect.

Of course, our association was a very, very happy one, and, I think, reasonably successful. Between 1957 and 1971, when we worked together a lot—and I think we shared the same instincts to a certain extent—and, of course, working for Hammer all those years, but not exclusively so—we also worked for Amicus, and I think other people, but I can't remember who—we naturally got to know each other extremely well.

Privately, I went to stay in his house in Whitstable, in Kent. Needless to say, he had an aquarium full of fish—I'm sure he made them, too—and all these wonderful lead soldiers that he used to make, models of aeroplanes he used to put together, the paintings he used to do. I mean, the man was incredibly able, talented—a great misused word—but, my God, did he have talent, in the *right* sense of the word. We, of course, refer to it today, in the industry, as "The Talent." Lovely phrase, but he was a brilliantly talented man, but he also was, more importantly, a wonderful human being. Very determined, got his way—oh, yes—but in a very different way than me.

I'm afraid I wasn't made that way. I'd say, "*No!*" if we disagreed about something or Terry Fisher would say to me, "That's terrible. Don't do it that way!"

"Fine. Here's another way."

Peter would say, "My dear fellow, what do you think"—and he looked at me—"if I was to do this and I was to do that?" That was his way of doing it, but that was the way he lived.

He always used to call me "My Dear Fellow," and I used to call him that.

Horror Express

He could do almost anything. I feel he should have been a priest, because the man had such loving kindness. It's a phrase we occasionally read in books, and it's even in the Bible: "loving kindness." He was a man full of love and affection, and he was the kindest, kindest man I think I've ever known. And he was never envious of other people's success. I never heard him once say a harsh word about anyone, *anyone*, in or out of the business.

Only once did he say something—of course, it was to me. We were making a film in Spain called *Horror Express*, which is a very entertaining movie. And there's this famous line where he and I are sitting in this railway carriage, in the compartment—you all know it, of course—and this investigating detective comes in and says, "We are looking for a monster"—or words like that—"There's a monster loose on the train"—and we both said almost the same line: "Monsters? We're British, you know," and so on. And we enjoyed making that movie.

His wife had just died, and so my wife and our daughter tried to spend as much time as possible with him—and it was quite unspeakable making that picture, because it was a so-called studio, which was like a warehouse, where the food, literally, was almost un-eatable. I got very sick, everybody did. It was quite appalling. It wasn't a proper studio. It wasn't a proper commissary or place to eat.

Peter—that's one of the reasons why he looked so gaunt, apart from his sadness—never ate anything. His lunch was always the same: an apple and a piece of cheese, year after year after year. And I remember going to his dressing room, which was a converted railway carriage. I said, "You know, I can't take this. I feel sick. This is *frightful* food, and we've got to go out there and work away, and our hours are very long," and he just looked up and he said, "Well, it's no good belly-aching about it," and I was shattered. I was absolutely stunned because that was the harshest thing I'd ever heard him say. Of course, I was the one who got it.

…After his death, I received a parcel in the post, and it contained a little snuff box made out of agate. And there was a note, which he had written long before his death, I think five, six, seven years. It said, "Dear fellow, when the time comes, I want you to have this, because this was the snuff box I used in *School for Scandal*, a play by Sheridan, when I first met Helen."

…I last saw him two months or so before he passed away in a hospice. I have no idea where he's buried and I don't want to know, and I would never ask—I would not be told. I know that people used to lay flowers on Helen's grave, which rather upset him, because he said, "Her soul is not there." Right, absolutely right.

And I know he made certain requests upon the Broughtons, who looked after him before, long before she died—and totally after she did, because he never got over it. He just lived to join her. And it was 23 years before he did. And I think I'm right in saying he left certain instructions. I really don't know what they are; and I have no idea where he's buried, or where she's buried, or even if they are buried—or were cremated, or with the ashes and so on. I really have no idea. I don't want to know. My memories of him are not of a dead man. Certainly not. Nor are yours.

What I miss most about him is what will happen to all of you one day: That one person in your lives. It doesn't matter who it is. There will be one person with whom you share a certain sense of humor, a certain feeling, a certain degree of memories. There will be that one person. You pick up the telephone, and you say something idiotic, and they know exactly who it is. You use a funny voice, they know exactly who it is, and so on. And you tell these stories, and they know who it is.

And you share this one thing or many, many things between you, which is what happened to us.

He was a great bird watcher. He had a great knowledge of birds—ornithologist. Again, it was one of the things that used to make me despair—this knowledge. And I was driving through the countryside and he suddenly said, "Look!" and name some sort of bird I'd never even heard of... And it had gone by then. But he knew. He knew... He knew the Latin name. He knew it all.

Absolutely despairing, I was, over those things—and so I used to send him postcards from all over the world, wherever I traveled, saying, "I just discovered the largest nesting... throstle-painted... whatever"—you know, I used to make up these ridiculous names. "Your ticket is in the post. What is keeping you? The room is reserved." He used to love this. He had 20 or 25 of these postcards from me.

Vincent [Price] used to send me postcards, too, from all over the world. And once he sent me a postcard which said, "This has got to stop. If anybody else comes up and asks me if I'm *you*—"

And as far as Vincent is concerned, he made the remark once—he made a great many—but he made the remark once, which I'll never forget. Helen Cushing died in 1971. She died basically of emphysema—a terrible story he [Peter] put in his book: She woke up at three o'clock in the morning, she was almost gone. And it was a dreadful story, absolutely dreadful. And it completely finished his life—totally. And that has happened to many people. He was totally lost, I mean *absolutely* lost, like a child. And he wouldn't see anybody. He wouldn't talk to anybody. He wouldn't write us. Wouldn't see anyone—wanted to stay in the house. It was a shrine. And gradually, gradually, over the years—with these idiotic postcards that I used to send him, these silly telephone calls I used to make, and so on—gradually he relaxed, I suppose.

Well, he never got over it, but he did lead a normal life. And, after all, there is a place on the sea front there where there's a bench: It's called Cushing's View. And when he died, his funeral took place through the streets of the town of Whitstable, and people were closing their shops in respect. And most of the town was foreign, of course. That gives you an idea, doesn't it?

I can't remember when it was, but I was having a conversation with Vincent, who called me from California. He said, "How is Peter?"

And I said, "Well, he's very frail—getting on. He's been very, very ill—very, very sick—but he has tremendous courage, and his brain is as

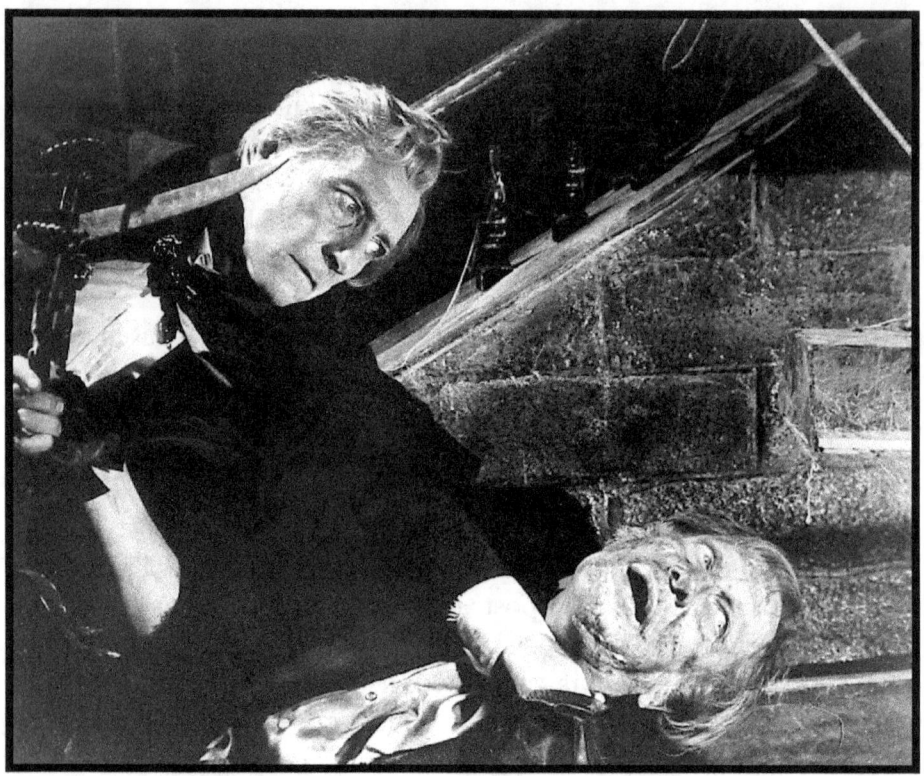

Peter Cushing and Vincent Price in *Madhouse*

sharp as a needle, and he's got all the guts in the world"—as, indeed, had Vincent toward the end of his life, because he had so many terrible things the matter with him, too.

But he said, "Well, how is he?"

And I said, "Well, I've just told you."

He said, "Does he really still believe that, when the time comes, Helen will be there, waiting?"

And I said, "Of course. *Absolutely*."

And Vincent said, "But what if she's *out*?"

And I said, "Only a man as tasteless as you could make that remark." And I said, "I am going to tell Peter."

So I rang him up, in one of my idiot voices—and he gave me one of his—and I said, "You know, Vincent was on the telephone this morning."

He said, "How is the dear fellow?"

And I said, "*Much the same*, you know," and I said, "He was asking after you. And he asked about Helen."

Silence, of course, on the other end of the line.

And I repeated what Vincent had said—and he roared with laughter. And he said, "Only Vincent could have said that. And only you could have told me!" And that made him very happy.

I don't suppose many people will believe this, but it is true—and I think the rumors have been going around, because... we loved the same cartoons... And I will never forget, by sheer chance, saying something to him, using Sylvester's voice from the Tweety-Bird cartoons, because I *love* Sylvester—one of my heroes. And he collapsed. He'd never heard—I don't think he'd ever seen any of these cartoons, you see. So, of course, from then on, he and I spoke to each other like that—not just on the telephone, but on the *set*. You can imagine what people thought, when one would say to the other, "Thstop thstanding there" or whatever it was. And people would look at us...

And, of course, we loved Spike, the bulldog...with his little boy... "Heh, heh, heh. That's my boy."

So I would ring Peter as much as I could, so he didn't feel cut off... He hated talking on the telephone, and he used to put on the most peculiar voices. And, of course, it was only him on the other end of the line. I knew that. And he would say, "Oh, ho, ho..." like that, and make the most peculiar sound. And I would just go, "Heh, heh, heh," and off he went. He roared with laughter. And then he said, "I'm going to take a bath, because I'm laughing so much," and I'd have to wait while he took a bath. And then he came downstairs again. In those days, of course, he couldn't move around much. It took him a long time.

How can I possibly say anything about him that doesn't take a long time?

The last time—ever—was in May of '94, when we did this commentary together, about Hammer. And I'd seen photographs of him, and I knew he was in a pretty bad way. I hadn't actually seen him in the flesh for quite some time. Talked to him, yes, but not seen him. And I had driven down to Canterbury in the pouring rain, from London—and he came from Whitstable, because he couldn't make the journey to London to do the recording. And the studio was a small one in Canterbury. There were actually a lot of people there, including some people who came over from the States.

I walked in there, and there he was, and I really did hesitate for a moment—fortunately he didn't see me—I really was so shocked. I must have shown it. Because here was a man I'd remembered as being

intensely vigorous, tremendously fast movements, very strong. He was a rugby player as a young man. I couldn't believe this was the same man. Many of you will have seen the pictures taken towards the end of his life. However, he didn't notice what my reaction was. And we sat down together and, of course, the rest of the thing was complete chaos, but we finally got through with it. Of course it was nothing but, "Do you remember when?" and so on. Peals of laughter and idiotic jokes which nobody else understood—and funny voices.

And then I brought two cartoons down with me. One was "Tom and Jerry" and the other was Sylvester, and we both sat and looked at them. He knew the words, he knew the lines and started to say them. And then we finished, and we went out of the doorway together, and many of you will have seen this picture of me standing in the doorway and he standing beside me, smiling.

Peter Cushing was six foot tall. This photograph: His head comes just above my shoulder, and he was so bent and so stooped and so thin and so gaunt. It was absolutely horrifying. Then he got into the car and drove away and waved at me. And I waved back, and that was it.

Coming to America

We all know what typecasting means. It's dangerous because, well, if you aren't typecast, if you're any kind of actor at all—you may be best known for one particular part or several. You try and get that through to the press, who love to put labels on people, stick us into little pigeonholes and so on... they'll never admit they're wrong. Some producers might admit they're wrong. Some of the casting directors might admit that you've proved them wrong. "That's life. That's show business," they say, is the phrase. I don't accept that.

And I was getting typecast in England, and it wasn't doing me any harm, but I was always getting offered the same kind of film—not exactly the same role, but I was always the bad guy... It was Richard Widmark, actually, who more or less told me when we were doing *To the Devil a Daughter*, which was ruined by the last five minutes by some genius at Hammer. And I mean that, because the last five minutes was absurd: Me disappearing... ridiculous, because we did have an alternative ending. I mean, it's there... the circle of blood... divine intervention, lightning and Father Michael Rayner on the ground in a sort of crucified position, dead, and so on. And they said, "Oh, no, he's done that before. So we'll change it." So they did, and so on.

Widmark said to me, "If you stay in Britain, you'll make a good living, but you'll end up being bored."

And I thought, "Well, if I get bored, so will the audience."

And so many people have said to me over the years, "If you want to expand. If you want to show them you can do something else—it doesn't matter what it is—you *must* go to America. You *must*. Because in America there is a huge amount of production. In America there are a lot of films being made. There are lots and lots of different parts, and some of them you could play. And you must go to the States because people know you there. People have seen your work. But if they ask you if you can do something, and you say, 'Yes,' you will be asked to do it."

I've got no argument with that.

"But you'd better *deliver*."

It's a ruthless business. I have no argument with that, either. Years ago, Mervyn LeRoy asked me—in *Quo Vadis*, which I didn't appear in—but he asked me if I could drive a chariot. And I said, "I'm licensed for all vehicles." I thought that was very funny. Very witty.

Well, the next day, I was there, dressed as a Roman soldier, in this sort of thing like a garbage bin with two... horses. And I lasted, I should think, less than a minute before I hit a tree... In those days, you said, "Yes" to everything. I couldn't do that now and wouldn't.

Widmark kept on saying this, and the people I knew in the film world—actors, producers, directors, writers—"It's the States for you, because you're known, but you'll be given the opportunity to prove you can do something else. *If* you can do something else, you will be given the chance—once. But you'd better deliver."

And so I came to this country in 1976 and, in my first film, I was 30 feet down [under water] for three days in *Airport '77*. I think I already mentioned the only reason I did that film was that I had a scene with Jack Lemmon. It didn't last very long, but I had a scene with him, and then, when the producer said, "You do realize you're going to have to *do* this. Your whole hold is flooded and you drown."

...And I said, "Oh, yes, yes, yes, of course." And I thought I'd be acting, you know, maybe four feet, two feet down. It would all be done with mirrors. And so I practiced in the pool at Universal, which is only 10 feet deep. I thought, "This is terrific. This is going to be the performance of my life." And then when the day came, it was 30 feet in the tank. That's a little bit different—and enclosed... I was a little bit taken aback, but I thought, "No. You said you could do it, you do it."

So I went down, of course, on what's known as the regulator, that's the breathing tube and the mask so you can see where you're going. That's that, I got into position. I could see the cameraman, Rexford Metz, who did *Jaws*. And I could see the stuntmen in their wet suits, all hovering, looking extremely dubious. And there were one or two of the crew, also, working under water. They were all hovering, and I could see them.

They had told me beforehand—written on a blackboard, actually—If you're in trouble, just do *that*, and they'll hand you the regulator and you can breathe and put the mask on. And then I got in position, and he did *this*, and we're rolling with the underwater camera. And I took an enormous breath, and being able to take enormous breaths, it was a really big one—and I took the mask off, couldn't see a thing. I took the tube out of my mouth—somebody took it from me—and I opened my mouth and I closed my throat, because if I hadn't, you could see the bubbles going up—and it was a live actor, you see, which takes away the credibility. I did that and I felt Jack Lemmon come over and thump me on the chest and put things over my face and everything. I just lay there. And eventually he tows me out, and I got past the window, and Lee Grant, my wife, *widow* actually, has total hysterics inside the plane. And so on and so forth.

I guess it was probably the most dangerous thing I've ever done, but I didn't know it at the time. Nobody told me if you've gone too far and you don't exhale, you get a bubble. *Bang*! That's it. You're dead...

Saturday Night Live

The thing that really mattered more to me than anything I think I've ever, ever, ever done, was hosting *Saturday Night Live*. It was a joyful experience. My agent said to me, "You've been approached by the most popular TV show in the States."

I said, "Who are they? What is it?"

"To host *Saturday Night Live*."

I said, "Never heard of it," and I hadn't. You see, I had just arrived, practically.

He said, "They want you to go to New York and do it."

And I said, "Well, what do I have to do?"

And he said, "You are the host. It's live television."

And I said, "Oh, *no*. Not live television." I'd had too many mishaps. If you read the book, you'll know what the first one was. I'm not going to go into that one here... But I said, "Oh, no. Live TV. Oh, *no*." I said I couldn't do it.

He said, "You've got to do it. Watch it on Saturday night."

I did. Well, it either works or it doesn't. The host either works or usually doesn't. The one I saw most certainly didn't, but I saw these

With Dan Ackroyd and John Belushi during a rehearsal of *Saturday Night Live*

extraordinary people—Belushi, Ackroyd, Murray, Radner, Curtin, Newman—all of them. And I thought, "This is lovely, extraordinary." I happened to watch the "Samurai Tailor." And I thought, "This is one of the greatest things I've ever seen in my life." I couldn't believe it. It was absolutely wonderful. It reminded me, of course, of Toshiro Mifune. Little did I know that in *1941* I would be working with him, under Steven Spielberg, in a submarine.

But I went there, with great misgivings. Arrived quite late, was taken straight to the studio, and walked into a room. It was the whole cast there, and 10, 15 writers. Lorne Michaels, the producer. And they all sort of stared at me, and I thought, "Oh, this is going to be a disaster." We sat down and we opened the script just to start with, started reading. And then we started rehearsing, and I spent the rest of the week rehearsing with these brilliantly talented people.

And I was a bit naive, I think, because I was a bit worried about their health. Every morning they would come in and blow their noses, all of this, you see. And after about three days of this, I said, "I think you ought to go to a drug store or see somebody. I'm a bit worried about you."

"What do you mean?"

I said, "Well, you know, you've got such terrible colds."

"We haven't got colds," you know. "We're fine." Sneezing, coughing, blowing their noses and everything. Eventually I caught on... Sadly, in the case of one person, it became very bad, which is a tragedy, in the case of John. An absolute tragedy...

We did the rehearsals on Saturday afternoon. Now, this was the worst audience imaginable... and doing scenes with James Bond. Dan Ackroyd was James Bond. I, of course, was the heavy. And John Belushi was playing Herve Villechaize. He had the voice down to a "T," speaking away, blowing bubbles. And Gilda Radner is chained to the wall, and I went over to her and said, "Are you sure you don't find me attractive?"

And she'd say, "Yecch" and so on. And we did these scenes and it was very funny... Then we did a whole scene with Holmes and Watson. And I played Holmes with a $10 bill stuck up my nose... And so they took those scenes out. Well, it came the night, many of you will have seen that show—it came the night, and it was just a unique experience for me, because in that kind of show, it doesn't matter what you do. You can fall over the camera. You can disappear out of the frame. It doesn't matter. And it certainly isn't easy. Nothing's meant to be easy. But when you've got these people around you—and I was very naughty, actually—I suddenly realized that I could almost do what I wanted.

The marvelous scene between Death and Laraine Newman, apologizing for taking away her puppy, and she says, "I hate you."

"Well, somebody has to do it" or "It's a living," or whatever the phrase was.

And then the scene with "Bawbwa Wawa" and so on...

I think it was the first television appearance of Meat Loaf and his group. And I was told that I had to introduce them. You know the host on *Saturday Night Live* doesn't do just that. You take part in some of the sketches and you connect. And I had an enormous mustache for some reason, some part I had been playing which required an enormous mustache. And I suddenly thought, "I'm going to throw them for a loop," and I said, talking to the audience, "And now, ladies and gentlemen, I'd like you all to meet—Loaf." I could tell instinctively there was instant panic—you know, "He's killing it. He's destroying the show. We're going to go in and murder him."

And then I had an imaginary conversation, you see. "Sorry. I beg your pardon? What? Oh, I'm so sorry. How stupid of me. I'm terribly sorry. I've never done this before." So I made a really big deal out of it. And then I said, "Ladies and gentlemen, Meat Loaf," and on they came. And he'll never forget it. I can tell you that. They were absolutely stunned. They thought, "How are we going to get on? We can't come on as 'Loaf'."

So that—suddenly someone said, "You know. That guy can be funny."

Hammer and Amicus

I would like to compare the people who ran Hammer with the people who ran Amicus. I have to be careful here. Some of them are still alive.

Hammer really revived the genre, resuscitated the genre. I can't help using those words, but they are the right ones. But they lifted the flag up that Universal had laid down, if you like, and kept it going for a long, long time. And Martin Scorcese, John Landis, Joe Dante, Coppola, Spielberg, Badham, DePalma—all these people all said to me, "If it hadn't been for Hammer, who knows?" Because it made the most difference in their lives. They said, "You know, we were all brought up as young men watching your movies."

It's like when people come up to you and say, "I've seen *all* your movies," and I say, "Oh, dear God, you haven't!" Because some of them aren't as good as they should have been.

However, you asked for a comparison. Hammer was really Jimmy Carreras. He was the live wire. His son, Michael, was the producer, and Tony Hinds was the producer and wrote some of the screenplays under the name John Elder—he's still alive. I occasionally talk to him—very much a recluse. Roy Skeggs is still around. He was their accountant. He is, so to speak, Hammer. All I can tell you is we are intending—we have a producer, we have a director, and I think we have the money—to remake, God willing, *The Devil's Bride*. When we think of the special effects we can call on today, it could be very stunning.

Amicus: That would be Milton Subotsky, of course, and Max Rosenberg. They were a different studio. I wouldn't say they were rivals. They made other films, some of which were extremely good. They made, as you know, films with four stories in them. I did one, I think—*Dr. Terror* [*Dr. Terror's House of Horrors*, 1965]—and *The House that Dripped Blood* [1971] too, and others. I don't think they were rivals, really, but

I, Monster

basically Milton Subotsky was a writer. Milton, who is no longer with us—Max is alive, at least I hope he is, but I haven't heard from him in years—Milton will go down in history, so I'm told—it was Bob Bloch who told me this—because he said, publicly, "The trouble with Christopher Lee is he has no sense of humor."

I didn't see him for many years, and I said, "Milton, you have been immortalized in the history of the cinema with that remark."

And he said, "What remark?" and I told him, and he said, "You were very intense."

And I said, "I *had* to be with your scripts!" Actually they were very good stories. They made one film, which I was in, which God knows what happened—but it was a film that some of you will have seen—with a rather weird title. I didn't like it: *I, Monster* [1971]. I didn't like that title. I thought, you know, the story is *Jekyll and Hyde*. Every single character in that film had the correct name from the story, except me. All the others—Utterson, whatever—all had the Stevenson names. But they decided that I would be "Marlowe" and "Blake." Obviously, this is silly, you know. First of all, the title is awful, in my opinion; and, secondly, you are doing *Jekyll and Hyde*, because you're using the other people's names. So it should be called *Jekyll and Hyde*. But, for some reason, they wouldn't give in on that—and then they said, "We've only got the money to make this movie because we're going to do it in 3-D."

And I think I said, "Why?" or something.

And they said, "Well, that's what the people who gave us the money wanted to do."

Well the result was unlike anything I've ever experienced, and the poor camera operator [Moray Grant] was one of the top people in the country. At the end of the first day—I remember the second day, he just walked away and said, "I can't do this," because something had to keep moving: Either the camera had to keep moving or you had to keep moving, even in a close-up, so you've got the definition of 3-D. So the result would be—the camera would start on you saying nothing, and it would move away from you, and then they would hear you say something but it wouldn't be on you, because it had to keep moving. So it started on Peter Cushing saying nothing, moved away or to somebody else while Peter was talking. And eventually it comes around to me and I'm talking, then it moves away and I'm still talking, because they must keep moving—certainly killed the movie.

I was rather upset about that, because I thought it was rather good.

The great directors

With [John] Huston it was a small part in *Moulin Rouge* [1952]. I was very conscious of his reputation, and I thought his father—and I still think his father—was the greatest screen actor I've ever seen in my life, Walter [Huston], when I went to see [*Treasure of the*] *Sierra Madre*. And I was engaged to play the part of this famous painter, Seurat. It was a very small scene. We did it at the real place, the cafe... in Paris on the Left Bank. It was unbelievable, because the whole of Paris was going past on the sidewalk, and all the tourists and the French police screaming and shouting and blowing whistles. You couldn't hear anything the other people were saying. And we brought a nurse.

And I remember Huston just bent over, patted me on the shoulder and said, "Just be yourself, kid" and disappeared. And the first assistant director said, "Action," and when somebody said, "Cut," we looked outside at the road, and there was John Huston sitting, reading *Time* magazine. I guess he felt, "Well, they can do it."

Orson [Welles]—another giant—that was a wonderful experience, for most of the time telling me stories about John Barrymore, which we encouraged, of course, because we didn't have to work too hard. And he would say, "This is the most talented company I have ever worked with," and you knew he said that to everyone. And when he finished a scene, he would say, "Print with enthusiasm." Wonderful phrases, and I remember one day, he strode in—because Orson strode—and said at the top of his voice, "Roll it!"

And the cameraman on the English crew... said, "Mr. Welles, I don't have a set-up yet."

"Find one. Surprise me." That was Orson.

Billy. Billy Wilder, who is still with us—93—he was everything you have heard. I was very nervous—very, very nervous—because I had heard some stories about Billy, that he would cut you right off at the ankles, and that he was a perfectionist, which I am, too, in a way, which is not a very satisfactory thing to be, oddly enough. You're never satisfied, but maybe that's a good thing.

Anyway, when I did *The Private Life of Sherlock Holmes* [1970], I was the last actor he saw, and among the other actors he saw were George Sanders, Laurence Olivier and James Robertson Justice and a few others, so I was in good company. And everybody, to say the least, was on their toes.

Here you have a man who is one of the greatest directors ever. Probably the greatest director of comedy ever. Here's a man who spent two years writing a script with I.A.L. Diamond. He was still on the set with the script. And his way of saying, "Action" was just to say, "*Go!*" which is slightly unnerving if you're playing a... scene.

And you spring into action, hope to God you've got the words right, because if you get one word wrong, you go again. One word.

"I spent two years writing this. You're going to get it right." And so on, and he's quite right.

And Bob Stephens, who is gone, who played Sherlock; and Colin Blakely, who is gone, who played Dr. Watson. I came in to do my first scene at the club, the Diogenes Club. Mycroft is the power behind the throne, Queen Victoria's right hand. And they were absolutely like this, rigid with tension and visibly shaky. And I said, "What's the matter?" and they said, "You'll find out." Because you had this feeling—you've got to get it right, otherwise God help you. Actually it was wonderful. If you did get something wrong, he said, "You're allowed one mistake."

Christopher Lee with Steven Spielberg and Toshiro Mifune in *1941*

And it was a beautiful picture, a beautiful picture. I enjoyed it enormously. He is, I think, really, the best director I've ever worked with.

And then, of course, there are the others, much the same level: Steven [Spielberg], marvelous director to work with, understanding, appreciative, encouraging, seems to have seen—alarmingly—most of my movies; and Joe Dante, another marvelous director to work with. It starts at the top, of course it starts at the top. If you have a director who likes actors—you'd be surprised at how many don't—who likes actors, you feel it and you do the best you can. "I'm going to do what he wants. I'm determined to do what he wants," or whatever. And somehow one does. It's a wonderful feeling, and if the crew is with you all the way, you can feel it, you can sense it. It's a wonderful feeling… "I got that for Steven. I got that, because I was making scenes with Toshiro Mifune, one of the great giants of the cinema."

And Slim Pickens was absolutely wonderful. There is a scene—it's not in the movie—when he captures me on the mainland. We shot it but it's not in the picture. And he captures me, the first Nazi captured on American soil. And he's in his nice pants, and escaped from the submarine, and he brings me there, and I'm shouting to Bob Stack, who plays Joe Stilwell, crying at a Disney movie. And I'm shouting, in German, of course, "Herr General! Herr General! I'm a German officer," and so on and so forth. "I demand this and I demand that." It's not in the movie. They had to cut a lot of things.

And Steven, again, a marvelous director—Joe, wonderful to work with. All of these that I've mentioned—if you feel they're on your side—and Tim [Burton], well, he's an actor's dream. I only had a couple days. It's only two or three minutes on the screen where I'm in the movie [*Sleepy Hollow*]. And he's cutting it now. I shall be seeing him in four days in London, because he's doing the music and the looping in London. An actor's dream.

The enthusiasm of the director and… the crew… starting in October of last year and finishing in July, right through winter, exteriors, night shots in the mud and everything, you know. Murder. But all the time, this tremendous enthusiasm, and you really feel it, and I think it's a tremendously important thing for an actor or an actress. It's a huge help.

And Johnny Depp. I gave him a copy of my book that I wrote—and Johnny Depp, a delightful companion, which he certainly is, and one who has revived my faith in the star system, and he has. This

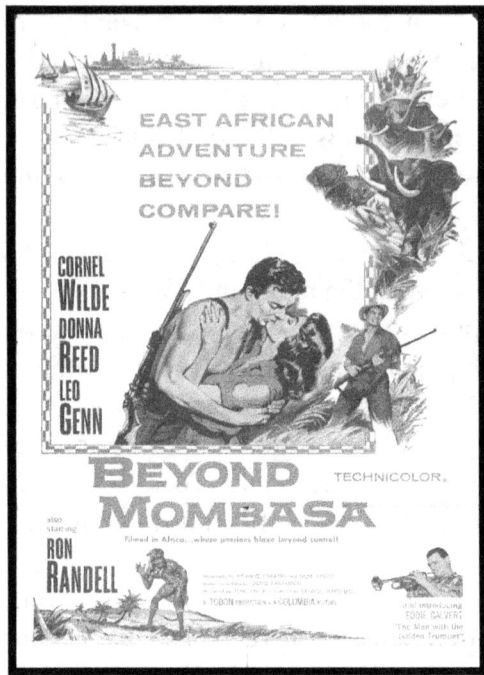

young man is remarkable. He is such a nice person. There is no star act, and he is such a good actor. And my comparatively small scene is with him—there are other people around, of course, but basically with him—and he's got the attention, he's listening, he's thinking, standing still, as I said earlier. I'm enormously impressed by Johnny Depp, and he is one of the few young actors around today who I think is really, *really*, as good as it gets. I am sure a lot of you in this room would agree with me.

But there are some directors who aren't quite so easy. And you still try to do the best you can. I remember doing a picture—you probably have never seen it—called *Beyond Mombasa* [1955], and a lovely cast—Donna Reed, Cornel Wilde—and I play the white hunter who got shot… And George Marshall was the director, and he must have directed more movies than any director in history—and he was a tough old guy. He was a lovely man. He was a terrific character, always smiling, flinging himself around in the river, singing the most unbelievable songs with different words. I loved him. I thought he was terrific. And there was a scene where I get shot in the back by a poison dart, and I happened to be standing at the top of an open cast mine, and George came up to me and in a very casual way said, "Can you go down there?"

And I said, "In what way?" you know, and he said, "Well, can you fall down there?"

And I said, "Yes." Those were the days when I said, "Yes."

He said, "Well, okay. Let's do it."

So, I didn't bother looking where I'm going to fall like that, on my only good arm, you might say, because the other one was in a sling. And there's a photograph, actually, I think it's in the book, of me actually doing it—landing, so to speak. It goes like that—it's a course, just like that.

Christopher Lee checks out Michael Ripper's autobiography from Midnight Marquee Press as Ripper looks on at the Monster Rally wrap up party.

And George says, "Okay, let's do it." And so: Action."

I did it. "Cut." I got up, sort of clambered back up to the top again. The producer arrived, literally green in the face because I'm pouring blood, and was absolutely green in the face because he thought I'd killed myself, you see—and this was only halfway into the movie. He was saying, you know, "Did he finish his part?" or whatever.

And so George came up to me and said, "That was okay."

And I said, "It wasn't any good?"

And he said, "All right, but you forgot to do that," which I did. I forgot to react to the dart, I was thinking so much about the fall.

And he said, "Okay." So we did it again, and I've got the scars to prove it.

That's one. That's Errol Flynn, in a sword fight, after lunch.

Family history

Doesn't exist anymore… Charlemagne, yes—named after, I'm told, an ancestor of mine. I wear his ring—it's the Holy Roman Empire, the emperor's crown and so on and so forth. Difficult to prove, but an archaeologist, fairly recently, came across some pottery in Lombardy, which is northern Italy, which is where my family comes from, on my mother's side, and the pottery had the name of the family painted on it in Latin. And I asked this man, who is a very distinguished archaeologist, number one in Italy—also happens to be my cousin—and I asked him, "Where does that put us?"

And he said, "Just before the first century A.D."

And I said, "Good Lord, that's rather a long time."

He said, "Yes, it is."

And I look back on the history of the family, and the one thing that I feel very strongly about—this applies to anybody in a similar situation: If you are fortunate enough, for whatever reason—it's got nothing to do with you—to be descended from a family that has achieved something at some time, you should try and live *up* to it, not live *off* it.

And there have been some quite remarkable people in the Carandini family over the centuries, and I mean remarkable: One of them was the cardinal who refused to attend Napoleon's coronation; and there was a papal secretary of state… a painting of him hangs in Windsor Castle. And there have been some most extraordinary people and that has nothing to do with me. I feel very strongly about that. I don't believe in inherited privilege *at all*. I think it's quite wrong. You've got to earn it.

And when he told me that, I was amazed. I said, "You mean the Romans?" and he said, "Yes. They were chariot makers, quartermasters, providers of food for the Roman armies. And the name was in Latin: *Carandinus. Carandini* is the interpretive of the Carindinus family.

So when I made this movie, the only one I've produced… way before its time, I think, I called it Charlemagne Productions, after the emperor who was crowned in A.D. 800 in St. Peter's on Christmas Day, the first Holy Roman Emperor. And if you walk inside St. Peter's in Rome—and I bet some of you have—there's a small circular spot that's inlaid in the floor, of colored marble or something like that. And I stood on it, and a man came rushing up to me and said, "You can't stand there."

I said, "Yes, I can."

He said, "No, you can't."

I said, "Yes, I can."

He said, "Only the heirs of the emperor are allowed to stand on that," and I said, "Look!"

YVONNE MONLAUR

We invited Yvonne Monlaur to Classic FilmFest 2000. Like Veronica, she is a darling who stole our hearts. She is very conscious of her English and doesn't realize everyone finds her French accent irresistible, and although she wasn't comfortable doing talks, she did brave it out for us. Yvonne has become a dear friend to us and our friends. This talk was hosted by Tom Johnson and Mark A. Miller.

Tell us how you began in acting.

My English is so bad. I started modeling. A French director saw me in a magazine and he asked me—first he wanted to know if I could speak French! I said *oui*. I made *Honore de Marseille* [1956] and *Mannequins de Paris* [1956], those were my first pictures.

How did you find yourself working in English productions?

It was very easy. My agent asked me to make a test for a series in L.A. called *Woman in Love*. I made it. I think it was a success and afterwards the producer of Hammer Films saw it.

Kevin Flynn watches over Yvonne Monlaur as she signs autographs for fans at FANEX 15.

Terror of the Tongs

Could you tell us about George Sanders?

He was the leading man, as you say. A perfect gentleman. Very helpful because my English was so poor.

Do you recall which Carreras you dealt with?

Michael, I didn't meet the father.

Tell us about Terence Fisher.

Terence Fisher was a very nice man and so kind and so helpful with me. I can't tell you much, he said I was free to do what I want.

Terror of the Tongs?

They asked me to make *Terror of the Tongs* [1961]. I was very happy because it was very different part for me other than Marianne [in *Brides of Dracula*, 1960] to do a Chinese girl. Christopher Lee was the lead, very commanding, very authoritative. And he looked really like a Tong. I didn't have many scenes with him, more with Geoffrey Toone.

Peter Cushing?

In French we say he was a *queen*, so sweet. He was very helpful, a very clever man, sensitive. We used to, for fun, talk Russian together [Yvonne's father was Russian]. He was really very nice.

What is your favorite film?

Yvonne Monlaur and David Peel in a publicity shot for *Brides of Dracula*

I made 20 pictures in France. It's difficult to say which is my favorite. My last picture was a German picture called *Rechnung - eiskalt serviert, Die* [1966], so that is one of my favorites.

What was David Peel like?

First of all, I remember, he was a very attractive and youthful Dracula. So blond and elegant. He didn't talk too much. He was a stage actor. He changed his destiny, he worked in antiques.
What types of movies do you like?

As a fan, it's unusual because I did a lot of films with violence, I like romantic films, comedies and old American musicals, dancing, that's my favorite.

What are your hobbies?

I play guitar and music is my hobby. So, I'm not too far from my activities in film, artistic.

You were a finalist for the lead in Thunderball *and came in second.*

I had to approach Sean Connery and all those people. It was an experience but very short. It was just a pleasure to know Connery.

Bray Studios?

In Bray everyone was very comfortable, people were a unit, they knew how to create.

Anton Diffring in Circus of Horrors *[1960]?*

Anton was terrifying, for the part physically, he gave that impression but he was a very nice man, very helpful to me.

What do you think of them remaking Brides of Dracula?

I think it would be an error to do a remake. We think we did it right.

Would you go back to acting?

I think it's better to retire and not do it again.

Do you watch your movies?

I watch and I say, "My goodness, is that you, that young girl?" But I watch and it makes me happy.

CAROLINE MUNRO

Caroline Murno was a guest at FANEX 11. She is very sweet and very shy, and we finally managed to get her to perform a song from her CD at the opening ceremony. She is a wonderful singer. It was another unforgettable FANEX moment.

What can you tell us about Peter Cushing?

In the other film I did with him—*Dracula* [*Dracula A.D. 1972*]—I didn't actually do any scenes with him, but I did a lot of scenes in *At the Earth's Core* [1976]. I felt he was very supportive to me. I suppose he became like my grandfather. He felt like my grandfather. It felt like that—it felt like a nice little team, and I could go to him and say, "What do you think about this, Peter?" and he would say, "Well, my child..." and he wore these little white gloves. This is when we weren't working, and he had these white gloves on, and he'd say, "I think perhaps"—and he knew I was relatively inexperienced—I'd done bits and pieces, but I was working with him and Doug [McClure], and they were old hands at it.

He gave me great guidance through the situations. And also, I remember this, though it's not really related to the film, but he was very, very comforting to me. My grandfather died during the making of the film, and his wife had died, I would say two years before... maybe three years before. So he

Peter Cushing in *At the Earth's Core*

knew what grief was. So during the making of that film he was extremely comforting to me. He was a lovely, lovely gentleman. I was talking to somebody earlier who was asking me about Peter, and I said, "I would have to describe him—there was not one person that had a bad word to say about him." He was just so special, and so funny. He kept to himself a lot of the time. He would have his tea, but he was always ready for a conversation if you wanted to chat. And I used to knit—I knitted a lot in those days—I'd sit on the film set, and I remember knitting all these squares for blankets... sew them and send them all off... and Peter would say, "How charming." He was just so sweet, and I miss him. I really do.

He had his trusty umbrella... in *At the Earth's Core*. He had this wonderful umbrella which he used to do a lot of business with. It really worked for him. It's actually a very good tip to have props... when you don't know what to do with your hands, which often happens with an actor... it props you up in a way, gives you something to latch on to.

JIMMY SANGSTER

Jimmy Sangster was guest at FANEX 11, where Midnight Marquee debuted his autobiography *Do You Want it Good or Tuesday*? This interview was conducted by Tom Johnson.

Mr. Sangster has been making a joke for the past couple of years about being a cult figure and how there's really no training for it—you either are one or aren't one. I'd like to say that I think there are two ways a person can become a cult figure. One is the Ed Wood way by making things that are so bad you become a cult figure and the other way is his way, by making things so good you become a cult figure.

One of the things you've said quite often in interviews that you've given is that you're not really a horror fan. Yet, at least, in the early part of your career, your career was made by horror films and the question that most horror fans have is how does someone who's not a horror fan know exactly what we wanted and how were you able to write what most of us would consider the best horror film [Horror of Dracula, *1958] ever made?*

Well, it wasn't so much of knowing what you wanted because most of you weren't even around then. It was a case of doing something and then you liking it. I didn't design it especially for you guys. I designed it as a movie, just a movie, and you guys like it—you were about nine or 10 years old. You were that age. You loved the movie. Going back to this cult figure thing—I only became a cult figure because the movies I wrote became cult movies. That's a bit stupid isn't it, what I just said actually? [Laughs].

I was working for a company, Hammer, who quite by accident, had made a science fiction movie which was a huge success called *Quatermass Experiment* [US title: *The Creeping Unknown,* 1956]. It was the first one they made and they said, "We must make another one of

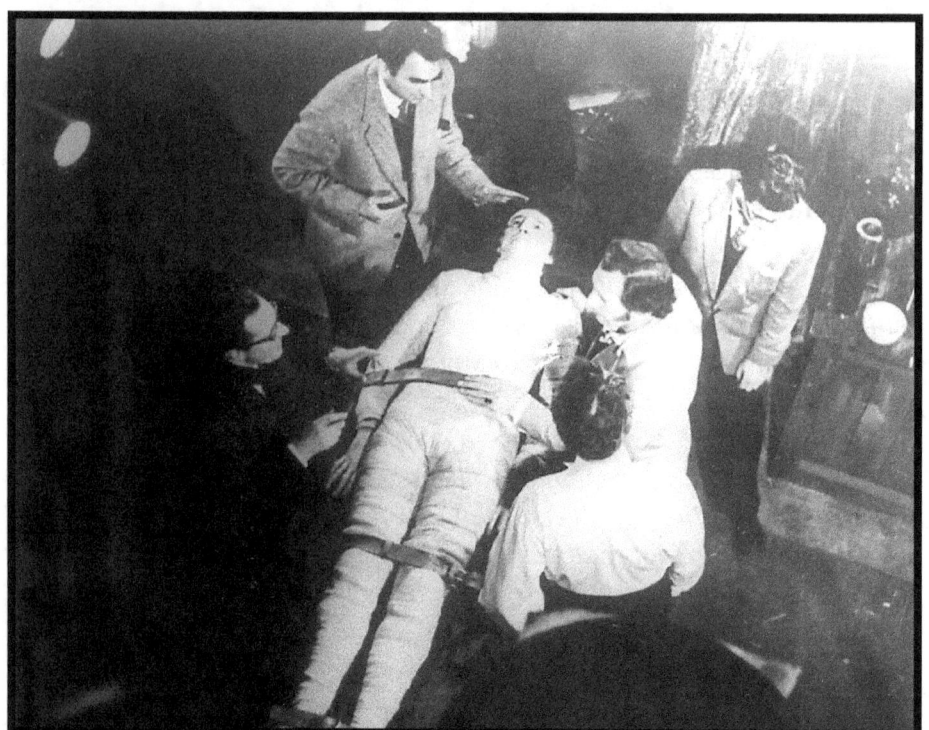

Terence Fisher, Christopher Lee and Peter Cushing on the set of *The Curse of Frankenstein*

these." I wasn't a writer, I was a production manager. We must make another one of these. There weren't any ones sort of lying around. They couldn't afford to buy one or anything, any property. So, they said to me, "Would you like to write one?" I said, "I'm not a writer, I'm a production manager," and they said, "Well, you can come up with a couple of ideas, and, if we like it we'll pay you. If we don't like it we won't pay you. You're already being paid as a production manager so you can't complain."

So, I went ahead and I wrote it and they paid me and we made the movie. So, when they suddenly decided—and I'm not sure why they decided to do *Frankenstein* [*The Curse of Frankenstein*, 1957]—but when they did decide to do it, being Hammer, it had to be done on the cheap and the cheapest way was to get Sangster to write it because he's production manager and we're paying him anyway and he'll do it for practically nothing. I did do it for practically nothing. I think they paid me £450, which, was slightly under $1,000. That's all I ever made out of it. We'll get Sangster to write it. Now what I'm saying is if in fact, instead of deciding to make *Frankenstein*, they decided to make *Carry*

Jimmy Sangster, Mary Peach and Val Guest sign for fans at FANEX 11.

on Sergeant or one of the comedy things, they would probably still have asked Sangster to write it and Sangster would have written it and I would be a comedy writer and I would never have become a cult figure. That's the whole genesis of me being a writer. I was cheap and I was there in the office. They didn't have to send out for anybody and, in fact, after *X—the Unknown* [1957] came out, some other company asked me to do a script for *The Day of the Triffids*. They never made my script, but they asked me to do a script for *The Day of the Triffids*. They said how long will it take? I said 10 weeks. They thought that was horrifyingly long. I couldn't tell them I was a production manager on the side.

I was sitting in the office one day sort of writing and Michael Carreras comes in.

"What are you doing?"

"I'm working out the budget for the next picture."

He said, "No you're not, you're writing aren't you?"

I said, "Yeah, I'm writing a script for somebody else."

He said, "You've got to decide what you're going to be, are you going to be a writer or are you going to stay working for us as associate producer."

I said, "But, I really would like to be a writer, but I have a brand new house with a mortgage and a new baby."

So Michael said, I'll always remember him for doing this, "I'll buy one script a year for the next three years. You know you'll get around $1,500 for the next three years." Believe it or not, I could live on that, I could pay my mortgage and bring up my baby. So I left Hammer and the first script I did, I think, it was *The Mummy* [1959], which was the first of those contracted scripts and the second year I was off and running... It was only because of that offer I became a writer. I quit my daytime job.

You once said in an interview in. I believe, Kintemagroph Weekly *in the United Kingdom that you described yourself as just a regular guy and what scares you will scare an audience.*

Yes, well what else do you go by? If you're writing a horror film, any film, that's the only judge you've got. If you're writing a movie which makes people cry, whatever makes you cry you hope will make them cry.

One of the things you know if you spend time around Mr. Sangster is that he's very funny, which comes as a shock maybe when you consider some of his movies. If I may be allowed to give a personal story, the first time I met Mr. Sangster was with Sue and Colin Cowie. We met Mr. Sangster in a restaurant near his house and we were going to have lunch, a fairly expensive restaurant. This is a fairly upscale restaurant and we were approached by the wine steward who was aware that Mr. Sangster was the guest of honor and opened the menu and angled it towards him and that there were fine wines available, one of which cost about $300 a bottle, and Mr. Sangster pointed to that particular wine and said we'll have two bottles of this. Now, it's understood that I'm paying for this. So he pointed to the bottle and said we'll have two of this. He looked at me and said I bet that scared you more than any of my movies. He ended up getting a coke and I ended up on the floor getting artificial respiration. How much do you think humor has played a part in your screenwriting?

I think it's very important, Especially in those horror ones. You've got to make people laugh where you want them to laugh, because otherwise they're going to laugh where you don't want them to. You give them an

Peter Cushing and Francis Matthews in *The Revenge of Frankenstein*

excuse to laugh, that's fine, and then the next dramatic bit if it goes slightly over-the-top or slightly ridiculous they won't laugh. It's the worst thing when you're doing a suspense film, horror film, whatever, if the audience starts to laugh. Nervous laughter, they do sort of laugh nervously, but if you give them a joke, a very subtle joke, whatever, then that gives them a chance to laugh and then you start to scare the shit out of them all over again, but you can give them a chance to relax. That parcel that was a line from *Frankenstein*, it was an excuse to stop that very, very nasty scene, to let the audience relax a bit. That sort of line, or that sort of trick, we called it "pass the marmalade" and the next script and the next one and the next one, when are you going to pass the marmalade, have you passed the marmalade yet.

So you're saying, as a writer going in, you're not trying to keep the audience on the edge of their seat for 90 minutes?
I don't think you can keep them on the edge of their seat for 90 minutes, they're going to fall flat on their faces. You've got the give them a chance to say whoa and then start lining them up again, I feel. But then again, I don't think our 30 films were all that horrible or horrifying. Were they?

I suppose they were. I mean you were kids when you saw them. I suppose, for a 9, 10 or 11 year-old kid, they were.

I think most of them still work today though as being frightening.

Do you?

I think they do. The one that still works for me quite a bit is The Revenge of Frankenstein *[1959]. I think that, in my humble opinion, that's your best writing. I think the way you took the Frankenstein story in a new direction was just incredible. Just the way you were able to center it on Peter Cushing's character and the character of the monster, that wasn't really a monster when he starts to realize that everything that had been done to him was all for nothing and he begins to revert back into the paralyzed condition he was before—that's terrifying and I think that's some of the best writing you've ever done.*

You've never told me that before, Tom.

Well you said you didn't quite remember the movie.

I still don't. All I maybe remember about the movie is this is the movie that Sir James Carreras took the poster, [*The Curse of*] *Frankenstein* was a big success and they were going to do another one and they had a very scary poster drawn up by a very talented artist, brought the poster to American and told all the honchos at Universal or wherever, that this is the next picture we're making, we start shooting in 12 weeks. And they just received the figures on *Frankenstein* and they all wanted to get in on it. The money arrived. He came back to me and he said, "Hey, you see this poster? Please write me a script on this poster, will you?" And I said but it's *Frankenstein*. He said, "Yeah," and I said, "But we killed him in the last picture." He said, "Oh come on, you'll think of something." And he said, "But we do start shooting in 12 weeks so I need the script in four weeks." So the first thing I had to do was bring him back to life. And that's about the only part of the picture I remember. You probably know much better than I do about it, but it had something to do with cannibalism.

Yes.

Frankenstein manages to return from the dead in the sequel of *The Curse of Frankenstein*.

I remember doing a newspaper article and them saying to me how do you write these horrible things, revolting things, they called them revolting in those days. How do you think of these revolting things? I said the things that really revolt me seem to revolt other people and cannibalism is pretty revolting, so I wrote in cannibalism.

You mentioned that you were going to have trouble bringing Frankenstein back since you killed him in the first movie but you never actually see him killed. I'm wondering whether some sixth sense told you don't show Peter Cushing actually dying, because we could come back with a sequel. Or was that simply something that happened as an accident?
I don't think it was an accident. As far as I remember, we saw Peter being led out to the gallows, the picture was over, there'd be no point in having him strapped down with the guillotine and seeing his head chopped off. I mean the picture was over. It's a bit like *The Scarlet Pimpernel* or whatever it was where the guy was topped at the end. The picture was over so you don't want to see him get his head cut off... You don't need to see the guy have his head chopped off.

Bette Davis in *The Nanny*

You've said that possibly your favorite movie of all was The Nanny *[1965].*

Yes.

And I'm just wondering off the top of my head if you had any amusing or grotesque experiences with Bette Davis?

Yes, I have. I won't tell you any of them, but yes I have.

I don't think you should tell us because I think it's very amusingly documented in your book which I think everyone should go buy immediately after this discussion.

That's not why I'm not going to tell you. Yes, if anybody's interested in Bette Davis stories, I've got a whole bunch of them. It wasn't *The Nanny*, it was the second movie that I did with her. After the first movie, after I'd done *The Nanny*, my wife, that's not Mary who's here but my ex-wife who died, she said if ever you do another Bette Davis movie I'm leaving the country the day that she arrives and I'm not coming back until she's gone. Mainly because Bette Davis used to call me at 9:30-10 at night and say come around. So I'd have to get in my car and drive round the house we rented for her and she'd be waiting for me at the front door with a glass of scotch in her hand and she'd start bitching about this, that, or the other. Anyway, so my social life really went to hell and Monica quite rightly said if she ever comes here again, I'm leaving. I said, "I'm never going to make another Bette Davis movie."

About a year later Tony Hinds came to me and said, "We're going to make a Bette Davis movie, want to write the script?" So I said, "Yeah, sure." So I wrote the script and he said, "Do you want to produce it?" I said, "No." He said, "Come on." I said, "No, I'm not going to produce it." Well Tony certainly wasn't going to produce it, he'd seen what I'd gone through the last time. So, in the end, I said, "Come on, make me an offer I can't refuse," so he actually made me an offer I couldn't refuse, and I had to produce the bloody thing. And it's true, the moment Bette Davis arrived, in fact I only did one trip to the airport. I drove Monica, we had this house in the south of France and I put her on the plane for the south of France and then waited an hour for Bette to arrive from New York, and I swear the day that Bette left, Monica came home. That movie [*The Anniversary*, 1968] was a very, very unhappy movie.

That was the one where a week into shooting, five days into shooting, well, previously on both movies, I had to take the director out to Los Angeles to audition because she had director approval We'd never had an artist who had director approval before. Most of our actors would say, "Yeah, I love it, I really want to do it. When can I see the script?"

Bette Davis, Jack Hedley and Sheila Hancock in *The Anniversary*

That's what most of our actors would do, but Bette Davis wanted director approval and got director approval. So I had to fly people out to LA. I did it with Seth Holt for *The Nanny* and that was fine and I did it with this very talented guy called Alvin Rakoff to see if she'd accept him for her director. I couldn't get Seth Holt, I tried to get Seth Holt, I couldn't get him and she saw him in L.A, and said. "Oh all right, we can't get Seth but Al would be fine."

So we started shooting the movie and four days into shooting she calls me up to her dressing room at the end of the day and said—she had this wonderful line, whenever she had anything to complain about, she'd always start out by saying, "I have starred in 68 movies." You can't argue with someone when they say something like that, especially Bette Davis, you know she starred in 68 movies, you've seen them all and they've all been great movies. And you know she knows what she's talking about. She said, "I've starred in 68 movies and I have never had to work for the camera, the camera has always worked for me." Which is a very logical thing and she said, "Alvin is making me work for the camera," in other words, Alvin would block out the scene, because Alvin is basically a television director, he would block out the scene before he even got the actors on the set, so, when Bette and the actors came down on the set he'd say, "All right Miss Davis, you come in here. You've a couple of marks here, you say your line then you walk across to a desk here where you light a cigarette, as you say so and so then you walk on..." She said, "Maybe I don't want to do that, maybe I can't light a cigarette there, maybe it isn't right. I've got to play the scene first." I said, "Fine, okay, I'll tell him. I'll tell him to change his style of directing." She said, "No, no he's got to go." I said, "What do you mean he's got to go?" She said, "Fire him." "I can't fire the director a week into shooting, I mean, we'd have to start all over again." She said, "Well that's your problem. But I will do you a favor, I'll get sick and go home so the insurance will pay for the hold up." So I called Fox, 20th Century-Fox and said, "I've got a problem here, Bette Davis wants me to fire the director." So Fox says, "What's your problem?" I said, "She wants me to fire the director." He said, "So fire the director. You don't understand, this isn't a Jimmy Sangster picture, it's not a Hammer picture, it's not an Alvin Rakoff picture, it's a Bette Davis picture. She wants you all gone, you're all gone, so fire the director."

So poor Alvin, I fired him, and the guy who came in to do it, a guy called Roy Ward Baker who had done some very good pictures in England and in Hollywood. Bette knew him personally so she accepted him as director. He wasn't stupid. We'd been shooting in this big set, a huge set with the main staircase coming right down the center where she makes her first entrance. He looked at me and said, "I don't like that staircase, can you make it so it comes down there?" I mean what he was doing was making sure that nothing that Alvin had shot would go in the final picture because there might have been a credit dispute, so we had to rebuild the entire set and then we shot. I thought, "Everything's going to be great, everything is going to be fine." I don't think I've ever been so miserable in my life.

All the other cast had loved Alvin Rakoff so they hated Roy Baker, they loathed Bette Davis for creating all this trouble and she thrived on tension, so if there wasn't any tension around she'd whip it up. I think I lost five or six pounds during that picture. I didn't have a woman to support me; I had to go home to an empty house every night. It was terrible. She did say at one time when we were looking for a new director, she did say, "Well why don't you do it?" to me. Tony Hinds said, "You do it. She'll take you as director." Fortunately I was wise enough to say, "No." I didn't want to do that, because then I probably would have died; I'd never make the end of the picture.

Socially she was also death, too. She was a very unhappy lady at that time. She had nobody in her life, her kids didn't like her much, and she was just a very unhappy lady. There was a lot of stuff written by other people in the movie about her. There was an actress called Shelia Hancock, who'd been in the original play of *The Anniversary*; she'd written that Bette Davis arrived with a huge entourage from Hollywood. Her entourage was one little nice gay guy who was a hairdresser. She never had an entourage. She disapproved of the fact that in England the studios are not dry, you can get a drink at lunch time. She thought this was wicked and also if the call sheet said Miss Davis on the set at 9:30, she'd be on the set at 9:30 and God forbid they shouldn't be ready for her. This was very different because I've been an assistant director and when you make up the call sheet for the following day you've got to work out how long you think the first scene is going to take before you're going to need the artist for the second scene, so you take a guess and you say ready on set at 10:30, and something goes wrong, and you don't need the artist till quarter past 11, then you send for them and that's fine. But if you had said 10:30 on the call sheet for Bette Davis, at 10:30 she would be sitting there. And a pall of gloom would settle over and everyone

The Anniversary

would go completely to pieces, and anyway, she was an experience to work with.

I'm very glad. I think I didn't like *The Anniversary* particularly, but I think *The Nanny* was the best picture I'd made. Seth Holt was a very good director and he'd done that other one for me, *Taste of Fear* [1961], *Scream of Fear* over here, which I also thought was a good picture.

You made it clear in many of your interviews and in your book that your relationship with Michael Carreras was not just a business one, he was a great friend of yours, and since he died not to long ago, maybe you'd like to tell us a few things about Mr. Carreras.

Michael. Well, Michael and I started to work for Hammer about the same week. I'd never met him before. I came out of the Air Force, he came out of the Army, we both went to work. I was a third assistant director, he was a location production accountant or something, so he got on better because his father owned the company, so he got promoted quicker than I did. And he became my boss eventually, quite soon actually around two pictures later, but we were instant buddies, we were both unmarried, we both liked swing and jazz and drinks and girls and we were best friends forever,

I'm godfather, I think I'm godfather, to one of his children. And, we had some incredible times. I mean some are far too rude for me to even begin to tell you about, but I remember one particular time there was a picture we were doing called *The Snorkel* [1958], and we had to find a location which had to be a big villa on the Mediterranean or Riveria somewhere, so we get into our car, we get a ferry across to France, we go

On location for *Maniac* with Michael Carreras

to Paris for a couple of days and whoop it up, and then we drive down. It takes us two days to drive down to the south of France where we whoop it up some more, we can't find our villa there [so] we drive across into Italy and finally one day we find this villa. And Michael said, "Well, this is dead right." He said, "But that scene where the girl climbs out of the window and walks across the thing there, you have to rewrite it because the stairs aren't [where] they should [be where] you've got them in the script, so you'll have to readjust that." I said, "Yeah." He said. "Aren't you going to write it down?" I said, "You've got a pencil?" He said, "I bring you a thousand bloody miles, my writer, I give you the best time you've ever had, and you haven't got a pencil?" He didn't have a pencil either, I had to memorize it all. Other stories, no they're all too rude, I can't possibly tell them.

You tell a story in your book about filming Maniac *[1963] which you wrote and produced and Michael directed.*

Yes.

That one of the actresses, not the lead actress, but the second or third billed actress came to you during filming and said a friend was going to be visiting and perhaps you could tell them that story.

We were filming in a place called Awl, which is a town in the south of France, in the wonderful ruins of a Roman arena where they still have bullfights, and Nadia Grey was an Italian, she was a star, believe it or not, but was an Italian star. She said one day to us, "I've got a friend who's sort of passing through town, can I bring him on the set?" I said to Michael, "Is it all right?" He said, "All right but keep him well in the background and let's not have any comments about what we're doing. Let's make sure he stays out of the way, bring him on if you like." So she brings him on, "I'd like you to meet my friend," it was Orson Welles. And not once did he tell us what we were doing wrong. He stayed for about an hour and a half and he didn't open his mouth once.

Could you tell us how you shifted from England to Hollywood?

I met this girl. That's true. I was single, I started going [out], [but] this is another story, I got an offer to do a movie of the week for Aaron Spelling, and I sold him the idea, I wrote him the script. What I did was take *Scream of Fear* and rewrote it in America, which was a big change, I tell you, because the language is basically the same. Of course, I thought nobody would have seen *Scream of Fear*, it was made a long time ago, and apparently, it was about four weeks before they started filming and they ran it on a late night movie and Aaron Spelling couldn't sleep that night and he saw it. And he called my agent who called me the next day and said, "Aaron Spelling called me this morning. He said this movie that you've written for him, which is about to start filming, is really quite similar to one you made called *Scream of Fear*." I said, "It's not similar, it's exactly the same." I said, "At least I changed the names."

But anyway that's the thing I did, and I was there, and there was this girl, so I stayed longer than I should have done, so I was about to come back to London with the girl who I later married, God, and I was about to come back and I got a call from Tony Hinds in London saying Columbia was looking for me. They were about to start a new series called *Ghost Story* [1972] and they wanted me as story consultant. I didn't even know what a story consultant was, so I called my agent and I said call Columbia and he called and said okay. And he called back and said, yes, they want you. Apparently the reason they wanted me because was because the executive producer was William Castle who used to make all those wonderful schlock horror movies. They made a movie about him with John Goodman playing the part anyway. Have you seen that?

Matinee.

That's it. He was the executive producer and he said let's get Jimmy Sangster as a script editor

on this and the producer, a guy called Joel Roberson, who was a very efficient line producer, he never heard of me and he was the one responsible for getting the scripts out and he said, "We better get somebody else because Jimmy Sangster doesn't know any at all over here." One of the arts of being a script editor was who you know, which writers you knew [and] could trust and rely on to give it to you good and Tuesday. No surprises. I used to ask my writers, "Please don't give me any surprises. Just do the work, no surprises please."

So Joel was really worried about employing me because I didn't know any writers in Hollywood. So he employed another story editor. There were two story editors in the beginning of the series, the first one left after the first 13 or 14 weeks, so the kept me on. Suddenly I was a member of the Writers Guild, I bought a house out there and a car and I stayed. That was a very good series, it should have gone on. There were some very good people in it, big stars. We had wonderful casting, Gena

Rowlands, Helen Hayes, but they were too expensive so they stopped it after the first season. My contract was I would stay on as script editor if I could direct two episodes, and they balked a bit, but they had to agree, so round about show 12 they said, well, you've better start choosing the two episodes you want to direct, but by then I was far too terrified to direct, they did everything so quickly, so fast, so efficiently. I'd been sitting in the theater every morning for 15-20 weeks listening to the comments people made during dailies. "Look at what he's done with that scene, how could we possibly employ that man as a director?" I'd been through all this and I thought they're going to do that to me. So I said, "No thank you, I didn't want to direct."

So I stayed on till the series finished and by then I was so established there I couldn't afford to leave. I stayed for 12 years, for which I was very, very thankful and grateful. I made a lot of money, it's that pension, the Writer's Guild pension, that I live on now. There was a story I told this morning, we were on strike and I was walking picket outside Paramount studios, about five or six of us with our signs. We'd drive to the studios in our Cadillacs and Mercedes every morning and asked the studios permission to park on their parking lot while we went outside to picket, and they always let us. Anyway I was walking picket that day and some young guy drives up, a delivery truck, he's union minded and he sees us and asks, "Can I cross your picket line?" We said, "Sure," he goes in and makes his delivery and comes out 10 minutes later and looks at us walking up and down and our signs saying unfair to writers and he says, "What do you guys do?" I said, "We're writers." "What do you write?" I said, "We write television stuff, the plays you see on television." "Oh, what are you striking for?" "More money." "You mean you get paid for that shit?" That's the honest truth. But we did, we got paid very well for that shit. Very well indeed.

I was involved in another strike. But the second strike, about four or five years later, they decided they didn't want to picket individual studios, they'd get the whole guild out and each day they'd choose a different studio and that was much more fun because you know you'd get 2,000 people wandering around the studio and you got to meet all your old mates and set up stalls and coffee things, that was fun, that sort of picketing. The other one was rotten. The Writer's Guild, were, they still are I imagine, very, very tough in Hollywood. The most powerful guild of the lot. And I can say because of them I got a nice pension and medical insurance, so I had a very, very profitable 12 years and then I got divorced. Don't get divorced in California, it's fatal. Oh, I tell you.

You are also a novelist.

Well, a novelist. I've written nine novels but nobody ever buys any of them.

I did.

Well, they're all out of print now. They're all out of print, it's ridiculous. The only two novels I made any money out of were the two that I made movie of the week of, *Private Eye* [*The Spy Killer*, 1969] and *Foreign Exchange* [1970]. There was a character, who was an Englishman, a really down-at-heel ex-secret service man who'd become a private eye in London, and in both these novels he gets dragged into something intriguing by his ex-secret service boss. A guy in Hollywood and I made a deal with ABC to make them. And I came back to London to cast them. I cast Trevor Howard, a very good English actor, to play the lead and I got Laurence Olivier to play the head of the secret service. He wanted to do something for television and all the scenes were in his office so it was about three days work, so he could afford to do it, so I signed Lord Olivier and Trevor Howard and I call ABC in Hollywood and tell them I've got this casting coup. They said nobody's heard of Trevor Howard and nobody likes Laurence Olivier, so they sent me for the Trevor Howard part an actor called Robert Hall who'd been a cowboy, he was a very nice man. For the Olivier part they sent me an ex-Englishman actor called Sebastian Cabot, who'd become

Sebastian Cabot and Robert Horton in *The Spy Killer*

very big over here in a sitcom where he played an English butler [*Family Affair*]. You know I had this down-at-heel detective and Robert Hall arrives with his wardrobe from Rodeo Drive and the director and I decide, what are we going to do, the man wants to play suave, he brought a suave wardrobe, and he's going to give us a lot of problems if he doesn't get to play suave. He doesn't get much money so let him play a suave. So he played his suave and it was awful.

I mean the whole thing was a disaster, but I made money from those because I sold the film rights and I produced them. But the actual novels no. It's a pity because it's really fun writing novels. You write a novel, it's straight from you to your audience. You write a movie there's 27 people get between you and your audience. The director, the actors, they all want to make changes, the producers, the story editors, they all want to make changes and they are usually rewritten too. So what comes out in the end has very little bearing on what you started out with. You write a novel, there's very little between you and your audience. And also, you don't have a deadline. Novel writing is fun but there's no money in it. I can't imagine John Grishim saying that or Tom Clancy, there's money in it for some, but not for me.

How did you prepare for the censors?

We used to have terrible battles with the censors because they had to have the script. We'd send them the script before we started shooting, and they'd say, "You can't show this, you can't show that, you can't have them say this." So what we used to do with the script was put in some really, really revolting scenes which we knew the censor would say, "Take them out" and we'd say, "Okay. Well, all right, if we take that out, can we possibly leave that one in?" So we'd deal with the censor to get stuff in. We used to say, "Well, what can we get away with?" Now there were two versions shot. There was the English version and the American version. The American version had a lot of stuff in it which we didn't put in the English version. Because we could get away with far more over here apparently, for some reason, I don't know why. And you should have seen the Japanese version of some of them. I mean they were really nasty. But we used to do them pretty fairly nasty and then expect to make some cuts for the censor and then censor would see the first cut and say, "You've got to take this out, you've got to take that out," and so you'd bargain with them, you'd take this out, you'd take that out. So we tried to make them as bloody as we thought we could get away with.

Were you trying to make any statements with your writing?

People say why did you write this and why did you write that and why didn't you do this? I did it for wages. That's what I did. I was a writer. There was nothing sort of inspiration about it, I'd go to my desk at eight and do my 10 pages or 12 or whatever I decided to set myself and that was it. It was also a lot of fun. But there was no sort of drive to get some wonderful sort of inspirational message down on paper, it was just to make a crust. I was a writer. I was a professional writer as opposed to a writer writer. It's how I made my living.

Can you tell us about The Night Stalker *[1974]?*

Darren McGavin starred in *The Night Stalker*

I did one script quite by accident, it's at the same time I was walking picket when that guy came up and said you mean you get paid for that shit. One of the people I was walking with was the line producer of *Night Stalker* and we were talking about this, that and the other, and he said, "When this is all over, come and write a script." I said, "Yeah," he said, "Well, see if you can come up with an idea; if you can't come up with an idea we'll give you an idea." So I came up with an idea and I did it. I met Darren McGavin last year, he now has a very big boat which he keeps in Paris on the Seine and I was in Paris with some people who knew him and we had drinks on his boat. He didn't know me from Adam but he was very polite. I said, "I wrote one." He said, "Which one?" I said, "[the one] about a rakshasa something or other" [The episode, *Horror in the Heights* which aired 12/20/74 is generally considered one of the best of the series]. He said, "Oh, I remember." He didn't remember.

Which Hammer films went through rewrites?

Which ones went through rewrites? The early ones didn't. The later ones did, yes. Some came back to me. As I say in my book, you know I look at a picture now and the credits are screenplay by Jimmy Sangster, so and so. Or so and so and Jimmy Sangster and I honestly don't know. A lot of people think that that means we all sit there working together; you don't. You rewrite things but most of them were so long ago and I don't remember if I was the first, the middle or the end writer. I really don't remember. *X–The Unknown, Frankenstein, Dracula, The Mummy*, the early ones, I don't think anyone messed with those. They might have done [minor rewrites], but they didn't mess with them enough to get them credited. That's what counts.

Did you screen any of the Universal films before writing The Mummy?

Denis Mikel wrote a very good book on Hammer, [and] he said I saw all three or four Mummy films; I remember seeing one Mummy film. But, definitely I saw a Universal Mummy film. I think it was only one I saw, because that was the source material, just like the Stoker book and the Mary Shelley book was the source material. In this case it was the film that was the source material, so I did see it.

Why did Dracula *and* Frankenstein *vary from the novels?*

This is a bit disappointing, this sort of applies to the *Frankenstein* as well. I'd been with Hammer for about 10 years as a production manager and one of the production manager's jobs is to do the budget. So I knew that we had £45,000 or whatever it was to make this movie. So I had to write the movie so that it wouldn't cost more than that much money and one of the ways was in the book he comes by ship to Whitby in England,

John Van Eyssen and Christopher Lee in *Horror of Dracula*

floating on the stormy seas, and they said, "You've got to be joking, a boat at night and sea, no, no, no, no, we'll put a board or post up on the driveway that leads down to the studio."

Basically it was condensing it for budgetary reasons, I suppose, but I don't think it suffered because of it, because the Coppola *Dracula* didn't have any budget problems so they had all the space and stuff in the world, but I don't think it was any better, it was different. Basically it was budget. The *Frankenstein*, you know in every *Frankenstein* movie there's always been the peasants storming the castle at the end. No peasants in Hammer. You can hear the peasants if you want to, you can see the torch light flickering in the back but you can't afford peasants, so basically one kept them tight and I think it worked. We kept them tight because of the budgetary restrictions.

We were incredibly lucky because we had Bernard Robinson who made these incredible sets out of nothing, I mean budget-wise. I know he had nothing because I did the budget. Sets £10,000, he made these wonderful, wonderful sets. He and Jack Asher used to make this whole thing. Hammer has risen from the grave, we should all be so lucky if Hammer

had risen from the grave. It hasn't risen from the grave at all, Hammer is sort of lying there very dormant and they keep on saying they're going to rise from the grave, but what are they going to do when they do rise from the grave? Because, the Hammer that us lot here, appreciate these, are those maybe 10, 12 movies all together, and Hammer could certainly remake efficient movies, television is all around, but Hammer in those days was Terry Fisher and Peter Cushing, and Michael Carreras, and Christopher Lee, and Bernard Robinson and Jimmy Bernard music and Jack Asher [photography] and Jimmy Sangster the writer and that was Hammer. That you can't re-create because most of us are dead. Apart from anything else it was the right people at the right place at the right time. You can set down and make another *Dracula*, but why bother? It wouldn't be nearly as good as the original one.

I was curious as to your decision to make Jonathan Harker a vampire. How did that come about?

I was afraid somebody was going to ask me that question. Doesn't he become a vampire in the book, I can't remember.

No.

Oh, oh. Well, I can't remember, I really can't remember.
Was X–The Unknown *envisioned as another* Quatermass *film?*

No, it wasn't envisioned as another *Quatermass* film. As I said earlier, we'd made *Quatermass* and everybody'd been amazed at how successful it had been and [someone] said let's make another science fiction-type film, and there wasn't anything around at the time, and we were sitting around the office one day, Michael Carreras, Tony Hinds, me, and I said,

A behind-the-scenes shot of the muddy set on *X—The Unknown*.

"What about a story, everything always comes from outer space, let's have something coming from inner space." So Tony said, "Yes, wouldn't it be a good idea if—" and Michael said, "Yes," and, "I think so, and so" and at the end of 20 minutes we had a rough story and apparently I'd come up with more than anybody and they said go ahead and write it. It was a follow-up to *Quatermass*, to try and do another picture in the same genre. I was production manager on it and that was pitiful. Joe Losey was supposed to direct [the movie]. I bet you didn't know that, and a week before we were due to start, Dean Jagger [who] was coming from Hollywood said I can't work with Losey because he's a Communist, he'd been blacklisted. So he conveniently caught pneumonia so we were able to get insurance so we got a guy called Leslie Norman to come in and do it. He was an absolute shit, I tell you. Quite a good director, we tried to get Freddie Francis, but he wasn't available. Hi Freddie [as Freddie Francis arrived for his talk].

That might be the note on which to end this. In closing I'd like to say that Mr. Sangster in person is as amusing and entertaining as his movies were, and I think it's people like him that make us all proud to be fans.

BARBARA SHELLEY

Barbara Shelley was the guest of honor at FANEX 15 where she received the prestigious Laemmle Award. Those attending have many fond remembrances of meeting this interesting and talented woman. She graciously appeared at each film we screened and delighted the audience with stories about the making of the film.

Since we do these conventions out of love of movies rather than love of money [our accountant can attest to that] and with a staff of dedicated volunteers, things always manage to go wrong. Barbara Shelley wowed the audience, speaking well over an hour, but, unfortunately, the camera's battery ran out, so this is all that is preserved. Hopefully, someday we'll see Barbara Shelley again and learn more about her fascinating years with Hammer. This talk was hosted by Tom Johnson and Dick Klemensen.

How did you first become involved in acting?

Have you got half an hour? Until I was 13, I was going to be a missionary/surgeon. That's what I wanted to do. When I was 13, I was in a convent school in London. One of the best baritones England had ever produced, a man called Herbert Langley—he was the greatest Faust we ever produced, used to sing at Covent Garden, and all those places. We were lucky enough to have him come to our school to start doing the Gilbert and Sullivan operas, and, of course, as a great big school, we had to rehearse for a year before we could do them. I was in the chorus but my friend Pamela, who I'm going to see when I leave here. If any of you know *The Gondoliers*, she was singing Gianetta, which is a prominent part. Because I was her best mate, I was in the chorus. All my family were musical. Some of them were opera singers. I used to sing the baritone part because I have a bass/baritone voice anyway. I used to sing the baritone part of Giuseppe to help her learn her quarters and trios and all of that. So, a fortnight before we were due to start, Herbert Langley came in to the hall one day with a face as long as two weeks and said—I'll never forget the girl's name—"Audrey has appendicitis, we have no one to do Giuseppe." If I ever write an autobiography I think I'm going to call it *We Have No Giuseppe*—"and what are we going to do?" Mother Helen, who was wonderful in theatre but a very shy nun, put her head down. She didn't know what to suggest. My friend Pamela put her hand

Barbara Shelley signs a poster at FANEX 15.

up and said, "Mr. Langley, Barbara knows the part of Giuseppe." It's her fault I'm an actress actually. So, he said, "Do you?" So he made me come up front and sing the bottom line to one of the quartets. So, he said, "Okay." So, we sang a trio. So, all I had to do actually was learn the dialogue and the patter songs. They come into my life latter on, the patter songs. I was a great success, much to my amazement. In the following years—I think it's the best box office I've ever been because if the parents knew that I was going to be the lead, which always was, then I played the Chancellor and the Major General and they used to... instead of doing it for three days we had to do it for a week. So, that was the best box office I've ever been.

So, when I left school the nuns were shocked. I wanted to be an actress. I wanted to go to the Royal Academy of Dramatic Arts. I had some very North Country, we're not North Country, but I had a very North Country sounding accent. So, that had to be [gotten rid of]. So, I went to train privately. My mother, who I don't know how they ever afforded it, she was just wonderful. I also became the resident model for a very big fashion house. That was her fault because she'd read in the paper when they had a competition. So, I blame her for that.

I was modeling, it was what they call private modeling, it was only in the fashion house [and] training at the same time. She said I'd rather you

Veronica Carlson and Barbara Shelley at the Laemmle Awards at FANEX 15

had a proper job. That's always youngsters, when they're starting out, parents say, I wish you had a proper job. They don't know just what a hard job it is. So, I was a dental nurse and I taught school, a private school which I learned a lot from the reactions of little ones about identity and never taking one's identity away. I learned a lot from those children.

...Nobody told me I needed an agent because I just wanted to be an actress. An American photojournalist came to one of the... shows. I'd put on about three pounds so I wasn't allowed to model that year, although models weren't as thin in those days. It was still considered to have too much puppy fat if you had hips over 35. Today if you have hips over 30, you're fat. I wasn't modeling but [they] said what are you going to do with the commentary? You can stand between the two salons and say this is dress 46 and costs £5000, whatever. So, I did, and he said he wanted to photograph me for *Vogue*. He did and so I became a freelance model.

Now, if you are photogenic, then they give [you] an acting chance, but in those days models can't act, period. Models can't act. So, I would go to an audition, a lot of... clients were married to producers or directors and they would book me up for these things because I had no agent. "Oh, what do you do?" "Oh, I'm a model..." "Models can't act."

It wasn't until I went to Italy on a holiday that—I was just on holiday with friends and we were all sitting at a table. This young man came over who knew some of the people we were sitting with and he was a fantastic comic. I don't know if any of you have heard of him over here, Walter Chiari, he was the biggest thing in Italy, terribly funny, improvisational comic. He was doing a small review and I was there with a friend. There were about four of us. We all used to model together. I used to do sportswear and [my friend] used to do the fashion glamour stuff. He said, "Do you want to be in my review?" And I said, "Oh yes..." So, he wrote the contract on the back of a menu. I stayed and did this review. I didn't sing, I didn't dance, didn't speak Italian, but fools rush in where angels fear to tread. So, there I was and I became quite a success because he was very clever. I just did one or two words in sketches there which I learned parrot fashion. I didn't know why the audience were laughing so much until I learned Italian finally. But, of course, as everybody knew in those days, soubrettes were just glamour girls who stood up and just were there. So, I used to say my line and because he was so clever he'd say something completely inappropriate and my answer would be completely inappropriate and the audience was rolling about. They thought I was very clever. I wasn't, it was like that.

Then, I got very ill, I got peritonitis. I had met Ava Gardner—she was absolutely wonderful to me. I might get a bit tearful because she was really wonderful. I did *The Barefoot Contessa* [1954]. I was an extra on that. I was kind of the mascot. I was very young, remember. Because I was working in the review, this is when I got ill, I used to be at the theatre until two and then have to be in makeup at six. So, I was always falling asleep on the set—I was only an extra. I'd feel a push on my shoulder and that would be Humphrey Bogart with a towel over his arm and a cup of coffee. "Excuse me, you're sitting in the middle of the director's main shot."

All of them, Eddie O'Brien, they were all wonderful to me. And they used to take bets that they couldn't smoke [Joseph] Mankiewicz' pipe. I used to smoke it, Mankiewicz was the director. I stood outside to be sick, they didn't know. That's when I got to know Ava Gardner and when we went up... to San Remo, where they were doing the scenes on the yacht. Now, Ava Gardner and myself were the only two that weren't seasick, it was very rough. So, we sat on deck and we talked. She told me things about her life, I think, she had never told anybody else. She was really a wonderful lady and so beautiful, just breathtaking with green eyes and completely down-to-earth. She taught me a lot about behavior on the set, because she would never have a row. You would see her leave the set and you might hear the dressing room windows rattle and I would say, "What were you doing?" "Telling them off." I would say, "Why did you leave the set?" She said, "Never do it in public Barbara. If you've got something to say to anybody, do it in private." So, that's how I met wonderful Ava Gardner and it was on the way back from San Remo that

I got very ill on the train and had to go straight to hospital. The review left town without me and I was left there with no money, nothing.

I got very thin. So, I went back to modeling. Of course, in Italy, it's, "If she's photogenic, let's give her a film test." When my picture started to appear on the magazines as a model about four people wanted to give me a film test. That's actually—I told you it was a long story—that's finally [how I got] from wanting to be a missionary/surgeon/nun [and] I finally started to act in Italy. I made about 12 films there. The person who taught me my technique as a film actress was one of yours—Marc Lawrence. You remember Marc Lawrence? He was the villain in a film that was written for me called *Ballata Tragica* [1954], which was a kind of modern *La Traviata*, I suppose. He used to tell me about the... things, and the lights, and he used to take me home at night and his wife, Fanya, who was a writer, used to cook a meal and Marc Lawrence used to go through all the lines. So, it was due—you see the Americans in my life. Ava Gardner, who I'll tell you more about later, and Marc Lawrence, taught me my technique, so from then on I lived in Italy for four years.

First, I used to learn the lines parrot fashion—they had guide tracks there so you'd have [an actor] speaking in German, somebody else speaking in French, someone else... So I thought, "Oh no, I've got to learn Italian because this isn't fair." So, I used to verbalize parrot fashion with the help of a lovely lady called Bianca Lattuada, the great director Lattuada's sister, but she was production line—she came to me laughing one day. She said, "The director says what language are you speaking—you're the only one he can't understand?" At least it's easier to dub my mouth because I used to dub Italian into English when I was in Italy, but little by little I learned Italian that way. That's four years of my life, really.

I don't know if any of you have seen *Cinema Paradiso* [1988], have you seen it? Isn't it a wonderful movie? Well, I knew about *Cinema Paradiso* all those years ago because I was making another film for a young director, it was his first film, and he became very famous after this, Sergio Corbucci. Sergio was producing this film, you didn't wear dresses cut down to there, but I had a strapless dress on. He came onto the set with this terrible black frock. I said, "What's that sir?" because by then I spoke Italian. He said, "You've got to wear it." I said, "Why?" He said, "Because if you don't—these films are shown in the parish halls, like *Cinema Paradiso*—the priest will put his hand in front of the projector." When I saw *Cinema Paradiso*, I mean it was absolutely true. But they were wonderful days.

By the time I came back to England, I was known as an actress abroad, so I had the chance of four different contracts and that's when I started acting in England.

The other story about Ava Gardner, after I came out of hospital, it was about maybe nine months, a year later. I was making a small Italian movie and she was making *The Little Hut* [1957]. A casting director I knew, we were all having dinner one night, he said to me, "You don't know anybody who can wiggle their little toe without moving the rest of their foot?" I said, "Yes, I can," because I had bad feet at one time and I can pick things up with my toes—it's scary. So, he said, "Would you do it for Ava?" "She can't do it?" There's a scene in the film where she says, "Look what I can do." So, that foot is mine. Remember, this is Ava Gardner we're talking about and she hadn't seen me for maybe nine months. As soon as I walked on the set, she dropped what she was doing. She came running over and said, "Barbara I'm so glad to see you. I tried to find out where you were when I heard you were ill, and I've been looking for you. Then I had to go back to the States." I said, "I'm going to waggle my toe for you." I always thought [she] was marvelous and she made absolutely sure—she took me up to the photographic department and made absolutely sure I was given photographs of everything I did, bless her heart. Ava Gardner and Marc Lawrence, thank you.

Your Hammer debut came before The Camp on Blood Island *[1958] but you probably didn't knew it was a Hammer film.*

Well, Tom [Johnson] told me something before we came down here and I said, "Oh yes, I'd forgotten." When I was a model, they asked for some models to do a show in a film called *Mantrap* [1953] with Lois Maxwell. So, we all tripped off, about six of us, of course it was Bray Studios, which I didn't know, that was before they built it. It was just a stately home, a falling apart stately home. Kieron Moore was in that. And we were hanging about, our pretty dresses on, waiting to do the thing and somebody said we need a fashion commentator. Alex Paul who was the producer, looked down the line, he wanted someone who was photogenic, and one of the girls said, "Oh, well, she's a trained voice." So he said, "You do it." I didn't know my professional name then, so they just gave me any old name [billed as Barbara Kowin] and I did it and it's Tom who told me this afternoon the director was Terence Fisher. I didn't know, and all those years later, I worked with him. I'm sorry I didn't know that when I

Barbara Shelley was the lead in *The Secret of Blood Island* (1965).

worked with him later, because I would have said, "Hey, it's not the first time we've worked together." That was the first Hammer film I made.

The first fantasy film you made, your co-star was a lion.

No, not a lion, a leopard. Now, I'm not silly about animals. I adore all animals. I'm a complete vegetarian, it started off for medical reasons, but it's become spiritual. I couldn't eat anything that had a face or could have looked at me in some time. When I was a model, they took me to the zoo and I was in the cage of the cheetah and I had boa constrictors around my neck and I fell madly in love with chimpanzees and the orangutans. I only give you that as a build up because I had worked with animals a lot before and I respect them. So, we come to *Cat Girl* [1957] and the leopard, Big Chief Horrible Noise was his name, and we called him Chiefy. Frank was the trainer and he was always there with a holstered gun and everybody was to work with a thick plate of glass between them. But I wanted to know what this leopard was. So I went up to Frank and said, "Frank, can I meet him before we start." He said, "Sure." So I went up to the cage and I did what I did with all animals, I follow what their body language is doing. If they look away, I look away, as you do with dogs. And Frank was watching me. I said, "Is he tame?" He said, "No, he's not viscous, but he's not tame." I said, "Any chance of scratching his head?" because I like cats. And over the next four or five days he taught me to put my hands around the bars of the cage so there was nothing sticking out, no thumbs, no fingers and Chiefly used to come and rub his head against my hand and in the end he would lick it. It was like sandpaper. After a while, Frank said, "Would you like to

Barbara Shelley in *Cat Girl*

work with him properly?" And, I said, "Yes, if you think it's safe." He said, "Yes, I do" and it came to the point he would bring Chiefly to my dressing room as long as you covered the mirror up. He didn't like to see himself.

Somebody heard about this and you know what a lot of the press are like, they like to make trouble. So, they said, "Oh you know this leopard has his fangs and his claws drawn [removed]." So, they said, "We're going to come down and see it." After a day's shoot I put on this evening dress. If you've seen *Cat Girl* it's the one with all the chiffon veils dragging in back. The studio was cleared. I don't know if they still do it but the studios in England then had like an air lock. There is one lot of doors and then another one to keep the sun out. I went into the studio and Frank brought Chiefy on this couch behind me so Chiefy's got his head on my shoulder. Frank was standing [about five feet away] and in comes the press. There was about eight of them, all with their cameras. Frank said, "Take it easy, take one picture at a time and he'll be okay." But Chiefy looked up and one technician had stayed in the gantry. They were all supposed to go, he was up high and that to Chiefy was another animal. He didn't recognize him. I felt him tense, up came his head and Frank, who was an old country man said, "Don't move, luv." I said, "Who's moving?" Chiefy went past me and he caught his paws in the chiffon veils and he bit them off. He was frightened. He sat on his haunches and he looked up at the gantry and he backpedaled, looking up and he sat on the gas tank. He turned it on. So, then he's got this man up there and this hissing under his tail and he didn't know which way to turn. It wasn't funny at the time. I stood perfectly still. Frank just went over to him, he had his hand on his gun and he just tapped him on the side of the head and said, "You big soppy thing, get off there." So, I looked up, Frank looked up—all gone. Every press man was gone, through the double doors and we couldn't get the outside door open, they were leaning on it. We got Chiefy's lead and put it on and Frank went out the other door, around the back. "It's all right, the leopard's gone out the other way." Well, they were all going toward their cars and I walked out with Chiefy on the lead, we walked around. Of course, they wrote [things like] "When is a beautiful girl going to get into trouble?"—oh give me a break. The animal was fine, it was them that were scared. So, that's the story of Chiefy. I don't know if he's still alive, but he was working not so many years ago. I would bet he was toothless by then, but he was a lovely animal. I loved him.

Blood of the Vampire *[1958] with Donald Wolfit, I believe he liked to be called Sir Donald and* The Dresser *was based on him?*

Yes, to go back a bit further, it's funny people talk about coincidence. I believe in synchronicity—that things have a meaning. The first thing I ever saw in a theatre, I was taken when I was six by a school party to the local theatre. It was Donald Wolfit in *Merchant of Venice*. So, that impressed me when I was six years old. When I stated interest in the theatre, I used to go see a lot of Donald Wolfit's work. In England he was thought of as a great ham, but those that know, will say that he is the best Lear that's ever been, because he was made for Lear. He was over-the-top as Hamlet, over-the-top as all the others, but as Lear he was magnificent. *The Dresser* [1983] was actually written by the man who did dress him for years. It was autobiographical. He was the old actor laddie who had a manager who made all the speeches and was quite sure there was nobody in the cast up to his standard and he got all the applause. But, when I worked with him, he was wonderful. We got along terribly

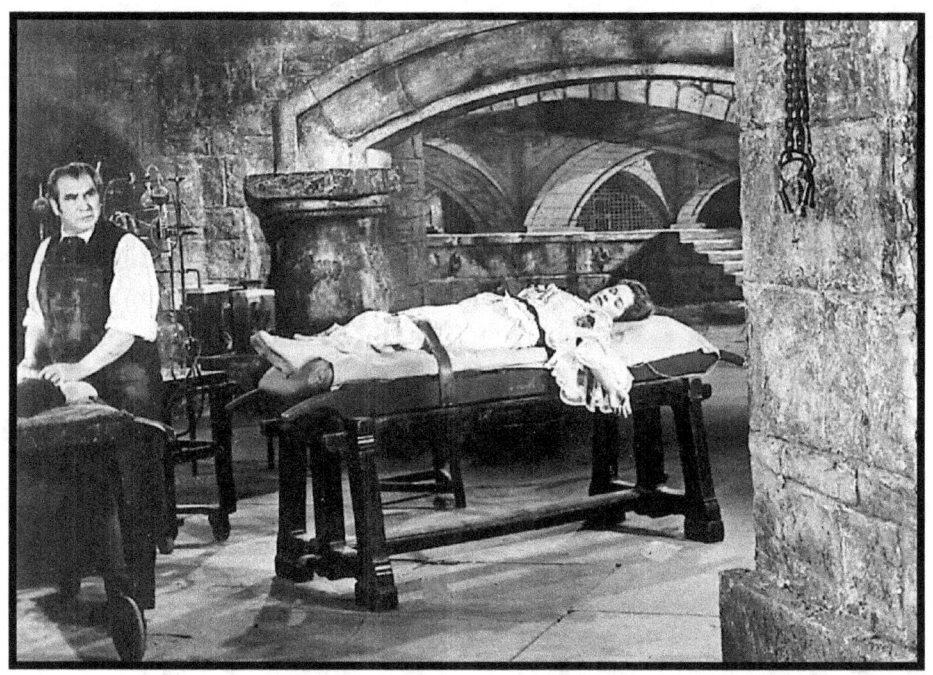

Donald Wolfit and Barbara Shelley in *Blood of the Vampire*

well and he'd just got his knighthood and he was so proud of it. Now, I was brought up, our elders were betters. When I worked with Shirley Booth, I couldn't call her Shirley, she asked me to, and I said, "No." We compromised and I called her Miss Shirley. That was all right. So, I automatically called Donald Wolfit Sir Don.

I'll you what a great [professional he was]—when you see the film you'll see the scene—he must have been in his late 60s, early 70s, he was quite a big man, and there's a scene when I can do nothing, I'm supposed to be a dead weight because I'm cut down from manacles and he has to carry me the length of the laboratory. Well, the length of the laboratory was quite a long way and I'm dead weight. So, Henry Cass, the director, said, "Donald pick her up, and start walking and then we'll cut." "No, dear boy," he said. "I can do that." Well, things go wrong with films, when there's a hair in the gate or a camera goes wrong or a light flickers. So, I think it was 11 takes and he would not give up. All I knew was when he put me on the table each time, I was dropped. I was bracing myself. But, I admired him for that. That was quite something. Remember, he wasn't used to filming, he was used to theatre, a completely different technique. But 11 times and he thought he'd only have to do it once as you would a performance.

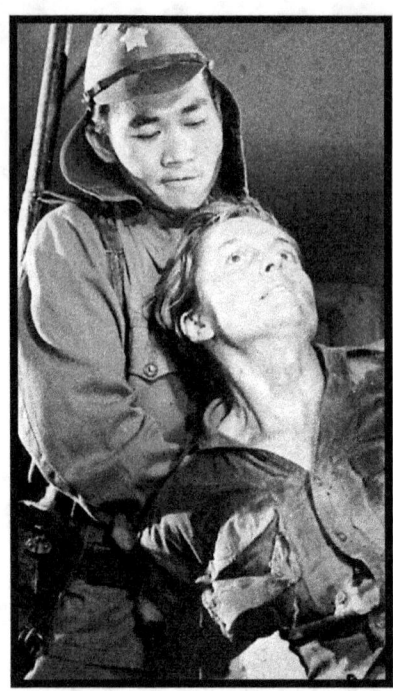

Ronald Radd and Barbara Shelley in *The Camp on Blood Island*

Your first real Hammer film The Camp on Blood Island, *you worked with Andre Morell, Michael Gwynn and Val Guest. Could you tell us about this controversial film?*

It's slightly difficult to remember a tremendous amount about the making of that film. Remember, I worked with Andre Morell later and got to know him better. But the story of the film was two segregated camps. I worked with the women and kind of only in passing, when there was a escape thing, got to know the men. There was a German actor called Carl Mohner, whom I remember because I had to escape with him. I loved the part because all I did for *The Camp on Blood Island* was go in in the morning and pour a bottle of oil over my head, so I looked greasy, My hair was greasy, I looked like I was sweating. I loved it. But, the point with Carl, he was a very good-looking young man. If you've seen the film you know that. It was incredible circumstances, we were rolling around in the mud and the rain and the cold, that sort of thing, in a thin cotton wardrobe. This is naughty, but Carl had to say stop, and they would get the mud and put in the shadows [on his face] so he had bone structure and there's us, our noses covered in mud, but Carl, bless his heart, and he looked beautiful, not quite as if he'd been in a prisoner of war camp. The thing I remember is... a great cartoonist during the war, he was in Malaya and he made a record, but the work he did in the Malayan prison camp was really quite distressing. I was saying to him one day, because he was an advisor, he was a big man. I said, was it really as bad as that? He just opened the book and he pointed to this picture and it was a man weighing six stone and it was him, it was a self portrait. So, it gave me pause for thought, it was strange, because [the film] did make a lot of money. Some people said it shouldn't have been made, some people said it should have been made. It didn't seem to cause any problems between the Japanese and

British government because the Japanese embassy used to send Japanese visitors over to the set. We were asked to cut out some of the swear words while they were there, but they would watch. I think the controversy was caused by the press.

But, I can't really tell you much about the actors. We never really saw them. It sure was nice—I used to have to get to the studio at six to be ready for 8:30 a.m. with all the stuff they used to do. But I used to get to the studio 25 past eight to be ready at half past eight. Bottle of oil.

Val [Guest] was lovely. I only made that one film with him. He was a lovely director. He knew what he wanted. Maybe a little too rigid because he used to make storyboards for each scene. There was no leeway for something good to happen. No room for improvisation, if I move that way or you move that way. Which, I found a little bit restricting. but I was quite happy rolling about in the mud with the others. He too gave me a very good piece of advice. While I was working with him, I was very upset. There was a magazine called *Picturegoer*, and they had come to interview me. It was a double page spread, it was only a small magazine, but it was a double page spread in the middle. We were talking about things, so out came this thing "Did you have an affair with Walter Chiari?" this man suddenly says. I said, "That's none of your business." So, he says, "Did Ava Gardner ever have an affair with Walter Chiari?" I said, "That's their business." Now, that's what was said. The headline of this double page was "Don't Be Jealous of Me Says Barbara Shelley" in quotes! I was very new to all this, so I went into the studio, it doesn't matter if I cried, I had no mascara on. Val said, "What's the matter with you?" I showed him this and he said to me, "Fine, you can sue them, they put you in quotes and you didn't say it. But, remember, this magazine goes to press six weeks ahead. This thing that's hurt you so much is going to be loo paper down in the privy at the end of the garden for most people by next week or by tomorrow. You dig it up and in six weeks time it'll come up again. What do you want to do?" I said, "Let them use it as loo paper, that's all it's worth." That taught me a lot about not getting upset. The only time I get upset and it varies all around, but if something true about my personal life is printed. I don't care if it's lies, because all my friends and family know. But, if it's true, I fell that my front door is open and I don't like that. I don't get upset anymore, but I always remember Val saying, "They'll forget it tomorrow, might hurt you for a few more days." So, I thank Val for that.

George Sanders, Barbara Shelley and Michael Gwynn in *The Village of the Damned*

You made Village of the Damned *[1960], we'd like to know about that and did you ever see the remake?*

We'll start with the remake. I can't say anything about it because I didn't see it. Not because for any reason, but I was at University at the time and not going to many movies, not doing very much except deadlines. Friends of mine in Canada went to see it and said it was silly to do the remake because the original was much better.

I think the first one was a classic and still goes round to festivals. It was a very happy coming together, certain things that make a good film. One of the main things I think about, and I've always said that about Hammer, that's why Hammer has it over a lot of other horror makers. But, it happens in *Village of the Damned* that what is real is more frightening, more deeply disturbing. I mean, you can be frightened silly getting out of the chair, I mean the monster Alien, brilliant, but, a child who is evil is more than frightening, it's deeply disturbing, the same as *The Bad Seed*, about the homicidal child. And, I think that it is also [better] they made it in England, because here in America they couldn't get an eye effect that they wanted. So, MGM made this glowing eye, but, I think

"VILLAGE OF THE DAMNED"

quite rightly, they decided when the film was made they wouldn't use the eye at all. Just all those dark-eyed children starring, all with blonde Hamlet wigs.

I loved that movie. Of course, if I was doing the part again, I'd do it very much different, but, I think all actresses think that.

One of the joys of it, not only Martin [Stevens] who was my child [in the film], who was a delightful young man. [He had] a mother who said, "You know, the only reason I let him act is he's going all over the world and getting a good education." And, years later when I was on a tour of England, his grandfather and grandmother came to the stage door and I had tea with them. He had actually redesigned their bungalow, he'd become an architect. He had made money in films and had done what his mother always hoped he would. But he was a delightful child.

Then we come to George Sanders. George, unfortunately, has left us now. There are two actors—if somebody said to me now here's a script and I said I have to read it and they said either George Sanders or Christopher Lee [is doing it], I don't even want to read it, I'll do it. I'll pay you to do it! Because, not only were they wonderful to work with, such communications and such lack of ego—probably the wrong word—but just to make a scene work, not to dominate the scene and if that happens

between two actors, then the right dominance will happen, because, it's what the writer wanted. Two actors really doing what is there—giving it the right balance. George was not only that, and like Christopher, the most wonderful gentleman. Sorry to sound like a Victorian prig, but it is nice to work with both of them–Christopher still does it—won't sit down till all the ladies are seated. That's old-fashioned but it's lovely. He opens the door and George was the same.

Lovely story about George, great sense of humor. Martin was sitting on the set one day. Martin was about nine or 10. He said to me, "Barbara, do you play chess? I said to him, "No Martin, I'm sorry." George came out of his dressing room on the set and said, "I do, come and have a game." And I went behind Martin [wriggles her finger], never play chess with a child, especially a clever child. Off they went into the dressing room and the silence, it was a long wait because we were waiting for something. George came out, "Dear God, he beat me!" I said, "Of course he did." He always played chess with Martin. He didn't mind, he said, "I'm learning." But, George was a lovely man and he always called me "dear heart."

Another lovely story about him, he was a great giggler and we'd always start giggling just before they put the boards–the clap—and we'd start giggling afterwards. The makeup man was called Eric Aylott. I don't know if you have them here but the first people to make good false eyelashes, that was Eric and his brother David. A very laid-back Englishman, a small mustache. He came up to me and said:

"Barbara,"
"Yes, Eric?"

"Don't make George laugh..."
"Well, I can't help it."
"No, dear, don't, 'cause I have to keep going in and mopping him up."

So, anyway, we start and I say something and George starts to laugh. This is [during] the first days of the movie, so we didn't know how George Sanders [would be]. I knew he was a giggler, but the rest of the staff didn't know what he was like. So, Eric came in with this look on his face and he gets his pad out and George bursts out laughing. "I know, dear boy, I'm a runny-eyed old bastard, aren't I?"

I was very sad when we lost George, a great gentleman. The other thing, if you remember when the baby makes me put my hand in the water and I get hysterical and George has to slap me to bring me around. It took him 10 minutes to even think of trying to slap me. He said, "I can't do it. I can not do this to her." I said:

"George, I'll move."
"Well, suppose you don't?"
"Well, that's my fault."

But, he did catch me with the top of his fingers, I think, that's why the scene goes so well. But, there again, he didn't want to hurt me. I loved George.

Shadow of the Cat *[1961] and Andre Morell.*

Andre was a man who was known to be very crusty. Expected people to be professional. I knew this about him, but he was wonderful. The first day I met him in the makeup room he said something.

Shadow of the Cat

Andre Morell poses for a publicity shot for *Shadow of the Cat*.

It was a very crude joke, but it was funny and I laughed. I couldn't help it and we became great mates because he was a great gentleman. He thought he might have offended me, but, if something is funny enough, I'll laugh, this was funny. Andre and I got along terribly well and he was a very, very nice man. It was a very difficult film to work on for many reasons. There are some funny stories, but there are some less funny. The man who wrote it, George Baxt, we've remained friends since. One of my dearest friends, he writes a lot of detective novels. He had written a completely different film, which was—the cat never appeared. It was a very subtle, psychological thing—*Cat People* and *Cat Girl*, all that are based on. The cat being the evil within us, the untamed that can hit you. The cat never appeared in George's script, it was implied that it was the evil in the family that caused all the trouble. But, the director [John Gilling] decided he would shoot it all through the cat's eyes. I think the movie is good, but if you see it and think, if you never actually saw the cat and weren't quite sure if there was a cat there at all, or if it was just people seeing things because they have a guilty conscience. This is what George wanted. Anyway, *Shadow of the Cat* brought me the great bonus of having George Baxt as a best friend. I know a lot of you, when I'm signing, have said it's one of your favorite movies. I'll tell George that.

Tell us about working with Peter Cushing and Christopher Lee.

Are we talking about *The Gorgon* [1964]? One of my favorites, by the way. The lighting man—[cinematographer] Michael Reed, who went on to do modern stuff successfully, like James Bond—if you look at *The Gorgon,* if you stop frame, it looks like a painting, wonderful photography. Lovely cast, Richard Pasco is a very good classical actor in England, and, of course, the time with Peter and Chris.

Peter, I used to call the propmaster. I used to put on his dressing room door when the film began, "Propmaster." He could make a fob watch jump out of that pocket into his hand, look at the time, and it would jump back. The watch knew where it had to go. Chris used to say to him, "My turn, this time. I want to use the fob watch in this scene." So, he'd try, he'd be [searching for the watch]. Peter wouldn't break up, I would. "Oh, give it up, Chris."

I remember there's a scene in *The Gorgon* where Carla is telling about the three Gorgons and the big head of Peter is in the foreground to me. I said to him, "Peter, no fiddling with the props," because he would do something so brilliant, he's the only one I know who could use a quill pen properly. You know, he was a great artist, a wonderful artist and he could just pick up a quill pen [and draw]. So, he said, "All right," and, of course, he steals the scene because he doesn't move. All you're looking at is Peter Cushing. I should have had him use the props! [Laughs].

Then we discover we go back to Gilbert and Sullivan, we both loved the patter songs. I don't know if he used them, but I still use them if my diction's getting sloppy., I go through Gilbert and Sullivan songs. So, we used to go behind the flats and see who could do them faster. We'd start off with the Gilbert and Sullivan, the Giuseppe

one—"Rising in the Morning"—to see who could get to the end of it first.

Chris, of course, has a wonderful singing voice. He used to sing with the Swedish Opera. So, very early in the morning, before anybody was there, he'd sing baritone and I'd sing bass-baritone, and Roy Ashton, his lovely tenor. We'd do a few trios from things.

Partick Troughton in *The Gorgon* plays a police officer and he clicked his heels Prussian [style]. The first morning I came on the set, I didn't know Patrick, and he said, "Guten Morgen, Gorgon." [Laughs] I fell in love with him straightaway. He used to come down in the early morning with the mists rising over Bray and you'd hear the sound of the pipe coming from his room. He used to play these wonderful pipes and the recorder. In the morning, Bray, if you weren't ready for it, could be pretty spooky with him playing the pipes.

I think *The Gorgon* is one of my favorites, it was the first one—of course, I met Chris and Peter through doing that. Peter used to go up to his dressing room, he never ate with us. The commissary at Bray was well-known for putting at least three inches on your waistline, because the cooking was wonderful, it was like cooking your mother did, it was a small restaurant—treacle pudding and bread pudding and all these things. But Peter used to go up to his room and I never knew why. I followed him upstairs one day and he had a bottle of milk for himself and a loaf of bread for the birds and he used to sit at his window and feed the birds and drink his milk. He was a lovely man and a great artist, water colorist and graphic artist.

Of course, Chris is Chris. You all know Chris. As I say, I'd rather work with Chris Lee than anybody else. The great thing about it was always trying to break each other up and he can't break me up and I can't break him up. The most he'll give me is, "You terrible girl." We never break each other up. I wish I was an actress again, talking about him.

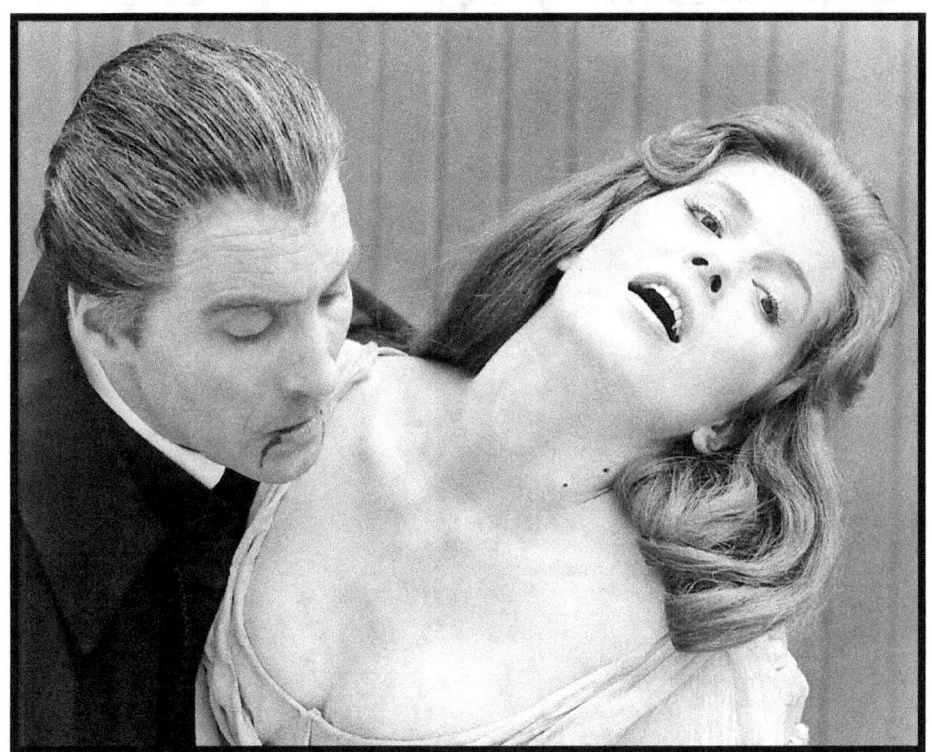

Christopher Lee and Barbara Shelley in *Dracula—Prince of Darkness*

Dracula—Prince of Darkness *[1966]*

I think I'll tell you some funny stories about *Dracula—Prince of Darkness*. Chris, of course, always hissed a lot. I think that he never had dialogue as Dracula and who needs dialogue with a face and presence like his! My character—I think that some great film buff in the audience is going to tell me I'm wrong—was the first live vampire ever staked. You know, okay, so they open the coffin and the vampire wakes up, the eyes open and the stakes go in. But, I was dragged screaming by four or two monks, and I think, I was the first live vampire and also the first vampire, certainly the first Hammer vampire, who ever spoke some dialogue. That scene I'll never forget—I'm going to spoil that scene—what happened in *Dracula—Prince of Darkness* was that they made the fangs, a wonderful Australian dentist, you know like having crowns or caps on your teeth. They were stuck in with fixative. And it's the scene where I come drifting down the stairs and I'm making a play for Suzan Farmer, having turned into a lesbian; of course, all vampires do. [Laughs] This rather beautiful

Barbara Shelley, with the notorious fangs, and Suzan Farmer in *Dracula—Prince of Darkness*

scene shot by Michael Reed, you notice coming through all the light... it really was the most wonderful shot. So, Terence said, "We don't need a rehearsal, do we Barbara?" I said, "Oh, no." He said let's rehearse on film. I drift down through the sunlight, my hands raised gracefully, the line was, "You don't need Charles." And I said, "Yew dan't neth charth, schlitz." You've got these teeth hanging down, you've got to practice. So, Terence said, "I don't think that will do, dear." So, I hid behind the plants [trying to speak]. It took me about half an hour to get it. They did something else. Don't let that spoil that scene, you promise.

One lovely thing about Terence was he enjoyed a joke as much as everybody did. With John Gilling, on *Shadow of the Cat*, it was an entirely different matter. *Shadow of the Cat*, you remember toward the end when the old house is falling down, and Conrad Phillips and I run up the

Barbara Shelley at FANEX 15

corridor. Well, I was wearing a black dress and black lace and hair up in the Edwardian style and Conrad had very dark hair, very long dark eyelashes and a black velvet collar. Dear Charlie, the prop man has got to run along the gantry and sprinkle little chips of plaster. He said, "I need a closing prop thing." "Oh, no, I can't wait for that, too expensive." So, we start and we do a rehearsal without the dribbles because we can't [get the costumes dirty]. So, Gilling says, "Okay, go for a take." Run a bit, trickle down, run a bit, trickle down a bit more, and suddenly the whole lot comes down, because poor Charlie couldn't get the thing closed in time. So, we got a shower full. Conrad and I are like good artists, trying to keep going, not realizing it was impossible because he had white eyelashes, hair, the lot, and so did I. And, through the cloud we're trying to keep on with this dialogue and suddenly we just stopped. As soon as we stopped and laughed the whole studio just broke up. Now, if that'd been Terence Fisher, you'd have to pick him off the floor. But, John Gilling was serious. The producer came running down from his office. "Whose fault was it?" He was going to fire Charlie. I said, "Then fire me too or get him a decent thing." "How long's it going to take to clean?" I said, "No, get the air hose and start." It took about 10 minutes to clean us up. But that was a good joke.

Terry had a great sense of humor. When you asked him something and, if it was funny, he'd go "heh, heh, heh." He was a delightful, wonderful man.

VERONICA CARLSON
SUZANNA LEIGH
INGRID PITT
YUTTE STENSGAARD

Veronica Carlson, Suzanna Leigh, Ingrid Pitt and Yutte Stensgaard appeared at Monster Rally in 1999. It was quite a moving experience to see the admiration the audience held for these ladies. This interview was hosted by Tom Johnson and Mark A. Miller.

One of the criticisms against Hammer films has often been that people went to see them not because of the stories, but because of the beautiful actresses who appeared in them. And this would seem to validate that criticism. How did you get into films?

Ingrid Pitt: It's very involved how I got into films. I was at a bullfight and I was photographed and that was it... Jimmy Carreras was very

Ingrid Pitt makes an entrance at Monster Rally

Veronica Carlson and Richard Svehla at Monster Rally

receptive and gave me all these Hammer films which I'm going to be eternally grateful for because he was the most wonderful friend I had and he did what he could for me. And I'm very grateful to you [the audience] because you keep these films alive. Without you, it wouldn't have been any point to making the films because nobody would see them and you keep seeing them again and again. I'm really grateful, thank you.

Veronica Carlson: I hate following Ingrid, she says it all beautifully. I got into films, well, it was Jimmy Carreras as well. I had a photograph on the front page of a tabloid on Sunday morning, and I was approached because of the photograph by Ben Gervis. I was rising up out of the water like Aphrodite and I had an audition for *Dracula Has Risen from the Grave* [1969] and that was it. As with Ingrid, he looked after me the same way, plenty of lunches, plenty of dinners, plenty of caring, he was a very, very dear, lovable man. He really was, and he was very anxious that you were going to be looked after and taken the best care of. So, like Ingrid, my introduction to the film world was one far removed from maybe today's introduction and I'm very grateful to Jimmy and I love him dearly. I always remember when he first met my to-be husband. We were at some Variety Club in Great Britain, a function in Bristol. I have a horrible feeling I'm just rambling on. And I came into the room and I looked radiant and he said, "You look wonderful." Then Jimmy said, "He's obviously arrived, please tell him to come and have a glass of champagne with us." And then he looked at me again and did a double take and said, "Veronica, tell him he can bathe in it." And, like Ingrid, I would like to thank all of you, because what you've done, I'm meeting your children and I'm meeting your grandchildren and they love these movies and they're starstruck by them, and that is our best reward that could be. Thank you all very much.

Suzanna Leigh: Oh dear, mine are quite different. I mean I started working as an actress when I was about 11 or 12. I didn't imagine ever doing anything else. When I was five or six I was just obsessed with movies and I was very lucky that my family knew lots of people in the business—so I went and knocked on Vivian Leigh's door and asked if I could change my name to hers, and she said, "Oh I've got so many Godchildren that I can't even remember, I've got over a hundred, none have come and knocked on my door. What about you, acting lessons?" I said, "Yes please." So that was very good news. It was fantastic. I was just incredibly lucky, I'd go out for a part and got it and then of course I used to lie like mad about my age and say I was 18 or 19 when I was like 15 or 16. I was just incredibly lucky. As for Hammer, that was amazing because I actually loved some of the scripts. I took them very, very seriously. I was a bit of a fan, anyway. So when *The Lost Continent* [1968] came along, it was a Dennis Wheatley [the film was based on the Wheatley novel *Uncharted Seas*], and I was a particular fan of his. Anyway Tony Beckley was my best friend

Suzanna Leigh signs at Monster Rally

and he said, "Have you read this?" I said, "Yeah." And then there was another friend of mine who was considering being in it, and anyway, we all got together and had lunch and said let's make it for real, we can really make this for real, Benito Carruthers. So that's what we did and we just loved making *The Lost Continent*. Of course, I got slightly carried away and said, well, I must design the clothes as well. Oh yes, yes, of course because Edith Head had taught me, supposedly, how to design when I

Suzanna Leigh in *The Lost Continent*

was in Hollywood. So there I was, and it's so mad because now I see everyone coming up and asking me for these crazy shots of me wearing these ridiculous outfits in the middle of nowhere in *The Lost Continent* with me in these skimpy little things designed by me.

We had a great time and then of course Yutte and I did *Lust for a Vampire* [1971], another classic masterpiece. But that story really is in the book [Leigh's memoirs] because it was a bit naughty because I really needed money. There was a big drama in my life and I phoned up Jimmy, because we were on the same committee at the Variety Club, and I said, "I really need a film starting on Monday." So he said, "Well right. We've got this one, there's no part for you." So I said, "I'm sure you could find something, because I really need it now." He said, "Well there's this gym mistress but I can't see you as the gym mistress." I said, "Fine, fine. Is she a little bats?" He said, "No, she's all right, she's the gym mistress, she's a goody." "Please, I must be cast, oh dear, I can't go into that now." "Okay darling, we start on Monday then, will you?" So I said, "Yes, thank you Jimmy." I never did discover who was going to play that part. That's my story on how I started.

Yutte Stensgaard: Well, when I was a little girl I was always interested in movies and musicals and I had pictures all over my bedroom wall of everybody who was famous at the time and I always used to think, "Wow, wouldn't it be great to be in that world?" And everybody always used to tell me, "Oh forget about that, you're just dreaming." So I kind of went, "Oh well, that's true" because I was living out in the middle of nowhere in Denmark so I just kind of forgot about it in the back of my mind. And, later on when I was about 17 or 18, I went to England as an au pair which is someone who works for the family in the house and helps out, doesn't get paid, but learns how to speak English. I did that for about a year and then I moved to London and I wasn't really sure what I was going to do in London and I was thinking, "People were saying you should become a model," and I thought, "That would be kind of neat to try that," so I decided I would give it a go and some said, "Don't do modeling, that's not a business to be in. You probably should go into acting." So I said, "Hey, that sounds like a great idea." "So I know this acting school you should go to, take some classes," and that's how I started taking acting classes. Then I fell in love with my art teacher's son which turned out to be very handy because he was also a casting director. And so I started doing some commercials and from there I went into doing some films, then television, then stage, when it's usually the other way around, commercials, stage, TV and film. I found all kinds of work and I had always been really fond of the Hammer movies and was always so excited when a new one came out and would always go and see it. I thought the girls were so gorgeous in them. I remember seeing Veronica, I thought you looked so

Yutte Stensgaard at Monster Rally

gorgeous. I guess that was two or three years before I went out for the interview and I'm not really quite sure how the interview happened, but whether Hammer called... but I had a lot of publicity, so anyway that doesn't really matter, but I remember walking into the Hammer office and was very nervous and seeing Raquel Welch all over the walls in there and Veronica who looked absolutely gorgeous, and I couldn't believe I was actually in there and just had a short meeting and apparently they had already decided, that was it, and I was going to do the part. So that's how that came about.

All of you at one time or another worked with some of Hammers top male stars including Christopher Lee, of course, and Peter Cushing, Michael Ripper and Ralph Bates. I was wondering if you could all reflect a moment on one of those gentleman that you worked with and just tell us what they were like to work with as professionals, what they were like between takes off the screen.

Yutte Stensgaard; Ralph Bates, of course, played the man whom I bit to death [in *Lust for a Vampire*]. That was a lot of fun doing that scene. He was very professional. He was really a nice guy to work with. He

Ralph Bates and Yutte Stensgaard in *Lust for a Vampire*

was easy to work with because he made it easy to respond to, which helps you do a better job. I didn't really get to know him much as a person because we were all so busy... because we didn't always have scenes together. Unfortunately, I didn't get to know him that well, but what I remember he was very nice. I'm sure that Suzanna can say some more things.

Suzanna Leigh: I actually did get to know him very well. In fact, he married a girl I was at school with, Virginia Wetherall. He and I just sort of really got on. He had a great sense of humor... he was a very funny guy. And of course the outfit he was wearing and the serious business with the glasses, it was so totally different. It was like he really climbed into that character. And then he could climb back out afterward. Obviously, it was awful when he died, leaving those children and getting that awful thing, cancer. It has no friends or enemies, it just takes who it wants, it was really, really sad. But Virginia has been fantastic and it's nice that he is being remembered so well. I'm sure he's here now.

Veronica Carlson: Wasn't it true that they dimmed the theatre lights in London for a while in respect of Ralph because he was adored by the community?

Suzanna Leigh: Yes. Nobody ever could ever say anything but lovely things about Ralph. He would go out of his way to help anybody. He was such an ace, ace person.

Veronica Carlson: We really all felt too, that he was just about to take off, this is the cruelty. Because Hammer wanted him as the future Frankenstein, didn't they?

Suzanna Leigh: Absolutely, he was groomed, he'd made the decision. He was an extremely good actor.

Veronica Carlson: And Peter approved.

Ralph Bates and Graham James in *The Horror of Frankenstein*

Suzanna Leigh: And everybody was really gunning for and he'd made that decision and real commitment; they were going to take this man along and it was going to be his thing and suddenly, to have this happen. It was absolutely terrifying, it was very, very serious because he took that mantle on.

Veronica Carlson: He thought about it very hard. He doubted his own ability to ever follow in Peter's footsteps or stand in his shadow. As Suzanna and Yutte attested to, he was a very funny person and he and Jimmy Sangster together, they were the best friends. It was worse because Jimmy was mischievous as well, so the two of them together were total rapscallions, we would go to lunch together, and Jimmy would have to calm us down at the end and say, now look, we have to go on back to the set. Very serious, we'd get over all the giggles, and get over them before we get back. And of course we did. We worked very hard on that film [*The Horror of Frankenstein*, 1970] but he, as Yutte said, he made it very easy for you to work with him and it made it easy to respond; just what she said, and he was faithful to himself and therefore he was respected by everybody. I regretted I only met Virginia because of his death, which was a terrible thing, and we had a wonderful thing at Bray to help the pancreatic cancer research fund and it went very well. In fact, they were able to get for £8,000, which is what, $13,000 or $14,500, which is what they raised at Bray. So it was a terrific thing.

Ingrid Pitt: One of the best paintings you have ever done was of Ralph Bates which we actually auctioned... at Bray on the 29th of May, and Veronica did the most wonderful painting. It was just great. But I didn't know Ralph at all well. I ran into him at a film festival just once, we were on the jury. But I think the man I most revere is Peter Cushing. I worked with him on various pictures and I loved him. I have traveled the world to find anybody who'd say something nasty about him and nobody ever did. He was just a complete angel. I met him, it was quite extraordinary, I had my wig fitted and it was the first day on *The Vampire Lovers* [1970] and the hairdresser said, "Good God, you should see what Peter's doing to you now." And I ran to the stage and I saw him raise his hand and he had this great big sword and in the other hand he had this cabbage. It looked like a cabbage and he went woosh and it was my head. And he came rushing up and said, "My God darling, what a terrible way to meet!" I said, "Yes, I'm a bit cut up too."

Veronica, out of respect to you and Jimmy Sangster, we're going to skip Horror of Frankenstein. *Perhaps you could tell us something about your experience with Christopher Lee in* Dracula Has Risen from the Grave *[1969]?*

Peter Cushing "went woosh and it was my head!" Cushing and Ingrid's head in *The Vampire Lovers*

Veronica Carlson: I was a little bit intimidated by Christopher. He has such a presence about him, he looks so aristocratic and regal and I was so immature and inexperienced, I didn't know what I was doing. But he was the first to put me at ease, actually.

Ingrid Pitt in *Countess Dracula*

We had the reading around the table at Pinewood Studios with Rupert Davis and Michael, it was a wonderful time. By the time I came out of that reading, I felt I knew the man a lot more and my feelings of trepidation had completely gone and from then on in I enjoyed his company. He was very helpful to me because he knew I was inexperienced and he gave me eye lines because he knew that a hand like this held by the camera didn't do much. So he said, "Freddie, Freddie, I'll give her an eye line." And he would react to me so that it would make it easy for me to be afraid. I loved him for that. I liked him. To show you how much he relaxed me, I had the nerve to say, "Would you sit with me for a portrait?" And this poor man sat for half an hour staring into space while I did a sketch of him. I wouldn't have the nerve to do that now. I was very fortunate and I look back on it with a lot of affection.

One of my favorite films is Countess Dracula *[1970], where you were working with one of my favorite actors, Nigel Green. Can you tell us about that?*

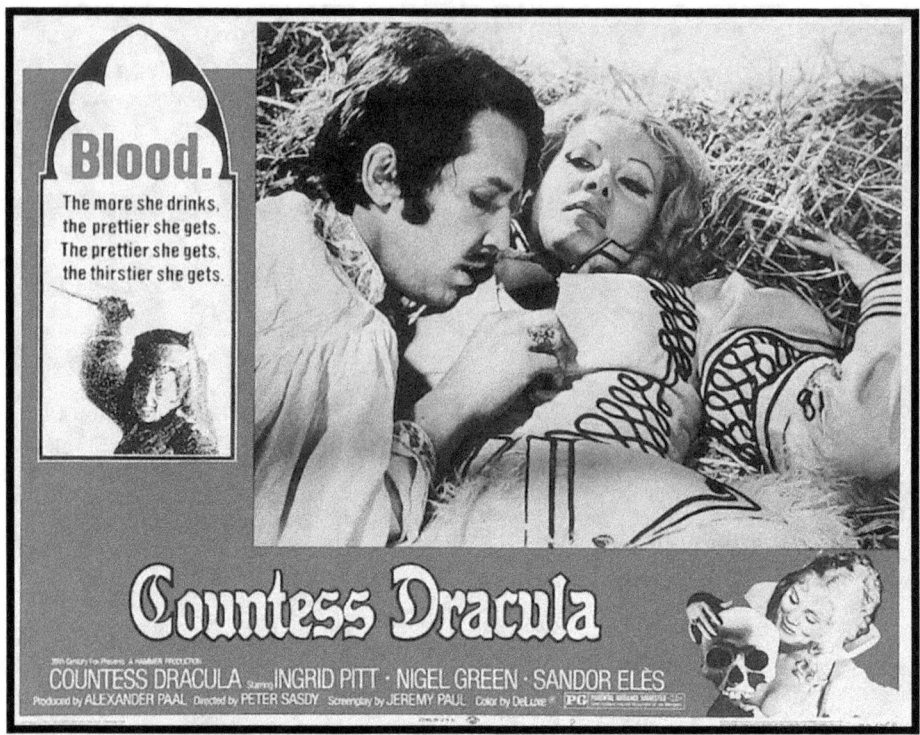

Ingrid Pitt: It's a very loaded question. I can possibly just glance over it. I think one of the funniest things that happened was that I called a limousine for Nigel Green to see Sam Spiegel to play Rasputin in *Nicholas and Alexandra,* and he refused to go, he preferred to kill himself. I'll never forgive him, because he would have been the most fantastic Rasputin. But I think the most funny thing that happened on *Countess Dracula* was that Sandor Eles was to nuzzle in my Tom and Jerry a bit and he raised his head and half his mustache was missing. So they said, "Cut, cut, cut." And Peter Sasdy, the director said, "Half of his mustache is missing." So I said, "Half of his mustache is missing, it's got to be in this haystack" and poor Tom Smith, the makeup man, did not have any more mustaches because Sandor couldn't grow the thing properly I suppose, so we called a halt while I went into my big Winnebago and I took everything off, which you know I love doing, I don't know how it got there, but that mustache was in my bellybutton.

I think the film was wonderful. I think it's on laser disc now. Today a lot of people came with the sleeve for the laser disc, and I wanted to keep them because the picture's my favorite on the cover and I think I could talk about it for a long time and about Nigel, but I can't really because, I can't forgive him, to top himself. It was so terribly wrong and I want to cry when I think about it. He shouldn't have done that [take his own life].

Can you talk about Elvis Presley?

Suzanna Leigh: Well, my memories as a fan go way back because my brother was 10 years old and we were brought up on Elvis records. He was the epitome of a major star to me when I was little, so my dream of going to Hollywood always sort [of revolved around starring] with Elvis Presley. You know how you have our dream and then you've got the next bit that goes with it. So when I got my Hollywood contract with Hal Wallis, of course Hal Wallis had Elvis under contract. I thought, "Could this actually happen?" And then I got a phone call, when I was in Paris making a film with Tony Curtis, *Boeing, Boeing* [1965], to say I was up for the next Elvis picture [*Paradise, Hawaiian Style*, 1966]. And there hadn't been a European make a film with Elvis, so I thought this is just a bit too much. So I completely ignored it although I finished *Boeing, Boeing* and I wanted to get back but I had an English boyfriend and we were going to go down to south France, so I just took off and went down to south France and suddenly there was a guy, a Paramount man, running down the beach with his hair all dressed up in his suit and everything saying, "You're supposed to be in Hawaii tomorrow." "All right."

So Elvis got to Hawaii before me. So the first impression I had of Elvis was incredible because I was sitting on the set and suddenly this sort of cup of tea was presented to me and this voice said, "I believe you drink a lot of these things over there where you come from." I didn't look up you know, I just said, "That's India tea, no I actually only drink China tea." And I look up, "Actually, I quite like Indian tea right now." So, of course, suddenly I'm drinking India tea all the time. He photographed so badly you see, that was the thing, there was this unbelievably tall, good-looking guy with these incredible eyes. Oh my God, you know. I had this little list given to me. You know when you're 19 and going to Hollywood, and your best friends were all sitting around saying, "This is who you're going to go out with," Steve McQueen, it's this, it's that, a little sort of shopping list. So it sort of all happened like that really.

So Elvis, we became really good friends, and he couldn't understand a lot of what I was saying at the beginning. We had a problem with my English and he had to keep saying, "Say that slowly. What was that?" It's a whole load of language, of course, here in America you speak... We turned an 18-day movie into three and a half months and Hal Wallis ended up flying over to Hawaii saying, "What's going on? Why are we still here? Why aren't we in Hollywood finishing this up?" So, Elvis said, "The good news, Hal, is, you know this little English girl here, well, we're going to make another film." Hal said, "I don't believe it, Suzanna you get a raise immediately." He said, "I'm making another Elvis picture, I've been dreaming about that." So we had a whole load of scripts, I had a script written for me. Yes, great, amazing guy.

Can you tell us about the fire during the death scene in Lust for a Vampire*?*

Yutte Stensgaard: The death scene, well they had, I can't remember the material they used but they are very good at controlling it. It's some kind of a gel that they put in the different areas where they want it to burn, so that they can control it very well.

Veronica Carlson: The fire department comes by as well.

Yutte Stensgaard: We didn't have the fire department, we had extinguishers there.

Veronica Carlson: You didn't have professional fireman. Oh.

Michael Johnson and Yutte Stensgaard in *Lust for a Vampire*

Yutte Stensgaard: I guess they didn't care so much. Then they had above me—I get this wooden stake right here in my chest and they had it rigged up in the ceiling and obviously it's done by cutting the film the right way so it looks as if it goes right into my chest. Of course, when it did go right into my chest, that was a dummy not me, luckily. So, most of it obviously was not really involved with me, they did that without me being on the scene. The only time I was there was when I had my scenes with Michael Johnson. So they faked it all, it's all fake obviously, but they're very good at controlling it. Something that I wanted to say before, I'm absolutely overwhelmed by the response I've had from you all this weekend. It's really been a thrill and very exciting for me to be here and I want to thank you all.

Can you tell us about Where Eagles Dare *(1968)?*

Ingrid Pitt: Perhaps I should start with the last day when we came driving towards London from where we were making the film. I was sitting between the two [Richard Burton and Clint Eastwood] and Clint leaned

Richard Burton posing as a Nazi officer makes contact with agent Ingrid Pitt posing as a barmaid. MGM presents A Jerry Gershwin-Elliot Kastner Picture "WHERE EAGLES DARE" PANAVISION and METROCOLOR

forward and he said to Richard, "Shall we tell her now?" And I said, "Tell her what?" Richard said, "Yeah, maybe we better." Richard said, "You go ahead Clint, you tell the kid." "Okay," he said. He turned to me and said, "We had a bet on you, you know." I said, "A bet, what was the bet?" He said, "Who would get you into the sack first, him or me."

I think it's always fantastic to work with the best. Those two men were the best. They were totally men's men and I became a man too, because they don't talk to women, they just lie them down. I had the standing up technique in my head and I didn't want to be laid down in the bloody snow, so we talked a lot and they taught me a lot, Richard especially about Shakespeare, I think. I'll never ever forgive him ever, either like Nigel Green, because there was one hell of an actor who drank himself to death. And he was going to work with me on the next day on *Wild Geese* [1978] too, which was a Euan Lloyd film we made in Berlin, and he never turned up because he died on the way to the hospital drinking himself stupid with John Hurt, and he had a hemorrhage in the brain and that was the end of him. The last time I saw him was in York when he played Equus and we had a long, long talk in his dressing room when he told me he wanted to be a writer. I told him what did you want to be a bloody writer for, it's a nightmare. You've got it all in your voice, you've got the talent, nobody has that I know. And he just didn't reckon it at all. He did reckon his voice, he didn't reckon his talent and I think it's so terribly diabolic that someone can have so much talent and not be aware of it at all and kill himself. I'm sorry I'm talking a lot about death today. At lunch someone asked me a lot of things about my childhood and we got to talking about England and spitfires and how England won the war and I'm here to tell you, If America hadn't come into the war, I don't suppose England could have won alone. Just want to say thank you.

Can you tell us about Michael Ripper?

Veronica Carlson: Oh Michael, he was irrepressible and he brought humorous scenes to the set. I would just sit and watch his every scene that wasn't involving me, just to see this man. Because I'd seen him in so many movies before and he always brought this wonderful effervescence to any character he played, and was humorous in and to the darker side of the movie, this was a wonderful sparkling moment, and made the dark darker for it. His characterization of the baker was so superb. I can still see him and Barry Andrews playing around [in *Dracula Has Risen from the Grave*] in the bakery, Barry clicking him around the ears with this tea towel. They were wonderful together and the sad thing now is the memories, he can't remember, and we can't share them with him anymore. I know that is Chris' sadness as well. I wish I had worked on more than one film with Michael. Let's put it that way.

Suzanna Leigh: Actually I worked on two pictures with Michael. One of the reasons I'm here actually, and thank you very much for letting me come here, it was my daughter's 18th birthday and that's why I was debating whether I could come. And I spoke to Michael two weeks ago and so he said, "Oh please come over, you know it's my first time I've been to America, going to America," because he has marvelous sort of spurts of being really together, anyway, "I've really got to keep my eye on you." So I said, "Right okay Michael, I'd better do that." So it's really Michael being Michael and he was so funny. In *The Deadly Bees* [1967] with his, "Something's happening up there." It's just unbelievable. Of course, in *The Lost Continent* [1968] with that scar. There was a time I think he must have been in every movie made in England. There must be like a million movies, Michael was there somewhere. Brilliant man.

JAMES BERNARD
MARTINE BESWICKE
VERONICA CARLSON
VAL GUEST
INGRID PITT

James Bernard, Martine Beswicke, Veronica Carlson, Val Guest and Ingrid Pitt, guests of honor at FANEX 8, participated in an audience question and answer session together. Since Gary was in a wheelchair and Jim Clatterbaugh, who was chairperson of the convention that year, was taken to the hospital with chest pains, well, I didn't get to see this panel either, but as I transcribed it, I knew I missed something special. John Stell hosted the panel.

Veronica, how it was to work with John Hurt in The Ghoul?

Veronica Carlson: That was very exciting for me. I had seen his work and I respected him greatly as an actor. I found that every time I worked with someone of that sort of caliber, I learned something. Although I

James Bernard, Martine Beswicke and Val Guest at FANEX 8

Ingrid Pitt, James Bernard and Martine Beswicke

rehearsed my lines in isolation, as soon as I was with that man, my reaction was tugged right out of me. I wish I could have worked with him more. He was a great guy.

Martine, are you currently at work?

Martine Beswicke: No, because I took a break and I'm assisting a director. I'm not an AD, I'm a personal assistant, keeping him together. Being a major organizer and really going behind the camera, that was really nice, just to kind of get behind the camera and see how things worked. It was for Carl Franklin who was doing *Devil in a Blue Dress* (1995) with Denzel Washington. It was a lovely experience. He's just a wonderful director. So, I've been working with him. I'm about to sort of get back into the ring when I get back. I have no idea what's going to happen when I get back, I'm about to go on another adventure.

Mr. Bernard, from the time you're about to compose a particular score, about how long did it take you to get the themes in mind, and about how long did it take you to deliver that score?
James Bernard: From the time you are asked to write the music, it might be seven or eight weeks and they send you a script. From that you start

to think of maybe a basic theme, you see what sort of music you're going to need. These are preliminary thoughts. Then of course you can't get down to the actual writing of the score until the film is in its final cut. So by the time you got that, you've had your music breakdown and decided exactly where you're going to help the image reel. One would be lucky to maybe have four weeks. It's always a round the clock job. So four weeks, it would be a luxury to have five.

Would you "spot" the film for the music with the director?

James Bernard: Yes, you'd have what you call a music breakdown session where you would go through the film reel by reel and you'd have the editor of the film [present]. The director and his interest was not always there, they just sort of trusted one another. It was the editor, sound editor and sound effects [who were most important here] because here they would remember there is going to be a tremendous clap of thunder or a lot of rain or bird song. So, that team was there and [so was] the music director. They sort of argued about where to have the music and it was the job of the assistant director to note all that down. So four to five weeks would be the typical thing. It's a terrible panic in my place.

So how long before you put it down?

James Bernard: They [Hammer] always had wonderful players of course. They always got top players for the orchestra. They'd [the musicians] probably go through a particular section maybe once only. So they'd go at it. The film is played behind the orchestra on the screen and the time is ticking by. Provided they keep to the tempo of the music that I've marked, all the sync points will click into place if I've done my maps correctly.

Would you lay the score down at one go?

James Bernard: What I liked to do, if I had time, I'd sketch everything first. I'd know exactly what I'd want to do with the orchestra, so I liked to get it all written down in short scores first. But then the copyist and the conductor would begin to bug you, "When will I get the section of music?" So, you'd have to abandon your basic composing to orchestrate some sections to keep them happy. That was how I did it.

Ingrid Pitt: Do you find that throws you when you go to do bits and pieces at different times?

James Bernard: Yes, I much prefer that because then you can build it up symphonically and make sure you have a standard there. But sometimes you have to go ahead, you're quite right. It's much better if you can do it in sequence.

Ingrid, I love your smile.

Ingrid Pitt: That's because I'm wicked.

Is there a Hammer blooper reel.

Martine Beswicke: I wish. I wish there would have been something.

Ingrid Pitt: This is very interesting. When I go home I will find out, I will dig about and find out. They should have something, somewhere in the vault.

Do you feel like in some of the movies the women were sort of exploited? Was it necessary for you to say that costume isn't necessary for that scene? Did you say enough is enough.

Martine Beswicke: Yep. I'm feeling that all three of us had the same thing. What is interesting about this is that all of us were in a period in Hammer where they actually wanted lots of—it was actually part of that period of time—but I notice that all of us are very strong women, very independent, very strong. Interesting that they chose such independent and strong women to try and exploit. And, we had, I know that I agreed to a certain amount [of nudity] because that was what the script said, however, when they went too far, I said no way. I mean, I had major fights on *Jekyll and Hyde* [*Dr. Jekyll and Sister Hyde*] because they wanted full frontal nudity and I said don't be ridiculous! I was actually nailed for a while, tagged for a while as being difficult, a diva. But I didn't care, because it wasn't right, you know, and in a funny kind of way they sort of pushed me to stand up for myself. Which, I did. That's my feeling about it. I don't know what the other ladies have to say about that.

Martine Beswicke and Gerald Sim in *Dr. Jekyll and Sister Hyde*

Ingrid Pitt: I find I can't be exploited unless I'm willing, and I was very willing.

Veronica Carlson: I was hoping that would slip right by me. Yes, I agree with Ingrid. You can't be exploited unless you want to be, unless someone really cheats on you, right Ingrid, goes behind your back. The only trouble I had, and I know you all know this, that's why I was hoping you'd slip by me, because it was a scene with Peter Cushing that they put into the film [*Frankenstein Must Be Destroyed*, 1969]. What was wanted was for Peter to take my gown right off me so that I was naked. That was the problem. The rape scene was bad enough between being stripped and exposed, like Martine said, to have the room looking at you. I wouldn't do it. I guess I threw a tantrum or a hissy fit, whatever you call it. And I know it upset a lot of people. The wardrobe lady tried to accommodate it and in the end Terry [Terence Fisher] stood up with me and said "cut" before Peter could take the gown away from me. It made everyone miserable. But, I'm glad I didn't give in. I'd rather have been miserable those few days than be miserable for the rest of my life.

Val Guest: I'd like to give a sense of balance here by saying at no time in my early Hammer days did anybody try to exploit my cleavage!

Martine Beswicke: You weren't wearing the right dress.

Yesterday's Enemy—*was it shot on location and could you give me some personal reminiscences?*

Val Guest: It was shot on location, a lot of it was shot in a sand pit just outside of Bray Studios. The others were built on stages not at Bray but at Shepperton Studios, because there wasn't enough room at Bray. Bernard Robinson, our art director, a brilliant man, created a complete—on one of the largest sound stages at Shepperton—a jungle with a river going through it and his jungle was all on wheels so he could change the format of that jungle by just reversing sections of it. The only location we did on that was locally around the studio.

Martine, what was the shooting schedule for the Bond films [*From Russia with Love*, 1963 and *Thunderball*, 1965] that you did?

Martine Beswicke: Well there were two months in Nassau, I think the shooting schedule was four months [for *Thunderball*]. Maybe even longer because they had a lot of second unit stuff. I really don't know [*From Russia...*], I think the schedule was between two and four months because they went to Turkey.

Was everybody friendly on the set?

Martine Beswicke: Absolutely, I suppose it was us and them, we were sort of the Bond lot, and there were all these other people outside of that, so we sort of stuck close together.

Ursula Andress and Christopher Lee in *She*

Mr. Bernard, on She, *I heard Christopher Lee was going to record some sort of chant for the film and you did quite a bit of work on that.*

James Bernard: That's right. They just got behind on schedule and they couldn't do it. I think he was rather disappointed because he really does have a very good singing voice of operatic quality. This would have been a good chance for him on screen. He was the wicked high priest, She's high priest. It was like a chant, really. He wrote some wonderful nonsense words for it. His wife is Danish, he speaks Danish, he speaks German and French and Italian. This was a real nonsense language. It was very convincing. We rehearsed it on the piano with Phil Martell, who was the music director, but then there was no time, so it was just never done.

Were there any particular actors or actresses who inspired you?

James Bernard: Well, I suppose Christopher really as Dracula obviously. All the actors were so good. There was never a bad performance in a Hammer film. It would be the characters they were playing who would

Christopher Lee and Carol Marsh in *Horror of Dracula*

bring out the music. That's why like Veronica being the heroine, there was a chance for something romantic. Veronica would obviously inspire my romantic feelings of music and helped me write that.
What about the lesbian scenes in the Karnstein trilogy?

Ingrid Pitt: I totally disagree that they were lesbian scenes. If you really study your vampire, you'd know that they have no sex. They simply don't copulate and be sexual, what they do is feed to exist. I think the part of Mircalla being in love with the girl, I can't remember her name [Emma Morton was the character's name in *Vampire Lovers*, 1970], Madeline Smith played her, it was a pure love, it had no sexual connotations. I think one of the reasons why the film [works] is because everyone is very innocent of the sexual aspect. It's only you lot who think about the lesbians, we didn't think any of that at all. We just had a purity of our lovemaking, if you know what I mean.

Ingrid Pitt and Pippa Scott in a scene from *The Vampire Lovers*

Do you have a favorite horror film that you worked on?

Martine Beswicke: I suppose the one that paid the most.

James Bernard: I don't have any favorite. I really can't put my finger on one. There's always bits in my scores that I'm quite pleased with and bits I thought I could have done better.

Martine Beswicke: I agree with James too. Each film has its own particular moments and each one, actually each film, has many favorite memories, especially the people and the characters. I have many fond memories of each one. I mean *Prehistoric Women* [1967] had Michael Carreras and me, and doing a dance and massive silliness, of course.

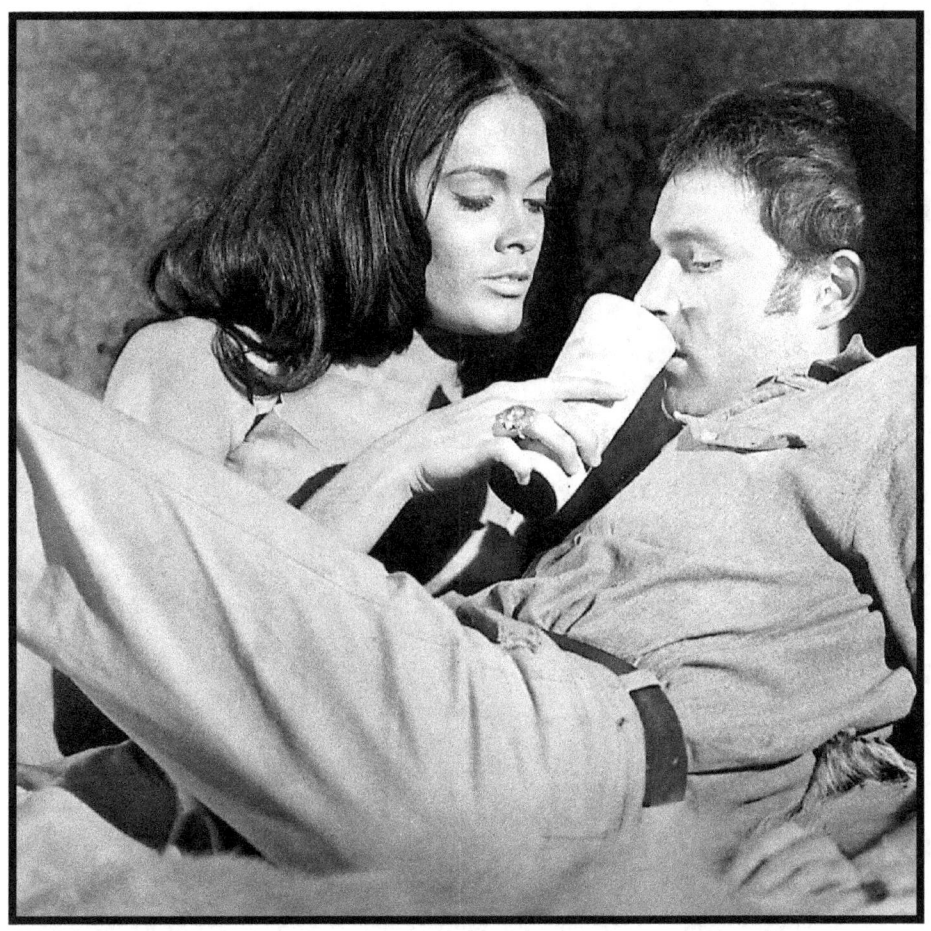
Martine Beswicke and Michael Latimer in *Prehistoric Women*

Val Guest: I would say they were all about the same to me. We had a lot of fun making them and I don't think you went away saying this is my favorite or that is my favorite. You may have an awful time on one picture but it doesn't become your favorite. We always had a lot of fun at Bray Studios, a good family outfit, you just did the best you could under the worst possible circumstances.

Veronica Carlson: Well, I have a favorite, *Frankenstein Must Be Destroyed* [1969] is my favorite. I think although I have happy memories I also have some awful memories, but the film with the most happy memories was *Frankenstein Must Be Destroyed*. Not only that, I adored and had a really special relationship with Peter. Nothing was better.
I hear Quatermass is going to be a big budget remake by Hammer.

Peter Cushing, Veronica Carlson and James Carreras on the set of *Frankenstein Must Be Destroyed*

Val Guest: I could have done with a few of those dollars! I have nothing to do with those. I would be fascinated to see what they would do with it. It doesn't necessarily mean if [studios] have all that money you're going to do a better picture. Sometimes the less money you have the more you have to dig and think and have instant genius. It's always much nicer to have it [a bigger budget], you can put more into special effects. I was thrilled to hear they are going to remake it.

Do you think if they approached you, you would do a cameo appearance.

Martine Beswicke: They'll pay.

Veronica Carlson: When they do the remakes, what studio would they be using?

Val Guest: I think Warner Bros.

Was it difficult to get past the censor board with color gore.

Veronica Carlson: I can remember on the first day of *Frankenstein Must Be Destroyed* we spent the first day shooting killing me. That was where Peter [Cushing] embraced me and the scalpel went into my heart and I said to Terry [Fisher], "Do you want me to die with my eyes open or closed?" And Terry said to me, "If you die with your eyes open we won't get past the censors," so I died with my eyes closed. I don't think he was joking.

Val Guest: You always had to, in any questionable scene at the time, you had to take two takes or two versions, one for America and one for the rest of the world.

Veronica, how was it working with Alexandra Bastedo on The Ghoul *[1975]?*

Veronica Carlson: Why do you ask me that? [Laughter] That's a difficult question for me to answer. I didn't get along with her very well, or maybe she didn't get along with me, I don't know. I'd rather not go into that.

What was she like?

Well, don't ask me. [Laughter]

Val Guest: Just read Veronica's memoirs.

Is there anyone you'd like to work with?

Val Guest: One person I always wanted to work with and almost did was Barbara Stanwyck. I don't think she would come down to Bray. That's someone I always wanted to work with. In fact, I actually wrote a movie for her, which she was going to do and we signed her and we had music and everything. The whole part of the deal was she could go to Rome

where Robert Taylor, her husband, was working and spend Christmas with him before she came back and made the movie with us. She called me from Rome and said, "I can't do it, I have to go back to Los Angeles." She had arrived in Rome unannounced and had found him with someone else. So, we were in a panic, we had studios, we had a script, we had everything. Doug Fairbanks, Jr. said, "I'll take the script back and see what we can do" and called me back and said, "Bette Davis wants to do it," a picture called *Another Man's Poison* [1951, produced by Douglas Fairbanks, Jr. and written by Val Guest].

But I always wanted to work with Barbara Stanwyck. I can't think of anybody in England that I'd say, "Oh my God, I'd have to work with them," there were so many of them [to name just one].

Martine Beswicke: I'd actually like to work with Sean Connery again. But, really work with him on a totally different level, not as a Bond girl, because, I just think he's really fabulous. He has an enormous presence.

Actually, there is somebody else I'd like to work with. There are directors I'd really like to work with very much so and Neil Jordan is one of my favorites. I wanted to do *Interview with the Vampire*[1994] actually, but they cut the part I wanted to do, so that was it. And Michael Caine, I'd like to work with Michael Caine!

Ingrid Pitt: I would just like to be working.

Could I get two different perspectives on working with Peter Cushing, one from the acting standpoint and one from the directing?

Val Guest: Peter is an old pal of mine. I adore him. Wonderful to have around. Enormous sense of humor, and after you'd done the most dramatic scene, he would suddenly burst into song and dance. He's a great person and a brilliant actor. He was in fact with the Old Vic, a Shakespearean actor.

Veronica Carlson: I found him to be the most sensitive actor that I have ever worked with. I found the change in Peter to be heartbreaking when

Maureen Connell and Peter Cushing appear in the Val Guest–directed *Abominable Snowman.*

his wife died. But, as Val said, he'd have us all in stitches. You know, I'd forgotten [his sense of humor] because the abiding impression I had in me was the grief the man had. I'd forgotten how funny he could be. He sent me a book not long ago called *The Bois Saga*. Have you seen it?

Val Guest: Yes.

Veronica Carlson: Isn't it wonderful. How would you describe that book?

Val Guest: Just wonderful, really.

Veronica Carlson: It's all misspelled words and jumbled history. He must be a brilliant historian. He's a brilliant artist. He's illustrated the book. It's a funny book, a satire. His wife was the inspiration for the book. When I read it I cried a bit because it was funny and touching at the same time. He had a nervous breakdown in 1951 and his wife had helped him get through it with a very funny remark. He used to sit on

> PETER CUSHING
>
> Like old Dracula himself, it would seem that Hammer Films are 'un-knockoutable'! - and it is thanks to the likes of you dear people that keeps 'em alive and kicking.
>
> How grateful all old Hammeronians must be, and may the recent revival of that Company give you even more pleasure in the years to come.
>
> From my 'rocking-chair-by-the-fire' I salute you, regretting that the toll taken by eighty-one summers prevents me from being at the Baltimore Convention.
>
> With my kindest wishes, and may God's be with you all always.
>
> In all sincerity,
>
> Peter Cushing, O.B.E.

The letter Peter Cushing wrote to us when his health prevented him from attending FANEX.

the john and just sit and worry about what it was he couldn't remember what he was worrying about. Well, that started the *Bois Saga*. He plays on words, he plays on history and he brings us through a certain point in history. And he says, "The book will never be finished because Helen was his inspiration and she's no longer with me." Peter is the nicest man I've ever met. Strangely enough, apparently his secretary's daughter is dyslexic and she can't easily read, and she understood the entire book. He found that to be very interesting.

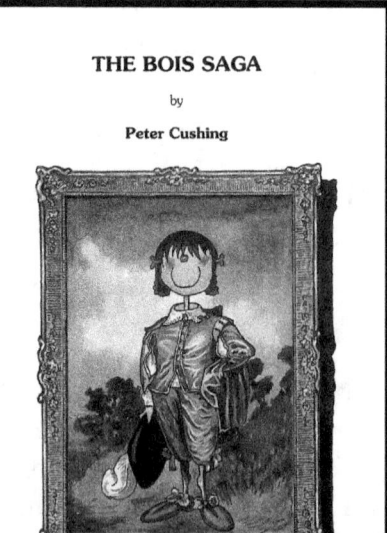

Ingrid, are the books you've written available in the US?

Ingrid Pitt: Quite a few people asked me about those books. They were mainly thrillers and some people have brought them for me to sign, which made my day. Actually I think it's quite nice to have someone present you with a book from another country. No, they were not published in America. One was about Eva Peron [*Eva's Spell: A Novel of the Perons*, 1985], just at the time when the Falkland war took place, so they decided not to publish in America, which I think was a great shame because it was a very good book. We've been told they will republish quite a few of my books now so I suppose they will shortly come to America. One of my books will be filmed now.

Mr. Guest, what part of Casino Royale *[1967] did you work on and what about* Space 1999?

Val Guest: You just want to know which section you can blame me for! I was contracted on that picture—there were two of us to start with, John Huston and myself. Then, Cy [Charlie] Feldman, the producer, who is a charming man but completely mad, suddenly decided he wanted to have four or even five directors all doing sections. John called me up one night and said, "He said he wants a compendium of directors."

I said, "Yes, that's what he told me."

He said, "Is it going to work?"

I said, "Of course not."

So he said, "What are we going to do?"

I said, "Go on with it and let's see what happens."

Each director would ask for a writer and write [the script] in sections. It was mad, of course, when they had all these four or five segments and then it didn't make sense. So Charlie Feldman said to me, "Will you write a linking scene? Will that help?" Well, anything would help. We tried it. I said I would only do this as long as I could write in my two

Ingrid Pitt, James Bernard and Martine Beswicke at FANEX 8

chums—Bill Holden [Ransome] and Ursula Andress [Vesper Lynd] had to be in all the linking scenes. It was the only thing that could keep me sane, which I could giggle about. This is how that happened. Then, slowly as the picture went on, various directors disappeared. [Directors eventually credited in the film include John Huston, Ken Hughes, Robert Parrish, Val Guest and Joseph McGarth.] Cy Feldman said it was him because of this and him because of that, and he ended up with John and myself—we were the only two left. By this time Charlie realized that all we needed was more writing. At the time I had only been asked to do the end third of it, the Woody Allen scenes. So we did what we could. [Writers credited in the film include: Val Guest, Ben Hecht, Joseph Heller, John Law, Wolf Mankowitz, Michael Sayers, Terry Southern and Billy Wilder.]

Then came the great day when John said, "I'm pissed off with this. I'm going to Wally's and play poker." So, I was left with this bag of whatever you'd call it, so we put it together somehow or other. Charlie Feldman said to me, "Val, I can't thank you enough. I'm going to give you an extra credit in the film as coordinating director." I said, "If you do that I'll sue you!" Technically it was the Woody Allen [scenes Guest

Val Guest directs Woody Allen and Daliah Lavi on the set of *Casino Royale*.

Val Guest with Dick Klemensen at FANEX 11

directed] but otherwise I had to finish John's stuff while he was playing poker.

What about Space 1999?

Val Guest: It was wonderful working with Martin Landau, he was a real pro. Barbara Bain—putz. We worked—Gerry Anderson, who was a very brilliant man, full of imagination, he had a wonderful special effects department and we had fun making it. We did it all around Pinewood Studios. There were some old chalk pits and iron pits we'd shoot around in [for] the lunar surface.

Is there lots of unused footage from Casino Royale?

Val Guest: Absolutely, because Charlie Feldman, who couldn't sleep very well, used to call us up in the middle of the night and say, "I don't like the color of Ursula Andress' dress in the sequence, so will you change it to peach?" We'd say, "Well, Charlie, you realize the sets have been designed to take a turquoise dress, not a peach one." "Well, redo the set."

Now, a lot of these sequences were junked. They were shot here but they were junked. Each time they were shot again they were shot a scientific way. There's an awful lot of material. I seem to remember being in the cutting room with about five hours of film, which had to be whittled down. But Charlie Feldman excused all this—"Don't worry, it's a psychedelic musical."

Is there any plan to bring it out on laser disc [these were the days before DVD]?

Val Guest: I don't know. I've severed the umbilical cord with that picture.

Ingrid Pitt: Did Charlie Feldman ever work again?

Peter Sellers in *Casino Royale*

Val Guest: Yes he did. He did one more picture and then died.

Martine, did you work with Vincent Price on The Offspring *[1987, AKA From a Whisper to a Scream]?*

Martine Beswicke: Oh, I did meet him. I fell in love with him. Actually, it's funny because when I met him, it was [a] special effect. He had a knife stuck in the side of his neck with blood all dripping around. I said, "I'm glad to meet you." He tried to kiss me [with the knife sticking out of his neck], so that was my meeting with him. I fell in love with him. He had such a beautiful spirit, really lovely with that dry humor. Just a lovely man.

Is there any particular film you would like to change?

Veronica Carlson: Every single one! Just like my artwork. I'd like to redo everything I've ever done.

Vincent Price in *The Offspring*

Martine, Ingrid and Veronica at the ladies tea on Sunday at FANEX 8

Val Guest: I'm sure we would all like to redo a lot of things that we've done. I'm sure there are a lot of things we wish we hadn't done.

Martine Beswicke: I don't dwell on it too much. Every so often, "That would be better if..." and then it's sort of gone. It's a very fleeting thing.

James Bernard: Yes, I feel very much the same. There's always bits you see and go, that's pretty embarrassing. I should do that over, and then you forget them.

Val Guest: We look every week hurriedly through *TV Guide* to see if we have to leave town!

Val Guest, Yolande Donlan and Gary Svehla at FANEX 8

Ingrid Pitt: Yes, I've done one or two films like that, but generally I think what's the point looking back. It's best to forget what you've done and [money you've made that] you've spent unwisely. Hopefully you're doing something better.

Did Richard Burton drink heavily during Where Eagles Dare *[1968]?*

Ingrid Pitt: No, it was Elizabeth [Taylor] who was drinking heavily during that film. How I got the film was really different because I only got to see the director [Brian Hutton] for three minutes on a day when he was editing at MGM. I was doing *Ironside* on the other end of Los Angeles. I got to see him finally for three minutes and then he left town for pre-production in London. I was living in Los Angeles at the time and I thought, "My God, how am I going to pursue this man across the big ocean?" So, I ran him up a couple of times and finally got him on the phone and said, "Would you mind if I came to see you in London?" Well, he said, "I never mind pretty girls coming to see me." I thought it was a bit vain to discontinue my habitat in Los Angeles, but I did anyway. I turned up and he said, "I think this is great, there are 299 other girls after this part that you want. Let's see who deserves to get it the best." He did a screen test with me and I stuck around although I went to live in Wembley after that. I thought, "My God, I must see how the screen test turned out,"

Ingrid Pitt

and when I saw it [by] sneaking into the projection room, I fainted. I thought it was awful. I really thought that I had no chance now to get the part [as Heidi], But, he gave it to me, which I thought was very nice. But, I think I got it because I was the first he saw and sort of fixed it in his mind that I shall play it [the role], and life has never been the same since.

MEMORIES OF HAMMER...
NOT A CONCLUSION!

Sometimes the end of FANEX conventions are the best times of the weekend. From the beginning we have hosted what is known in convention cycles as "dead dog" parties, intimate little gatherings of convention staff and guests, where the staff gets its chance to speak to the guests after working on the show the entire weekend. The early convention "anyone for pizza" bare-bones party soon developed into catered convention dinners with staff and guests seated around large banquet tables. This event became *the* event to crash as we found out to our amazement. Many times fans would find out where the dinners were held and sit outside in the hallway for that one last chance to get an autograph.

It is always interesting to watch the Hammer celebrities at such functions, because, as stated earlier, the Hammer people really know how to enjoy themselves, but strangely enough, they seem to bond and have a desire to keep in contact long after the show. Thus we have actresses who worked during the classic early Hammer period exchanging addresses with directors who worked over a decade later in Hammer films. We have stars, who never worked together in the same Hammer film, swapping stories and swearing they must keep in touch. And these celebrities really mean it! Many times, when hosting convention dinners or lunches, Sue and I or the staff must work overtime to keep conversation moving along, introducing the spouse of one guest to the spouse of another. But we never have this problem with the Hammer folk, who seem to mingle easily and fit right in as just regular people. Perhaps it is the British upbringing, but in all the years of doing the conventions, most of our warmest, kindest and most enthused guests have come from the ranks of Hammer Film Productions. Perhaps it was the low-budget nature of Hammer that encouraged collaboration, or perhaps it was the family atmosphere sparked by the familiarity of using the same directors, producers, writers, production designers, cinematographers, set designers, etc. Hammer, for many of these celebrities, was very much like high school, and our convention very much like a high school reunion. Some of these celebrities peaked with Hammer and these experiences became the zenith of their professional lives. While others looked upon their Hammer experiences as training, as a start, before wider success developed after "graduating" from Hammer. With so many limitations that Hammer had to tolerate in order to survive, all our Hammer guests, from so many different conventions, look very fondly upon their Hammer years.

And Hammer guests never forget a kind gesture. When Sue and I do other conventions and meet former FANEX Hammer guests at other shows, these people always stop to hug in the halls, join us for lunch or drinks and make sure to spend quality time with us. Not that other guests blow us off, but there's a genuine appreciation of being remembered and of being treated the FANEX way that Hammer guests never take for granted. We still receive books, letters, Christmas cards and even warm telephone calls from our Hammer guests. Once a perplexed Val Guest called me and said he was away, but upon his return home he had a phone message to call Susan. After exploring every immediate Susan in his range of relatives and friends, he phoned us to inquire if we had phoned.

In closing, reflecting upon all the Hammer memories revealed in this book, remembering all the classic movies and riveting sequences burned into our consciousness, recalling those wondrous compact sets, the lush Technicolor or stark monochrome photography, the intense and professional acting all these years later, it is amazing to realize that working at Hammer must have been an amazing opportunity. Hopefully, these intimate conversations and panel discussions shared within these pages will reflect the glory that was Hammer and reveal the warmth and charm of the personalities involved in the making of such important movie history.

Long live Hammer, and long may its virtues be sung.
—Gary J. Svehla

For more information about the careers of these Hammer stars check out their autobiographies available from the publishers or Amazon.com:
Peter Cushing: An Autobiography and Past Forgetting [Midnight Marquee Press, Inc.]; *Val Guest: So You Want to be in Pictures* [Reynolds & Hearn]; *Christopher Lee: Tall, Dark and Gruesome* [Midnight Marquee Press, Inc.]; *Michael Ripper Unmasked* [Midnight Marquee Press, Inc.]; *Jimmy Sangster: Do You Want it Good or Tuesday?* [Midnight Marquee Press, Inc.]; *Ingrid Pitt: Life's a Scream* [Midnight Marquee Press, Inc.]; *Midnight Marquee Actors Series: Peter Cushing* [Midnight Marquee Press, Inc.]

*IF YOU ENJOYED THIS BOOK
PLEASE CALL OR WRITE OR E-MAIL FOR A
FREE CATALOG*

*MIDNIGHT MARQUEE PRESS, INC.
9721 BRITINAY LANE
BALTIMORE, MD 21234*

410-665-1198

WWW.MIDMAR.COM

www.ingramcontent.com/pod-product-compliance
Lightning Source LLC
Chambersburg PA
CBHW071227080526
44587CB00013BA/1526